# Vladimir Odoevsky and Romantic Poetics

**Studies in Slavic Literature, Culture and Society**

General Editor: Thomas Epstein

**Volume 1**
Neil Cornwell, *Vladimir Odoevsky and Romantic Poetics. Collected Essays*

**Volume 2**
Rosalind Marsh (ed.), *Women and Russian Culture*

**Volume 3**
Michael Epstein, Alexander Genis, and Slobadanka Vladiv-Glover (eds.), *Russian Postmodernism: New Perspectives on Late Soviet and Post-Soviet Literature*

# VLADIMIR ODOEVSKY AND ROMANTIC POETICS

## Collected Essays

Neil Cornwell

*Berghahn Books*
Providence • Oxford

First published in 1998 by

**Berghahn Books**

© 1998 Neil Cornwell

### Library of Congress Cataloging-in-Publication Data

```
Cornwell, Neil.
    Vladimir Odoevsky and romantic poetics : collected essays / Neil
Cornwell.
       p.   cm. -- (Studies in Slavic literature, culture, and society
; v. 1)
    Includes bibliographical references.
    ISBN 1-57181-907-X (alk. paper)
    1. Odoevskiĭ, V. F. (Vladimir Fedorovich), kniâz´, 1803-1869-
-Criticism and interpretation. 2. Romanticism.   I. Title.
II. Series.
PG3337.03Z62   1997
891.78'309--dc21                                        97-28797
                                                           CIP
```

### British Library Cataloguing in Publication Data

A catalogue record for this book is available
from the British Library.

# CONTENTS

# PREFACE

In 1986 I published *V.F. Odoyevsky: His Life, Times and Milieu* (Athlone Press, London; Ohio University Press, Athens, Ohio). Presented neither as a biography, nor a literary study as such, but as a 'life and times', this – the first book on Odoevsky in English and the first full study of him in any language since 1913 – was largely a thematic biography, designed to provide as full coverage as possible of Odoevsky's literary and multifarious extra-literary activities. The book was in the event excerpted from my doctoral dissertation (Belfast, 1983), the two versions having been written in tandem (and having considerably outgrown my original plan for a short biographical study). It did contain a fifty-page chapter on Odoevsky the writer; however this was perforce confined to a summary of his literary career and a fairly brief survey of the main characteristics of his prose fiction. Further discussion of certain fictional works occurred in the chapters on Odoevsky as a thinker and musician. In my 1986 preface, I drew the attention of those readers whose main concern lay with the literary side to the existence of a range of articles of mine, in which many of Odoevsky's literary works were treated in much greater detail. This did not prevent a number of reviewers, whose comments otherwise were in the main generous, from regretting what they saw as a relative paucity of literary attention per se in that study.

Since then I have republished an annotated Russian text of one of Odoevsky's rarer main works (*Pestrye skazki/Variegated Tales,* Durham, 1988) and have also translated a selection of his stories (*The Salamander and Other Gothic Tales,* Bristol Classical Press, 1992), most of which appeared in English for the first time; John Bayley listed this last volume as one of his 'books of the year' (*TLS,* 4 December 1992), claiming that Odoevsky's fiction was 'more interesting than anything by Poe or Hoffmann'. I also pressed for a revised republication of the 1965 translation of Odoevsky's most fundamental work, *Russkie nochi (Russian Nights)*. Fortunately this project has recently been realized. The first serious Russian biographical study of Odoevsky was published in 1991. A paperback collection of *Povesti i rasskazy* (Tales and Stories) was published in Moscow in 1988 with a print run of 2,700,000 – lending credence to the view that Odoevsky was achieving, in the last years of the Soviet Union, something like cult status. Most, if not quite all, of his romantic-Gothic works of any substance, denied to earlier generations of readers for their excessive 'mysticism', have now been republished. However, there still remains a lack of a full and satisfactory literary study in any language and, as yet, any further work of substance in English. Moreover, despite the documentation now available of Odoevsky's labyrinthine biographical and literary connections with the major figures of his era, studies of Pushkin, Gogol and Dostoevsky (to name but three) still appear with little (or, all too often, no) mention of him. His place in Russian thought also remains still very largely undetermined and unacknowledged.

It therefore seems an appropriate time to collect my earlier Odoevsky articles, together with some new thoughts and updated material, into book form. I assume (possibly wrongly) that the essays in this volume are more likely to be read singly than as a whole. Imagining that to be the case, I have therefore allowed a certain amount of biographical and other detail to overlap or recur from essay to essay, to preserve a modicum of self-sufficiency, although more glaring passages have been omitted or reduced. I trust that readers interested enough for total immersion will not find this excessive. It is hoped that, as a whole, this will serve as not an exhaustive, but at least a reasonably full basic, albeit (hopefully) interim, literary study, giving at least some attention to most of his essential works. There will, of course, remain no shortage of byways to investigate – of lesser known Odoevsky works, still not reprinted or never published – or, for that matter, of highways to subject to more specialised analysis. Odoevsky's real day of recognition is yet to come!

Neil Cornwell, Bristol, 1997

# ACKNOWLEDGMENTS

With the exception of Chapter 1, which was written for this book, these essays are based, to a greater or lesser extent, on articles or essays published previously and now collected in revised and updated form to constitute the present volume. They are printed, following the introductory chapter, in the chronological order in which they were first written. Acknowledgments and thanks are therefore due to the following journals, editors and publishers:

Chapter 2 and its Excursus are based on material which first appeared in *Quinquereme: New Studies in Modern Languages*, vols 2 (1979) and 3 (1980). Chapter 3 (written in 1981) is condensed from my essay in the volume *Problems of Russian Romanticism*, edited by Robert Reid (Gower, Aldershot, 1986). Chapter 4 appeared first in *Essays in Poetics*, vol. 8 (1983). Chapter 5 is based on an article published in *The Slavonic and East European Review*, 62 (1984). Chapter 6 is adapted from an essay written for *Renaissance and Modern Studies*, 28 (1984). Some of the material in Chapter 7 is taken from my study *V.F. Odoyevsky: His Life, Times and Milieu* (The Athlone Press, London, 1986) and from my introduction to V.F. Odoyevsky, *Pyostryye skazki* (Durham Modern Language Studies, University of Durham, 1988). Chapter 8 is revised and expanded from my introduction to *The Salamander and Other Gothic Tales* (Bristol Classical Press, London, 1992), itself condensed from a short essay published in *Rusistika* (1991). Chapter 9 is a reworking of papers given to the Leiden October Conference (1991) and a symposium on Fantastic Realism at the University of Nottingham (1994), as well as my essay published in *Exhibited by Candlelight: Sources and Developments in the Gothic Tradition*, edited by Valeria Tinkler-Villani and Peter Davidson (DQR Studies in Literature, 16, Rodopi, Amsterdam and Atlanta, GA, 1995).

I am also grateful to the administrators of the Faculty of Arts Research Fund, University of Bristol, for a grant to assist in the preparation of this volume and to technical assistance from Sally Steen.

# NOTE ON
# TRANSLITERATION

The transliteration system used in this volume is that of the Library of Congress, without diacritics. An exception is made for Russian surnames ending in '-ii' and '-oi', for which the more customary '-y' or '-oy' has been retained (e.g., 'Odoevsky', 'Dostoevsky', 'Tolstoy'); the soft sign at the end of names is omitted (e.g., 'Gogol', rather than 'Gogol'); and occasionally well-worn English usage has been retained ('Tchaikovsky', rather than 'Chaikovskii'). In the case of quotation or bibliographical reference to other sources, of course, the original spelling or usage is used.

# Chapter 1

# VLADIMIR FEDOROVICH ODOEVSKY

## Career, Personality, Reputation

Prince Vladimir Fedorovich Odoevsky (1804-1869), to give him
his full name and title, was a central figure in Russian culture
over a period of nearly half a century. From being an 'angry young
man' of Russian literature in the early 1820s, when he edited the cul-
turally rebellious almanac *Mnemozina* (together with Wilhelm
Küchelbecker [Kiukhel'beker], soon to be arrested as one of the
more hot-headed of the Decembrist insurgents), he went through a
florid period as a leading romantic writer of Gothic and mystical
leanings, before maturing into a conscientious public servant and
indefatigable philanthropist. At the end of his life he was a Moscow
senator, a leading musicologist, a keen amateur scientist and would-
be court historian. Meanwhile, he had also been an enthusiastic the-
orist of romantic aesthetics and cultural thinker, Russia's first
important music critic, a prominent popular educator (the predeces-
sor in certain respects of Lev Tolstoy), and even a culinary columnist
(or 'crafty cook', under the pen name of 'Doctor Puff').

He has been dubbed by a range of commentators, and at various
times, 'the philosopher-prince', 'the Russian Hoffmann', 'the Russ-
ian Faust' and even 'the Russian Goethe'. Another major figure
with whom Odoevsky had much in common, in terms of their cul-
tural ambitions, their formal experimentation and their interests in
the limits of language, was Denis Diderot. It could equally be said
of Odoevsky, as it recently has of Diderot, that he is now renowned,
amongst other things, 'for having been incapable either of com-

pleting his grand encyclopedic scheme, or of repressing his frag-
mentary ejaculations'.[1]

He was close to the major historical events of his period, from the
Decembrist uprising of 1825 to the reforms of the 1860s, and was
well acquainted with virtually all the leading Russian cultural per-
sonalities, from Griboedov, Pushkin and Glinka, to Turgenev, Tolstoy
and the young Tchaikovsky, as well as playing host to Berlioz, Liszt,
and Wagner on their visits to Russia. His salon flourished for some
thirty years in St Petersburg and again in the 1860s in Moscow – as a
centre for literary and musical discussion and cultural exchange.
According to his friend, the critic Shevyrev, on Odoevsky's divan
could be found seated the whole of Russian literature. Indeed the lit-
erary salons, at this point in time and place (or, in Bakhtinian terms,
'chronotope') of European cultural intersection, held a position of
considerable importance and influence. As a recent commentator
has written:

> It was in the salon that writer and potential reader came face-to-face as
> interlocutors, that an oral culture of wit, anecdote and improvisational
> repartee arose to rival the system of written genres. Writing would have
> to address itself to the pleasure and attention of the reader, who as often
> as not was an educated woman.[2]

Although this passage was written with figures other than Odoevsky
in mind, at the same time it appears to resonate with significance in
the light of his social and belletristic activities.

Further particularities of Odoevsky's life and career are noted in
the essays which follow. A full account has been attempted in my
'life and times' study, published in 1986. Here, in this introductory
essay to the present volume, I wish to focus briefly on some of the
more enigmatic features of his personality and reputation, both per-
sonal and literary. In fact, the more closely one looks at Odoevsky's
life and career, the less clear many details and aspects become.

## II

The hagiographical tone adopted by contemporary memoirists in
the volume published following Odoevsky's death in 1869 soon gave
way to more variegated accounts and opinions.[3] The myth fostered
of peasant origins on his mother's side, traditionally seen as nicely
balancing the 'Rurikovich' princely status inherited from his father
(and thus rendering him a perfectly balanced 'man of the people',
descended from aristocrats and serfs) has turned out to be a consid-
erable exaggeration.[4] His year of birth has never been certain: both

1803 and 1804 were cited by him on different occasions (the latter year now being accepted by most commentators).[5]

Even his name and title are a matter of some (albeit needless) dispute. As a *kniaz'* whose family could trace its ancestry back to the Varangian prince Rurik, Odoevsky was an aristocrat equal in seniority and birth to any in the realm, including the Romanov family: indeed, in later life he accordingly became Russia's 'premier nobleman'. The title *kniaz'* has normally been rendered by generations of historians into English as 'prince'. However, there remains the possiblity of confusion with the title *velikii kniaz'*, given to sons of the Tsar, and traditionally rendered as 'grand duke'. Nevertheless, it comes as a considerable surprise that so illustrious an historian of Russian literature as Victor Terras, in his recent history, should refer to a 'Duke Vladimir Odoevsky'.[6] Even more erroneous, perhaps, is the misuse in Odoevsky's case by another eminent critic, Joseph Frank, of the title 'count' (from the Russian *graf*, as in Count Lev [or 'Leo'] Tolstoy).[7] Furthermore, the present writer was taken to task by at least one reviewer of his 1986 book for privileging the formulation 'V.F. Odoyevsky'. Transliteration apart, it was suggested both that the title 'prince' should have been prominently highlighted and used and that the name 'Vladimir' would be somehow preferable to the austere initials 'V.F.' (as favoured by Soviet critics). The mere 'Odoevsky' would, of course, have been inadequate, given the existence of Vladimir's cousin, the Decembrist poet A.I. (Aleksandr Ivanovich) Odoevsky. I have since chosen to try exploiting more prominently the 'Vladimir' variant, though I find myself unable to rationalise this decision. In any case, all of this would have caused Odoevsky himself no small amount of ironic amusement, given his own eccentric propensity for the use of pseudonyms.

Given that he was arguably the most highly educated man of his age, it might seem incongruous that the impression that persists of Odoevsky the man should be, above all, that of the self-deprecating eccentric. His dress frequently reminded observers of an alchemist of old and his interests and pursuits were as extraordinarily wide as many of them were bizarre. He had the air of an idealistic dreamer, yet one with a serious cultural and civilising mission. Many saw him as caught, or torn, between his position in society and his artistic temperament and aspirations. Aleksandr Herzen, never exactly close to Odoevsky, once remarked of him: 'notwithstanding all his charm of spirit, one can see the gentleman-in-waiting key in his back'.[8] He could be described by one memoirist as colourless in appearance, yet by another as Byronic. To some he was saintly, to others a figure of ridicule: a universal encyclopedist know-it-all, or a genuine renaissance man.

After December 1825 he ceased functioning as a virtually professional *littérateur* and lapsed into lower profile dilettantism. Accounts of him as a young man refer to a quality of staidness; he was deemed a pedant and already senatorial in bearing. He is sometimes characterised as 'feminine' in appearance. However, a number of commentators have described him as resembling Chatsky, Griboedov's sharp-tongued protagonist from the classic comedy *Gore ot uma (Woe from Wit)*. This seems to accord ill with later descriptions of a modest and gentle personality and may derive rather from that of his own fictional invention, Arist, of the 1820s; or perhaps he indeed mellowed after his marriage and entry into government service in 1826. His domestic situation, we now learn, in the 1830s was much unhappier than has previously been assumed. One commentator even asserts that Odoevsky was the prototype for Goncharov's first hero, Aleksandr Aduev (Odoev-Aduev?).[9] Whatever the case, Odoevsky retained a private and discreet veneer and his personality is not easily pinned down. He features in many memoir accounts over a long period of time; dubbed a 'man of three generations', he was obviously capable of creating and leaving a variety of impressions.[10]

Odoevsky's own romantic theory of artistic biography, brought out most clearly in his tale from *Russkie nochi* 'Sebastian Bach', intimated that the real biography of an artist was to be found only within his works. It was long ago suggested that this very story may have been based at some level on Odoevsky's own domestic life; recent research would, if anything, tend to support this fascinating, if at first sight implausible, conjecture.[11] Although Odoevsky was, throughout his active literary career at least, an inveterate romantic, it would be difficult to say of him, as Tomashevsky wrote of the romantic poet: 'The Romantic poet *was* his own hero'; Tomashevsky goes on to argue that what is important to literary scholarship is not a writer's 'actual curriculum vitae, but his ideal biographical legend'.[12] This legend, it is claimed, is created by the author himself. An attempted re-creation of this, from Odoevsky's published and unpublished works and fragments, is one possible entry into his literary biography.

Another way in is to jump, from the Formalist critic Tomashevsky (writing in 1923), over Western theories of authorship – its demise or its return – to the biographical implications of Iurii Lotman's semiotics of behaviour. This system, which seems to cope equally with (or be equally happy to confuse) historical and fictional personalities, has been directed largely at the eighteenth and early nineteenth centuries, and in particular at the Decembrist period.[13] Lotman produces a diagram, constructed like a family tree, to illustrate 'the behaviour patterns of the gentry' in the eighteenth century.[14] It would be a fascinating exercise to extend this into the nineteenth century and to apply it to the multiple parallel careers and activities of Odoevsky: one can only here conjecture that something resembling a monkey puzzle tree might result!

Although a fully Lotmanesque treatment of Odoevsky's life and occupations must remain beyond the scope of the present study, we can make a few further points. According to Lotman, 'the Decembrists cultivated seriousness as a norm of behaviour'; 'all forms of society entertainment – dances, cards, flirtations – are severely condemned by the Decembrists as signs of spiritual emptiness'.[15] These qualities, clearly observed in the young (and, to some extent, the not so young) Odoevsky, clearly owe something to the Decembrist ethos, which must have influenced him both through personal contacts and by general codes of behaviour – despite his personal lack of what Lotman considers the 'crucial' military background.[16] A general aura of theatricality permeated social and public life in this period:

> Convention, ritual and the arbitrariness of the sign were stressed; and thus the closed culture of the nobility, as part of its rapid development, cultivated etiquette and the theatricalization of life-style.[17]

This can go as far, in some cases, as 'the culture of the dandy'.[18]

'Romanticism prescribes forms of behaviour', remarks Lotman, with the result that 'a whole phalanx of imitators' arises from the ranks of military and government servants, adopting 'the gestures, the expressions and the manners' of characters from literature: 'in the case of Romanticism, reality itself hastens to imitate literature'.[19] Furthermore there occurs a separation between 'routine behaviour' (received from society) and 'semiotic behaviour' (adopted by choice); the non-semiotic can become semiotic in the eyes of the casual or unfamiliar observer, such as a foreigner or outsider.[20] This phenomenon by itself could help to explain, at least in part, the disparate memoir accounts of Odoevsky.

'At the beginning of the nineteenth century', argues Lotman, 'the dividing line between art and ... everyday behaviour ... was expunged':

> Examples of how people of the late eighteenth and early nineteenth centuries constructed their personal behaviour, their everyday speech, and in the last analysis their destiny in life, according to literary and theatrical models are very numerous.[21]

This can be observed in literature itself, from Pushkin to the early Dostoevsky, and appears to be evidenced within cultured society by a plethora of memoir material.[22] While we cannot here compare the

paradigm of Odoevsky's behaviour – overall or in its particularities
– against 'the mythology of everyday and social behaviour' of his
epoch, we can nevertheless still see the outline of his life 'as a text
which is organised according to the rules of a particular plot'; par-
ticularly striking in this regard is the last Moscow period of
Odoevsky's life, or what Lotman would call 'the theatrical category
of the "ending", the fifth act'.[23]

Under romanticism, Lotman avers, 'the biographical legend [he
evidently follows Tomashevsky in using this phrase] became an
essential condition for the perception of any text as artistic'. He also
dates 'the disappearance of the poetics of behaviour' to that of 'the
last of the Romantics in the 1840s'.[24] It may therefore be seen as no
coincidence that Odoevsky's literary swan song went largely unap-
preciated in 1844 and almost totally so for many years thereafter. By
1844 Odoevsky's brand of romanticism was already seen as passé
and his retrospective of collected (though, in reality, 'selected') works
(including *Russkie nochi*, the bulk of which was an old wine now
rebottled) had been too long delayed: his biographical legend had
already faded.


# III


Thus the reception of Odoevsky's collected works in 1844, which
included *Russkie nochi* as an entity for the first time, was on the whole
disappointing, although respectful attention was paid in serious
reviews written by Belinsky and the young positivist critic, Valerian
Maikov. One appreciative contemporary, a voice from the wilder-
ness of Siberia, was the exiled Decembrist (and former co-editor
with Odoevsky of *Mnemozina*), Wilhelm Küchelbecker, according to
whom Odoevsky had now become 'very nearly the best prose writer
in our country'; 'you have written a book', he wrote to Odoevsky in
1845, 'which we can boldly place against the most serious ones in
Europe'.[25] Then, for the rest of Odoevsky's lifetime (furthered, of
course, by his own failure to reprint his works), and indeed for the
rest of the century, came what amounted to critical oblivion.[26]

A succession of critics, whenever periodic minor revivals of inter-
est occurred – the turn of the century, the 1920s, the 1950s, and
finally the contemporary period (which we can date from the late
1960s) – have complained that *Russkie nochi*, which they recognise as
an important work of Russian literature, has been little appreciated
and little understood. Their cumulative efforts have done much to
rectify this. At the same time, a number of Odoevsky's best roman-
tic tales have only been reprinted in very recent editions (see those of

1977, 1981 and 1988); the cycle *Pestrye skazki* (*Variegated Tales)* made its reappearance in Russia in 1991; the fragmentary *Segeliel* only in 1994. Odoevsky's children's tales remained popular throughout; his reputation from now on, though, will rest on his romantic-Gothic tales – very much back in vogue in both Russian and Western tastes – but in particular on that unique compilation entitled *Russkie nochi.*

*Russkie nochi,* then, is a quintessential work of Russian literature and a key source-book, both for Russian romanticism and for Russian social and aesthetic thought of its epoch, written, for the most part, in a high post-Pushkinian prose style, fully recognisable as modern literary Russian. It is also a work of deep European erudition in the fullest sense, its references ranging from the Pythagoreans to the American slave trade. Like Coleridge, De Quincey and other prominent European romantics, Odoevsky spotted the significance of Piranesi as an archetypal figure. His interest in Giordano Bruno and Jakob Boehme was to be taken up later by the Symbolists and James Joyce, among others. Most of his concerns still confront the modern world, many of them with a vengeance: the conflict between the environment and utilitarianism; the resurgent monetarism of Adam Smith and the morality of free-market economics. There is even a passage in the anti-Benthamite story, 'Gorod bez imeni' ('A City Without Name'), which seems to anticipate Pol Pot: 'And everyone whose hands were not used to coarse work on land was driven out of the city'. Now once again, for the first time since 1917, Russians are looking back to nineteenth- and early twentieth-century discussions and blueprints for solutions to those old 'accursed questions': the future, the role and the direction of Russia.

It is also fitting indeed that *Russkie nochi,* the Russian book which is, perhaps above all Russian books, a book based on other (almost, one is tempted to say, on *all* previous) books, should appear again in English at a time when not only the West is 'perishing'. Books and culture, one is tempted to say, seem under threat as never before – above all from a media avalanche of instant trivia. Odoevsky, for all his 'encyclopeadic dilettantism' and occasionally excessive pedantry, is needed now more than ever.

*Russkie nochi* may also appeal more to the fragmentation-conscious postmodern age than to certain earlier epochs. Odoevsky's mysticism and his Gothicism may be, if anything, better displayed in certain of his other works (see *The Salamander and Other Gothic Tales,* translated in 1992). However, *Russkie nochi,* Odoevsky's single completed *magnum opus,* with its mixture of genres and styles, mingles fiction with non-fiction, romanticism with social reality, philosophical dialogue with historical reportage. It will perhaps be the twenty-first century that will finally make Odoevsky's reputation.

## IV

In the interim, Odoevsky scholarship continues to make advances, especially in Russia. The main development of recent years is the publication in 1991 of M.A. Tur'ian's biographical study, entitled *'My Fate is Strange ...'*.[27] This is a detailed biographical study, confined, though, very largely to the period up to Odoevsky's withdrawal from the literary scene. Based on new archival research, as well as the familiar published sources, many details are filled in, though plenty of 'white stains' (as the Russians call lacunae) still remain, both in the realms of curriculum vitae and biographical legend. Tur'ian's study now takes its place as the most important Russian book on Odoevsky (eclipsing in most respects – except for its immense documentation – Sakulin's huge, unwieldy, unfinished and almost unreadable study of 1913). The two main areas on which new light is shed are firstly, the question of Odoevsky's origins on his mother's side (which turn out to be less lowly than we had previously been led to believe), together with Odoevsky's relations with the Filippovs (his maternal relations) and his step-father Sechenov; and, secondly, the saga of a protracted unhappy love affair, involving a certain Nadezhda Nikolaevna Lanskaia.

Other recent publications include a catalogue of Odoevsky's library (see the bibliography to the present study). There has also been an interesting article on *Russkie nochi*, by L.A. Levina.[28] This emphasises the drama of the four disputants (Faust and his friends), and sees the work as a diachronic and synchronic drama of themes, motifs and ideas. It concentrates on the narrational scheme and, unusually, the frame-tale itself: the embedded stories are thereby relegated to the background (as must have seemed the case, indeed, to Odoevsky's readers of 1844, who were already familiar with the earlier published stories). The overall stress of Levina's article is on the reversals and parallels of this inimitably 'philosophical novel'.

Apart from anything else, it will be apparent from this study that the history of the reception of Odoevsky's works serves as a useful paradigm for the fortunes of romanticism throughout both Russian and Soviet criticism.

Meanwhile, back in the West, it has now emerged that at least some of the warnings given to Odoevsky by friends, concerning the alleged piracy of his works and urging him towards the never to be fulfilled second edition of 1862, had a certain foundation. What the Irish-American story writer Fitz-James O'Brien made of Odoevsky will be explored in Chapter 9. There is, no doubt, a more innocent answer to the question of George Eliot's *Silas Marner* (1861). The motionless fits of her eponymous protagonist seem to link him with the unhappy figure of Odoevsky's 'The Tale of a Dead Body, Belonging to No One Knows Whom' (from *Pestrye skazki*, of 1833): 'But there might be such a thing as a man's soul being loose from his body, and getting out and in, like a bird out of its nest and back.'[29] Given the apparent lack of a nineteenth-century translation of this story, it would seem that Eliot could not have known it, other than by word of mouth, which seems unlikely, or by means of the time-honoured process of 'ideas in the air', recently intellectualised by Lotman and Uspensky under the concept of the 'semiosphere'.[30]

Odoevsky's full importance to Russian culture, let alone his European significance, has still to be evaluated. Much remains to be done, for instance, in the exploring of his impact upon Dostoevsky. Even if no further O'Briens come to light, it remains highly likely that intertextual studies to come will reveal that Odoevsky, whether communicating through the semiosphere or otherwise, may well yet have a few surprises in store for us.

## Notes

1. Monika Greenleaf, *Pushkin and Romantic Fashion: Fragment, Elegy, Orient, Irony* (Stanford, CA, 1994), p. 22. Odoevsky's sceptical views on language may be compared with Diderot's 'Lettre sur les sourds et muets'.
2. Ibid. p. 23.
3. See *V pamiat' o kniaze Vladimire Fedoroviche Odoevskom* (Moscow, 1869).
4. See M.A. Tur'ian's biographical study, "*Strannaia moia sud'ba ...*": *O zhizni Vladimira Fedorovicha Odoevskogo* (Moscow, 1991).
5. Neil Cornwell, *V.F. Odoyevsky: His Life, Times and Milieu* (Athlone Press, London, 1986), pp. 2-3.
6. Victor Terras, *A History of Russian Literature* (Yale University Press, New Haven and London, 1991), p. 249.
7. Joseph Frank, *Dostoevsky: The Seeds of Revolt, 1821-1849* (Princeton University Press, Princeton, NJ, 1976), pp. 160, 398. When I pointed this error out to Professor Frank some years ago, he courteously replied that he would then correct it in the Spanish translation. Odoevsky's name has not, as yet at least, reappeared in the index of the subsequent volumes of this massive literary biographical study.
8. Quoted from Cornwell, *V.F. Odoyevsky*, p. 25; see this study for the sources of a range of memoir comment on Odoevsky.
9. P. Mizinov, *Istoriia i poeziia. Istoriko-literaturnye etiudy* (Moscow, 1900), pp. 488-91. There seems little or no evidence that Goncharov had Odoevsky in mind here; they seem barely to have known one another and Goncharov's Aduevs are held to be autobiographical projections (see Galya Diment, *The Autobiographical Novel of Co-Consciousness: Goncharov, Woolf, Joyce*, University Press of Florida, Gainesville,

FL, 1994). Diment writes (pp. 28-9) of the names Aleksandr Fedorovich and Petr Ivanovich (Aduev) as combining names from 'Ivan Aleksandrovich (Goncharov)'; as it happens they also involve four names to be found in the Odoevsky family tree (see Cornwell, *V.F. Odoyevsky*, pp. 280-81). Nevertheless, even accepting this, together with the phonic similarity of Odoev-Aduev, the evidence is at best flimsy.

10. Ch. Vetrinsky, 'Chelovek trekh pokolenii', in his *V sorokovykh godakh – istoriko-literaturnye ocherki i kharakteristiki* (Moscow, 1899).

11. Vetrinsky, 'Chelovek trekh pokolenii'; see Tur'ian, *"Strannaia moia sud'ba ..."*, p. 370.

12. Boris Tomaševskij, 'Literature and Biography', in *Readings in Russian Poetics: Formalist and Structuralist Views*, edited by Ladislav Matejka and Krystyna Pomorska, Michigan Slavic Contributions, No. 8, (Ann Arbor, 1978), pp. 49, 52.

13. See the essays collected in Ju.M. Lotman and B.A. Uspenskij, *The Semiotics of Russian Culture*, edited by Ann Shukman, Michigan Slavic Contributions, No. 11 (Ann Arbor, 1984).

14. Lotman and Uspenskij, *Semiotics* p. 236.

15. Ibid., pp. 79, 107.

16. Ibid., p. 153.

17. Ibid., p. 136.

18. Ibid., p. 136.

19. Ibid., p. 87.

20. Ibid., pp. 101-2.

21. Ibid., p. 145.

22. Lotman singles out Pushkin's Silvio, from the story 'Vystrel' 'The Shot', as an imitator of the characters of Byron and Marlinsky. Furthermore, he comments, 'it is interesting that the heroes of Gogol, of Tolstoj or Dostoevskij, that is, of texts which themselves imitate life, aroused no imitation among their readers' (Ibid., p. 147). This last statement may well be moot in several respects.

23. Ibid., p. 245.

24. Ibid., p. 252. The phenomenon did make a comeback, though, in the Symbolist period and again in the twentieth century (at times, arguably, of a revival of interest in romanticism and in the critical fortunes of Odoevsky).

25. Quoted from P.N. Sakulin, *Iz istorii russkogo idealizma. Kniaz' V.F. Odoevsky. Myslitel'-pisatel'*, vol. I, part 2, pp. 439-40.

26. For a full account of Odoevsky criticism up to the mid-1980s, see Neil John Cornwell, 'The Life and Works of V.F. Odoyevsky (1804-1869)', Ph.D. thesis, The Queen's University of Belfast, 1983, Chapter 11. I have resisted the temptation to publish this chapter in the present volume, on the grounds of its being overly thesistic and long-winded (and perhaps Odoevskianly 'pedantic'!).

27. Tur'ian, *"Strannaia moia su'ba ..."* (see note 4 above).

28. L.A. Levina, 'Avtorskii zamysel i khudozhestvennaia real'nost' (Filosofskii roman V.F. Odoevskogo "Russkie nochi"), *Izvestiia Akademii nauk SSSR: Seriia literatury i iazyka*, 49, 1, 1990, pp. 31-40.

29. George Eliot, *Silas Marner* (T. Nelson and Sons, London, no date), p. 9.

30. Lotman and Uspenskij, pp. xi-xii: 'Just as life on earth forms a biosphere, the single mechanism of inter-dependent dynamic life structures, so the different semiotic phenomena come into the researcher's view not as separate isolated phenomena but forming a vast picture of a single *semiosphere* ... [which] because it possesses memory which transforms the history of the system into its actually functioning mechanism, thus includes also the whole mass of texts ever created by mankind as well as programs for generating future texts.'

Chapter 2

# V.F. ODOEVSKY'S RIDICULOUS DREAM ABOUT THAT?

Although the case for an awakening of interest in the works of V.F. Odoevsky has been made from time to time in recent years, a full study of his work is still awaited.[1] In an article published in 1966, Simon Karlinsky drew attention to Odoevsky's importance as a thinker and outlined a number of areas in which Odoevsky scholarship might usefully be pursued, suggesting influences or resemblances between Odoevsky and later Russian writers, such as Turgenev, Dostoevsky, Tolstoy, and Chekhov.[2] The purpose of this chapter is to examine just one of Odoevsky's extremely varied stories, 'Zhivoi mertvets' ('The Live Corpse'), to consider it from the point of view of genre, and to relate it in terms of themes and underlying philosophical ideas to works by Dostoevsky and Maiakovsky: in particular 'Son smeshnogo cheloveka' ('The Dream of a Ridiculous Man') and *Pro eto (About That)*.

Dated 1838, but not published until 1844, 'Zhivoi mertvets' was written towards the end of Odoevsky's main period of creative literary activity, which extended from about 1830 until the early 1840s. His output of fiction ceased altogether after 1844, following the publication of his most important work, *Russkie nochi* as part of his 'Collected Works' (which managed nevertheless to leave many of his works uncollected).[3]

The plot, such as it is, is unusual, but simple. A middle-aged, successful civil servant, Vasilii Kuz'mich Aristidov, awakes one morning to find that he has died: 'What's this? – it seems I've died? ... really' (p. 306).[4] This is the very beginning of the story, which continues in a colloquial, humorous style of first-person narrative,

breaking from time to time into a form of dramatic dialogue remi-
niscent at times of Gogolian comedy: 'It's strange, very strange – the
soul's splitting from the body!' (p. 306). The 'spirit' departs from the
body, together with the soul, and observes the body lying on the
bed 'as if nothing had happened'. Looking in the mirror, it finds its
mirror image has also departed (a Hoffmannian motif). Gradually
the 'spirit' acclimatises to its new-found state, and discovers it is
able to move around and observe other people, but not to be seen
or heard by them. Having been a man of regular habits, the 'spirit'
steps out to the office as usual, and on the way is run down – rather
run through – with no ill effects by a carriage bearing down on it at
great speed (the motif of the carriage here suggests possible parallels
with Gogol's *Mertvye dushi [Dead Souls]* and with Dostoevsky's
*Prestuplenie i nakazanie [Crime and Punishment]* ). The 'spirit', becom-
ing aware of its ability to transport itself by flight to wherever it
wants to go,[5] is cheerful at first in its new-found freedom, but grad-
ually becomes more and more depressed with, on the one hand, the
loneliness and sense of alienation of its new state, and, on the other,
the remarks and actions of its erstwhile colleagues, friends, and fam-
ily, which it is unable to influence, despite attempted interjections.
A series of picaresque wanderings and scenes involving the clerks at
the department, the head of the department, Aristidov's friends,
mistresses, sons, niece, and another town where he had previously
worked and lived in gay abandon, reveal first to the reader, and
then gradually to the 'spirit' of Aristidov himself, the falsity and
shallowness of his self-satisfied complacency, and open to view the
sordid reality of a self-centred materialistic life of bourgeois provin-
ciality, based on squalid intrigue, lying, betrayal of trust, bribe-tak-
ing, and the ethic of accumulating a personal fortune at the expense
of others.[6] More and more despairing as self-awareness comes on,
the 'spirit' finds that everyone is talking about him and exposing
some aspect of his past life, or the consequences of his actions.[7] Try-
ing to escape this, he takes refuge in his grave and even flies round
the world.

Time and space are distorted, events are nightmarishly tele-
scoped, and finally, after Aristidov's son Petr poisons his brother,
and his niece Liza, who has been swindled out of her fortune by the
brothers acting under the inspiration of Aristidov's example and
upbringing, has landed in jail and gone mad, Aristidov is assailed in
an apocalyptic finale by the spirits of all those he has wronged. Pre-
sumably the abyss is to follow.

At this point, Aristidov wakes up, exclaiming 'What a stupid
dream!', berates the authors of tales such as the one he was reading
the night before: 'They don't even let a man get to sleep peacefully!'

(p. 331),[8] and ends by wondering which of his mistresses he should go and see.[9] The dream has obviously had no effect on him whatsoever.

Basically a 'society tale' with romantic trappings (the fantastic element of a 'ghost' telling the story), 'Zhivoi mertvets' is, like many of Odoevsky's stories, an amalgam of styles and devices, written with a number of intentions, to be read at a number of levels.

The Gogolian influence, strong throughout Odoevsky's fiction, has already been mentioned, and the links with the prose of the rising 'natural school' are obvious. Elements of parody are also present, both of the Hoffmannian type of fantastic tale itself in the sharp, prosaic ending, and of the Sentimentalist tale.[10] However, closer examination is warranted of the way 'Zhivoi mertvets' operates as a fantastic tale, as social satire, and as a philosophical tale, before going on to determine its possible influence on, or relation to, later works.

The immediate level on which 'Zhivoi mertvets' strikes the reader is that of the fantastic tale. What exactly constitutes the fantastic in literature? Perhaps the clearest statement of this has been made by Tzvetan Todorov:

> The fantastic is that hesitation experienced by a person who knows only the laws of nature, confronting an apparently supernatural event.[11]

The question of the fantastic arises when an unfamiliar or unexplainable event occurs in the real world. The person experiencing the event must opt for a solution based on either natural or supernatural causes. It is this hesitation between a natural and a supernatural solution that comprises the fantastic:

> The fantastic occupies the duration of this uncertainty. Once we choose one answer or the other, we leave the fantastic for a neighbouring genre, the uncanny or the marvellous.[12]

The application of Todorov's framework to 'Zhivoi mertvets' reveals considerable grounds for applying the adjective fantastic to Odoevsky's story (as indeed to a number of his other tales). The crucial question is that of hesitation between the real (uncanny) and supernatural (marvellous) alternatives which the story poses. Uncertainty is clearly felt by the 'spirit', acting as first-person narrator, who is continually questioning, and often forgetting, his state, and even asking the reader whether he would believe it. It is also, to at least some extent, felt by the reader (if the title is not too much of a giveaway). From the very beginning there are two possible explanations for the story: either the narrator is experiencing a dream or some other illusion, or the voice actually comes from 'the next world'. This is not finally resolved; in other words the doubt in the reader's

mind may persist until the very end of the story, the abrupt revela-
tion of which may, as already remarked, represent an element of pas-
tiche, and the suspicion quickly grows that Odoevsky is in fact
exploiting the genre, by presenting his overall didactic and philo-
sophical intentions in a fantastic framework.

The fantastic, then, begins with the very first sentence,[13] and con-
tinues until almost the end, when the story is finally pushed firmly
and sharply into, to use Todorov's term, the genre of the uncanny.
Other features which fit the genre of the fantastic are the use of a
familiar or 'average man' type of narrator – the world of the *chinovnik*
of course being widely portrayed in literature of the period –
designed to appeal to the average reader, who is meant to be able to
identify with the narrator (especially so in this case, in view of
Odoevsky's moralistic intention). The use of dream is also a typical
feature, as are the themes of metamorphosis (in this case purportedly
of a man into a 'spirit'), of spatio-temporal distortion (distortion of
time gradually builds up as the story goes on, and distortion of space
and distance takes place by the use of 'flying'), and of sexual desire
(in this case, as is usual in Russian literature, reduced to a very minor
role, but nevertheless present when the 'spirit' is contemplating the
sleeping Natal'ia Kazimirovna).[14] Moreover, the theme of death, with
the ultimate stress here on the finality of death ('there's no return
from the grave'), even if the spirit does drag out a miserable purga-
torial existence, is obviously an important part of fantastic literature.

The importance of fantastic literature as a precursor of psycho-
analysis has been amply stressed by Todorov,[15] and Karlinsky makes
strong claims for Odoevsky's thought in this respect too, as a pre-
cursor of the later Dostoevsky, and of Freud and Jung.[16]

The next most obvious level at which 'Zhivoi mertvets' may be
read is that of social satire. Whatever else Odoevsky may be doing,
he is quite evidently poking fun at a particular social type – the com-
placent functionary – and at his social values. Aristidov's continually
proclaimed assertion, 'I am a simple and straightforward man', is
patently the exact reverse of the truth, and he reveals his hypocriti-
cal philosophy quite early on:

> I hardly ever, so to speak, troubled my conscience – naturally, some-
> times, according to circumstances, I stretched it a bit ... Yes! Of course, I
> did stretch it a bit – but only when it was all right to stretch it ... Who is
> an enemy to himself?(p. 308)

This seems to be the way everyone else lived, and it brought
material success. In fact, apart from 'Poor Liza', who suffers disas-
trously from being too trusting, all the characters in the story live the

same way, to a greater or lesser degree (even Valkirin is ready to believe the worst of Liza). Everyone deceives Aristidov and/or each other, by lying, stealing, telling tales, or betraying trust. Odoevsky is attacking all forms of unprincipled action, compromises with expediency, and kow-towing to *obshchee mnenie* (public opinion).

> Before, I thought that conscience was something more or less like decency, I thought that if a man was careful about his behaviour, observed all social stipulations, did not fall foul of public opinion, said what everyone else said, then, that was all there was to conscience and morality. (p. 329)

Odoevsky sees the successful vulgarity of the aspiring bourgeoisie and lower aristocracy of the day as being worthless in itself and falsely based on utilitarian ethics and materialistic values. One of the objects of his satire and attack in a number of stories is the Western-based system of education. Aristidov, in 'Zhivoi mertvets', educated his sons himself, and bears full responsibility for the way they turned out:

> I wanted to make my sons into *men of reason*; I wanted to preserve them from weakness, from philanthropy, from everything that I called trifling. (p. 329).

After hearing Petr's plans to get his hands on Liza's money, Aristidov remarks, 'It's both very sensible and bad, and yet, it's very sensible ...' (*blagorazumno*).

Odoevsky's anti-Utopian stories and his attacks on the worship of reason can be seen as early blasts in the Dostoevsky-Chernyshevsky debate that was to rage in the 1860s.[17] Odoevsky saw rationality and culture as being responsible for the weakening of what he called 'instinctual energy' in man, resulting in the loss of a whole side of man's former knowledge and awareness (reflected earlier in alchemy, magic, the occult, etc.).[18]

A discussion of Odoevsky's ethics, which appear to have been based largely on Fichte,[19] and of his hostility to the overstressing of rationality and the values of traditional education, merges with the philosophical level of 'Zhivoi mertvets'. Fantastic tale and social satire 'Zhivoi mertvets' may be, but closer examination shows it to be, like many of his other works, ultimately a fictional vehicle for the illustration of Odoevsky's philosophical ideas. The first indication of this is in the epigraph:

> I wanted to give expression ... to that psychological law by which not one word pronounced by a man, not one action, is forgotten or is lost in

the world, but without fail produces some kind of action: so that respon-
sibility is connected with each word, with each apparently insignificant
action, with each impulse of a man's soul.[20] (p. 306)

The relationship between this and the story which follows is per-
fectly clear. Towards the end of his purgatorial Odyssey, Aristidov
exclaims:

> Judged from any reasonable point of view, I was no upstart, never tried
> to appear too clever, didn't exactly work my fingers to the bone, and
> achieved precisely nothing – and look at the traces I left behind me! And
> how oddly all these things are strung together, one after another! (p. 326)

The main body of the story thus emerges as a chronicle of the con-
sequences, either direct or through cause and effect, of the deeds,
example, or even thoughts, of a seemingly inconsequential man. This
stress on the examination of such a behaviour pattern over a whole
life may derive in part from Schopenhauer,[21] but is perhaps more
profitably seen as the relationship of the parts, however apparently
insignificant, to the whole. The importance of 'the whole' was funda-
mental to Odoevsky's thought from the 1820s, when as a member of
the 'Liubomudry' (wisdom lovers), he was involved in the publication
of the literary and philosophical journal *Mnemozina.* Here he empha-
sised the need to start from the 'harmonious structure of the whole' in
investigating particular aspects of being, applying this equally to the
sciences and to aesthetics.[22] The idea (the part) was to be deduced, as
was aesthetic theory, from the Schellingian Absolute (the whole) – the
point of departure for most of his ideas of this period. [23]

As a concomitant to this philosophical principle of the parts and
the whole, Odoevsky was particularly fond, like Vladimir Solov'ev
after him, of devising triads, both aesthetic and cognitive, and then
seeking an overall synthesis. With regard to aesthetics, 'poetry is the
number, music the measure, and painting the weight' of a common
truth.[24] Truth, beauty, and goodness were regarded by the 'Liubo-
mudry' as the three harmonising powers. With his later interests in
anthropology and the philosophy of history, Odoevsky stressed
again the three elements that are fused in man – the believing (rep-
resented by religion or faith), the cognitive (by science), and the aes-
thetic (by art). This crops up again in Odoevsky's critique of the
West in *Russkie nochi.* It is therefore perhaps not surprising to find a
comparable triad in 'Zhivoi mertvets'. Aristidov, on his visit to the
opera during a performance of *The Magic Flute,* and with the benefit
of hindsight from his new state beyond the grave, remarks on light,
rest, and love *(svet, pokoi, liubov'),*[25] these are the rewards for virtue
and great deeds – 'the fulfilment of all desires'.

The scene at the opera is interesting in a number of ways. It is an example of a kind of *ostranenie* technique, in which mysterious or exotic things are seen for what they are: 'the water's cardboard, and the fire is too' (p. 322). The make-believe of the theatre is thus exposed as being 'the same here as everywhere'. Aristidov attempts verbally to assail the audience (an echo of Gogol's earlier *Revizor*). Furthermore, believing in the Schillerian idea of man's restoration from 'the fall of nature' through the aesthetic sphere, and hence in the derivation of moral life, too, from the aesthetic principle, Odoevsky saw Aristidov's complete lack of aesthetic perception as a measure of his moral worthlessness, and consequently of the utter impossibility of his ultimate redemption.[26] In Odoevsky's view, there is present in art a particular kind of 'instinctual energy' which has been lost to non-artists through rationality: 'We seek to participate in art by means of this energy'.[27] There is no hope of restoration for anyone who does not.

This element of pessimism in Odoevsky's thought (he disagreed with Rousseau's idea of the excellence of man's nature in itself), may also owe something to Schopenhauer's view of human nature, the lack of conscious rational choice in everyday conduct, and the under-lying primacy of the will. In any case, the quasi-comic ending of 'Zhivoi mertvets', with Aristidov's awakening and resumption of a 'normal life', thinly conceals a basic philosophical pessimism, as well as what Belinsky called 'the rejection of a dead reality'.[28] Odoevsky's greater emphasis in the 1830s on an anthropological approach to the investigation of man's being and the many-sided life of the 'inner man' (determining outward behaviour), paralleling Schelling's later advance from nature philosophy to philosophic anthropology, is strongly reflected in this story. Aristidov's dream is a vision of immor-tality, or at least of an indeterminate period following death, as a jour-ney through one's own conscience, during which the consequences (actual or possible) of a whole life and all its component actions unfold. The whole truth has hit Aristidov like a bombshell:

> So this is life, and this is death! What a horrible difference! In life, what-ever you may have done, you can still put it right, but once you cross that threshold – your whole past is irretrievable! (p. 328.)

Feelings of guilt take over, with a demand for retribution. This is answered by a vision reminiscent of Dante's *Inferno*. However, before the apocalyptic ending of the nightmare (for such, in reality, is all it is), there is a questioning of the human condition and the pur-pose of existence, again during the scene at the opera, when Aristi-dov tells the audience:

Believe me, I have really passed through water and fire, and nothing
came of it; I lived, had money – it was good, but now what am I? Noth-
ing! (p. 322)

The existential tendency here echoes Schelling's later development,[29]
and may be a case of influence, parallel development, or indeed (in
1838) of anticipation. Furthermore, the state of spiritual 'survival'
after death is, in its determined nature and complete absence of
choice, a vision of eternity not unlike that of Sartre in *Huis Clos*.[30] It
is this extremely modern quality of aspects of Odoevsky's thought
which provokes comparison with the existential tendencies of later
writers, particularly Dostoevsky and Maiakovsky, and perhaps also
Bulgakov and Abram Terts.

It is now proposed to examine similarities between Odoevsky's
story and works by Dostoevsky and Maiakovsky. We have no evi-
dence as to whether Maiakovsky knew Odoevsky's work,[31] but we do
know that Dostoevsky did. The fact of his having known Odoevsky
personally and admired him has been documented,[32] and we know
that he knew 'Zhivoi mertvets', and that this story must have made
some impression on him, by virtue of the fact that he used the fol-
lowing lines from the end of 'Zhivoi mertvets' as the epigraph to his
first published work of fiction, *Bednye liudi (Poor Folk)*:

Oh, these story-tellers! They can't write something useful, pleasant,
soothing! They have to dig up all the dirty tricks under the sun! ... They
ought to be forbidden to write: Well, I mean to say! You read and think
about it for a bit – and then all kinds of balderdash enter your head;
really, I would forbid them to write; simply forbid them altogether.[33]

Certain of Dostoevsky's pre-exile works contain fantastic or roman-
tic elements, such as *Dvoinik (The Double)*, 'Khoziaika' ('The Land-
lady'), and *Netochka Nezvanova*, and a number of critics have pointed
to the influence of Odoevsky, as well as Hoffmann, on these works.[34]
However, there is a comparative lack of these elements in Dosto-
evsky's later work[35] until they re-emerge in somewhat different form
in the trio of 'fantastic stories' written in the 1870s: namely 'Bobok'
(1873), 'Krotkaia' ('A Gentle Creature') (1876), and 'Son smeshnogo
cheloveka' (1877). Of these three stories, only 'Bobok' and 'Son
smeshnogo cheloveka' approach the fantastic in Todorov's sense,
and even these remain safely rooted in reality, in so far as 'Bobok' is
explained from the outset as attributable to demented ravings
induced by alcohol or fever, while 'Son smeshnogo cheloveka' pur-
ports to be, as the title indicates, merely a dream.[36] This being so, it
may be more appropriate to impose another framework – that pro-
posed by Bakhtin, namely Menippean satire, which has in any case

many elements in common with fantastic literature as defined by Todorov.[37] There has never been any doubt about the philosophical nature of 'Son smeshnogo cheloveka', and it is hoped that the above discussion has established that the same may be seen also to apply to 'Zhivoi mertvets'. Major elements common to both fantastic literature and Menippean satire, and present in both stories, include the prominence of dream, an artistic conception of space and time, and an element of self-parody.

At a cursory reading, neither 'Bobok' nor 'Son smeshnogo cheloveka' may appear very close to Odoevsky's story, but closer examination of themes and ideas reveals a number of parallels.

In 'Bobok' the similarity seems to be little more than a comparable treatment of the continued consciousness and consequent conversation of the dead (in Dostoevsky's story, inconsequential chit-chat, continuing the preoccupations of inconsequential lives – an interim state of a few months before the final expiring of consciousness and the onset of we know not what – presumably nothing). In a reversal of Odoevsky's vision, the voices are heard from within the tomb by a mortal (until they are frightened off by his sneeze), and converse with each other, whereas Odoevsky's Aristidov is a solitary figure who cannot make contact with mortals or, until the end of the dream, with other of the dead. Other similarities include objections to the state of being 'dead', the importance of consciousness, and the stress of the truth ethic ('only I don't want there to be any lying').[38]

In the case of 'Son smeshnogo cheloveka' the resemblances are rather more widespread and complex, operating on three levels: similarity, inversion, and development (ideas or motifs which are to be found in Odoevsky, but which are developed or enlarged by Dostoevsky).

The most striking similarity is the use of dream in the structure of each story to highlight consciousness and to facilitate psychological penetration (in each case with results verging on psychoanalysis). In Odoevsky, Aristidov continually questions whether he is really dead; in Dostoevsky, the Ridiculous Man's awareness of being dead is greatly stressed. (In both cases, following death, the 'spirits' are able to observe what is happening in the life they have left behind, their own burial, and so on – Aristidov's observation of this is from an objective standpoint, that is, external to the body, the Ridiculous Man's subjective.) Similar too are Odoevsky's (perhaps lesser) stress on the role of falsity in the downfall of human life, and Dostoevsky's insistence on the primacy of lying in all human and social failings. The motifs of flight and distortion of space and time also figure in both, the scale of these being considerably enlarged by Dostoevsky.

Everyone is talking about Aristidov (in death), while everyone laughed at the Ridiculous Man (in life, both before and after the dream); this is accompanied by a feeling of alienation and loneliness (Aristidov in death, the Ridiculous Man in life).

Two main inversions can be picked out. Aristidov develops a feeling of guilt and conscience only after death, and this has vanished on his return to life, after the dream; the Ridiculous Man, on the other hand, starts to feel responsibility and guilt before his death, at the time of contemplating suicide – these feelings play an important part in his dream, and they are felt even more deeply after the dream. Based on this, we can say that Aristidov's dream has no ultimate effect on him, and therefore displays a pessimistic element in the philosophy of the author; the Ridiculous Man, on the other hand, is transformed by the intensity of his vision, by its essential *truth*, and is led to a position of (albeit irrational) optimism ('In one day, *in one hour*, everything could be arranged at once!' [p.441]).

We have already mentioned Dostoevsky's enlargement of the scope and scale of flight, and of temporal and spatial distortion.[39] There are a number of other instances in which themes or ideas to be found in Odoevsky are given similar treatment by Dostoevsky. In the first place, the Utopian aspect of 'Son smeshnogo cheloveka' may well owe something in origin to Odoevsky's futuristic and anti-Utopian tales. Also in the realm of ideas, Odoevsky's attack on the cult of rationality in 'Zhivoi mertvets' has been remarked on above; Dostoevsky's comments on 'a modern Russian progressive' (p. 432) and the final stress on the 'living image' (p. 440) of what the Ridiculous Man has seen, as opposed to the abstract concept (as arrived at by reason), are a demonstration of his well-known stand on this issue. Allied to this, and carried further by Dostoevsky, is Odoevsky's idea of the loss of 'instinctual energy' caused by the development of reason and culture. The people visited by the Ridiculous Man in his dream 'knew how to live without science' (p. 433), they knew how to talk to the trees, they communed with the stars, lived in harmony with nature and appeared to communicate with the dead: they had 'a certain awareness of a constant, uninterrupted, and living union with the Universe at large' (p. 434). This was just what mankind, according to Odoevsky, had lost (his view of the cause of original sin was man's taking from nature of the means to live) and should strive to reattain, though not by obviating science and reason. What was required was a new synthesis, a fusion of knowledge and culture with an all-embracing new and poetic type of science, in which the aesthetic would play its part, and nature *as a whole* would be grasped.

Aristidov's gradual realization of guilt in 'Zhivoi mertvets' is developed in the case of the Ridiculous Man until he takes on the responsibility for the wholesale corruption of the entire paradise he is visiting, the complete wrecking of a Golden Age, and in a somewhat grotesque reversal of the role of Christ – in fact as no less than an Antichrist – he demands to be crucified. This demand is treated with contempt, and he is labelled a madman. At the same time, the concentration on the examination of a single life in 'Zhivoi mertvets' is expanded to gigantic proportions in 'Son smeshnogo cheloveka' to cover not just the life of the Ridiculous Man himself, but as an allegory of world history.

The hints of existential speculation in Odoevsky take on much greater prominence in Dostoevsky's story. Before the dream takes place, the Ridiculous Man explains his feeling of its making 'no difference' ('vse ravno') 'whether the world existed or whether nothing existed anywhere at all' (p. 421). This idea he carries to the point of ultimate nihilism, denying all existence – past, present, and future:

> I began to be acutely conscious that *nothing existed in my own lifetime.* At first I couldn't help feeling that at any rate in the past many things had existed; but later on I came to the conclusion that there had not been anything even in the past, but that for some reason it had merely seemed to have been. Little by little I became convinced that there would be nothing in the future, either. (p. 421)

A⁻¹ ·'m·m·n¹ ·f in'·nd·d ⁻ i·id·· ~~·· ·hes, he speculates that, when the world ends for him, maybe the world will end altogether (p. 426). He then, approaching the point of relating his dream, says:

> What does it matter whether it was a dream or not, so long as that dream revealed the Truth to me? Once you have recognised the truth and seen it, you know that it is the truth and there can be no other, whether you are dreaming it or living it. (p. 427)

The question of the nature of dream as a transcendental mystical experience, in which 'death' is a way to a new 'life' and back again to 'reality', suggesting the possibility of parallel lives, probabilities, and visions of an alternative reality, albeit schematised or allegorical, present first in Odoevsky, is developed almost forty years later by Dostoevsky in an extremely modern manner, posing some of the same questions on the nature of reality, the illusory *maya* of this life, and a transcendental alternative, that were to be raised in the twentieth century by writers such as Hermann Hesse, for example in *Steppenwolf* and in 'The Indian Life' from *The Glass Bead Game*.⁴⁰

Strong links between Dostoevsky's works and Maiakovsky's *Pro eto* (the reference to Raskol'nikov, line 1137, is immediately striking)⁴¹ are well known,⁴² but it is only comparatively recently that similarities have been pinpointed between the last section of Maiakovsky's poem ('A request in the name of ...') and 'Son smeshnogo cheloveka'. E.J. Brown talks of 'the union of selfless and universal love' being linked with 'the golden age of human happiness' in both works and points to a number of comparisons.[43] What this essay seeks to suggest is that certain motifs and ideas that can be located in stories by Odoevsky and Dostoevsky undergo further expansion and development in fantastic poetical form in Maiakovsky's *Chelovek (Man)* and *Pro eto*.[44]

*Pro eto* (1923) stands somewhat apart from much of Maiakovsky's poetry of the Soviet period, and can be seen, in many ways, as a second part, a thematic continuation and a reappraisal of *Chelovek* (written some seven years earlier, in 1916-1917), the most important and the most complex of Maiakovsky's prerevolutionary works. For present purposes the two can be considered together.

In comparing these poems with the other works in question, the first problem that arises is the nature of the fantastic in relation to poetry. Poetry, in Todorov's view, is a genre in which normal representation is in any case rejected, and therefore the fantastic, in the sense in which we have understood it, cannot arise.[45] This lack of the possibility of the fantastic in one sense leaves the poet completely free in another, by virtue of the genre, to introduce at will 'fantastic-type' elements without having to concern him (her)self, as has the writer of prose, with questions of artificiality in the placing of the boundaries between the fantastic and the realistic. Maiakovsky exploits this possibility to the full in his poetry, by the introduction of fantastic elements, vast expansions and contractions of scale, hyperbole, and surrealistic imagery. Maiakovsky is therefore able to insert a fantastic motif such as flight without of necessity having recourse to a framework of dream, death or illusion, immune from concern about hesitation or credibility with regard to the reaction of the reader. When the suicide theme comes to the fore in *Chelovek*, the hero, Maiakovsky himself, looks for a chemist to obtain poison, but then immediately claims that as man, 'your fantastic guest',[46] is immortal, poison is not necessary – in other words death is not a prerequisite for the introduction of fantastic events, such as the passing from one 'life' to another:

> A dim realisation came over the fool,
> Gapers seen through windows.
> My hair stands on end.
> And suddenly I
> Sail lightly past the counter.
> The ceiling opens up by itself.

> (vol. I, pp. 257-8, lines 436-41.)

There then proceeds a fantastic ascent to heaven without death having to occur first even nominally.

There are a number of features common to 'Son smeshnogo cheloveka' and the Maiakovsky poems which are not shared by 'Zhivoi mertvets'. The most obvious of these is the suicide theme. Others include the presence of Christ figures, the motif of the star (present in *Chelovek* in the 'The Birth of Maiakovsky' and at the very end of the poem), and the Ruler of All *(Povelitel' vsego)*, the origin of whom may owe something to Dostoevsky's similarly named figure *(Vlastitel' vsego)* to which the Ridiculous Man makes an appeal (Dostoevsky, vol. X, p. 428).

Apart from the obvious motif of 'flying' and the persistent use of dream-reality (particularly in *Pro eto* it is often difficult to pinpoint exactly when one dream sequence ends and what passes for reality begins), there are a number of elements common to all three works under consideration. Spacio-temporal distortions, present in Odoevsky, and expanded to cosmic proportions by Dostoevsky, are continued in the same vein by Maiakovsky, with, in addition, vast projections forward in time. On a more minor level, the paranoia arising from the feeling of everyone talking about Aristidov, carried on through the Ridiculous Man, crops up again in *Pro eto*, when Maiakovsky, eavesdropping at a party, thinks everyone is talking about him (vol. IV, p. 168, lines 1179-92).[47]

The comparatively veiled attack on reason in Odoevsky, somewhat more explicit in Dostoevky, is replaced in *Pro eto* by the attack on *byt*, a word of complex connotations, including, in the context of the Maiakovsky of the 1920s, the following: the tedious detail of everyday life; detested or ridiculed aspects of bourgeois lifestyle (symbolized in *Pro eto* by tea drinking); everything Maiakovsky had been railing at in his pre-revolutionary poetry, from *Oblako v shtanakh* (*A Cloud in Trousers*) and before, to *Chelovek*; plus, and in particular, the survival or re-emergence of all these elements in the new Soviet state (bureaucracy, petty-mindedness, philistinism etc., as exemplified in the spirit of NEP). Maiakovsky's attack on the all-pervading concept of *byt*, the creeping philistinism rising again from within, and the final recognition of its presence in himself, bear a close resemblance to, and may be seen as an expansion of, Odoevsky's attack on the demon of materialism and the worship of money in 'Zhivoi mertvets' (although the class orientation of the two writers leads to an essential difference of emphasis – Maiakovsky's demon attacks humanity as a whole, especially the poor and working classes, whereas Odoevsky's strikes at the comparatively rich and powerful). The significance to Maiakovsky of the phenomenon of *byt*, together with his at least partial disillusionment with aspects of

the situation at this time (*Pro eto* is also Maiakovsky's defence of him-
self as a poet under siege from the new philistinism, in the person of
the proletarian poets, which was to destroy him in the poem, as,
eventually, in life), takes on an almost metaphysical force when com-
bined with his preoccupations with the human condition in the form
of what Stahlberger called 'cosmic alienation', leading in *Chelovek*
and *Pro eto* to a state of existential and metaphysical rebellion.[48] Thus
the existential musings present in embryo in Odoevsky and devel-
oped by Dostoevsky find their fullest expression here in
Maiakovsky, in his search for 'the man on the bridge', the
Maiakovsky of 1916, who, suicide-prone then as later, had been left
suspended in cosmic revolt, refusing to accept either the idea of
progress in this world or a bodiless existence in the next.

Maiakovsky is not hostile to reason as such, as are, in varying
degrees, Odoevsky and Dostoevsky, but he does have extreme diffi-
culty sustaining any faith in progress, sinking into ultimate despair in
*Chelovek*,[49] rising again to a new-found scientific and Utopian opti-
mism at the end of *Pro eto*, only for this to pale somewhat in *Klop (The
Bedbug)* (1928), and, tragically, to disappear altogether by the end of
the decade. The 'rational optimism' of *Pro eto* is perhaps best seen as
a kind of 'ultimate Futurism', by which all hopes – namely the triad
of faith, hope, and love – are placed in a new ᵍ olden Age of the thir-
tieth century, in which man not only will be able to, but *will* by sci-
entific means effect, at least in selected cases, a physical resurrection
of the dead. This startling idea probably derives from the views of
the philosopher N.F. Fedorov (1828-1903), and it may be noted that
Fedorov's stress on the application of science to moral problems,
indeed a new approach to the idea of science (harnessing it to the
'common cause') is not far removed from, and may well owe some-
thing to, Odoevsky's ideas on science.[50] In any case, there is certainly
common ground between the overall synthesis sought in Odoevsky's
ultimate philosophical aims, Dostoevsky's final goal of love and uni-
versal brotherhood, and Maiakovsky's Utopian optimism at the end
of *Pro eto*, when love will abandon its former sordid state, and, rang-
ing far beyond mere personification in Maiakovsky's beloved Lilia,
will cover the universe in brotherhood and harmony (Maiakovsky,
vol. IV, pp. 183-4, lines 1761-1813).

The problems arising from the question of what exactly consti-
tutes influence, or the borderline between influence, resemblance,
parallel, and anticipation, are outside the scope of this essay. Had it
been written a decade later, the term 'intertextuality' would have
been unavoidable. It is, however, hoped that the above discussion
has established links in terms of structure, themes, and ideas between
the works discussed, and that these works have been shown to be,

ultimately, vehicles for the imaginative anticipation (Odoevsky), expression (Dostoevsky), and development (Maiakovsky) of broadly comparable existential preoccupations.

## Notes

1. This was the case at the time of writing the first draft of this essay (1976) and of its publication (1979). Since then, see Cornwell (1986) and Tur'ian (1990).
2. Simon Karlinsky, 'A Hollow Shape: The Philosophical Tales of Prince Vladimir Odoevsky', in *Studies in Romanticism*, vol. 5, no. 3 (1966), pp. 169-82. Links are made between various works by Odoevsky and the following: Turgenev, 'Prizraki' ('Phantoms'); Dostoevsky, *Zapiski iz podpol'ia (The Notes from Underground)* and the whole Dostoevsky-Chernyshevsky debate of the 1860s, and subsequently *Idiot (The Idiot)* and *Brat'ia Karamazovy (The Brothers Karamazov)*; Tolstoy, *Smert' Ivana Il'icha (The Death of Ivan Ilyich)* and *Zhivoi trup (The Live Corpse)*; and Chekhov, 'Chernyi monakh' ('The Black Monk') and 'Skuchnaia istoriia' ('A Dreary Story'). On Odoevsky's possible influence on *The Notes from Underground* see the previously unpublished fragments in the first Soviet edition of *Russkie nochi* (Leningrad, 1975), pp. 236-41, which include speculation on the implications of 2 x 2 = 4; see also R.G. Nazirov, 'Vladimir Odoevsky i Dostoevsky', in *Russkaia literatura*, 1974, no. 3, pp. 203-6. There are also, of course, links with Gogol' (see notes 5 and 8 below, and references in the main text).
3. *Sochineniia kniazia V.F. Odoevskogo v trekh tomakh*, (St. Petersburg, 1844).
4. Quotations from 'Zhivoi mertvets' are from my translation, which appears in *Russian Romantic Prose: An Anthology*, edited by Carl R. Proffer (Ann Arbor, 1979), based on the text of V.F. Odoevsky, *Povesti i rasskazy* (Moscow, 1959), pp. 306-31; page references are to the Russian edition.
5. The motif of flight might suggest comparison with Turgenev's fantasy 'Prizraki' ('Phantoms'), but there is little other similarity, and a particular dream of Turgenev's own has been identified as the probable source for his story (see Marina Ledkovsky, *The Other Turgenev* (Würzburg, 1973), p. 81). Indeed 'Sil'fida' ('The Sylph') (1837), has been suggested as a more likely contributory source for Turgenev's story (see I.S. Turgenev, *Polnoe sobranie sochinenii i pisem v dvadtsati vos'mi tomakh*, vol. IX (Moscow and Leningrad, 1965), p. 476. Nevertheless, the motif of flight can be traced from Gogol, 'Strashnaia mest'' ('The Terrible Vengeance') and 'Vii', through Odoevsky, 'Zhivoi mertvets' and Lermontov, *Demon (The Demon)*, to Turgenev, 'Prizraki', and Dostoevsky, 'Son smeshnogo cheloveka', on to Maiakovsky, *Chelovek (Man)*, and Bulgakov, *Master i Margarita (The Master and Margarita)*.
6. This can be compared to Odoevsky's own story 'Brigadir' ('The Brigadier') and in certain respects to Tolstoy's 'Smert' Ivana Il'icha' (see again Karlinsky, quoted above). A connection can also be seen with Tolstoy's story 'Fal'shivyi kupon' ('The False Coupon'), with its karma-like spreading of evil through a chain of cause and effect (this may also be relevant to the possible Schopenhauer influence – see note 21 below).

7. The only good word said of him comes from his obituary in the paper, which has been identified as a dig at *Severnaia pchela*, the conservative paper edited by Bulgarin and Grech, with whom Odoevsky had a long-standing feud (*Povesti i rasskazy*, quoted above, p. 487).

8. This passage may be compared to the last two paragraphs of Gogol's 'Nos' ('The Nose'), published in 1836 in *Sovremennik*, of which journal Odoevsky was a co-founder and editor, with Pushkin.

9. The question of Aristidov's mistresses and the discrepancy in the name of one of them (pp. 314 and 331) will be the subject of a separate short excursus, which follows this essay.

10. The figure of Liza, seeming also to prefigure some of Dostoevsky's female characters, clearly looks back to the Sentimentalists – and in particular Karamzin. The words *bednost'* and *bednaia* are continually associated with Liza and her *kvartirka*, eventually leading to her being labelled 'Bednaia Liza'. This is then repeated twice within a short space.

11. Tzvetan Todorov, *The Fantastic: a structural approach to a literary genre* (Cleveland and London, 1973), chapter 2, 'Definition of the Fantastic'. Todorov also quotes a very similar statement on the subject by Vladimir Solov'ev (pp. 25-26). Although recognizing Todorov's definition as 'an acute and useful insight', Eric S. Rabkin allows a somewhat wider cross-genre application of the fantastic, which he defines as 'a quality of astonishment that we feel when the ground rules of a narrative world are suddenly made to turn about 180 degrees' (*The Fantastic in Literature* (Princeton, 1976), pp. 118n and 41). For the purposes of this paper, Todorov's framework seems the more applicable. For subsequent references to Todorov's theory, see Neil Cornwell, *The Literary Fantastic: From Gothic to Postmodernism* (New York and London, 1990).

12. A natural or rational explanation thus delivers a work over to the genre of the (merely) uncanny (the strange, the coincidental, the contrived, or the imagined, as may be the case), while a supernatural or inexplicable (by the laws of our world) solution leads on to the genre of the marvellous (the world of fairy tale, the 'next life' or a mystical but purportedly existing dreamland, such as the 'distant lands' of the German Romantics). The hesitation between these two alternatives will normally be on the part of the fictional protagonist (usually a first-person narrator for reasons of structural or psychological convenience), but may very well also be on the part of the reader, if the work is at all convincing. Furthermore, a work of the fantastic will normally contain a number of typical themes, about which more will be said shortly. (See Todorov, op. cit.)

13. This may be compared to Todorov's analysis of Kafka's *Metamorphosis*, in which the fantastic also enters in the very first sentence, and in which adaptation on the part of the protagonist to an inexplicable event (just as the 'spirit' in 'Zhivoi mertvets' is largely concerned with adaptation to its new state) takes over from hesitation as the main preoccupation. This, in Todorov's view, is to be seen as a 'modern' feature (Todorov, op. cit., pp. 169-73).

14. *Povesti i rasskazy*, p. 315.

15. Todorov, op. cit., pp. 160-1. Rabkin goes even further in this respect, and concludes by demonstrating the fantastic to be 'a basic mode of human knowing' and development (Rabkin – see concluding chapter 'The Scope of the Fantastic').

16. Karlinsky, op. cit.

17. Ibid.

18. For an account of Odoevsky's philosophical ideas and importance, see V.V. Zenkovsky, *A History of Russian Philosophy*, translated by George L. Kline (London, 1953), vol. 1, pp. 134-48. The fullest account of Odoevsky's philosophy

(most of which remains unpublished) is, however, in P.N. Sakulin, *Iz istorii russkogo idealizma. Kniaz' V.F. Odoevsky* (Moscow, 1913). Sakulin sees the epigraph to 'Zhivoi mertvets' (p. 306) as a constant 'law' ('zakon sokhraneniia idei i dukhovnoi energii') throughout Odoevsky's work, and the basis for his sociological ideas of the 1840s and 1850s (Sakulin, vol. I, part 2, p. 156). From a literary point of view, however, Sakulin followed Belinsky's somewhat blinkered reception of the story by describing it as 'ochen' slab' (vol. I, part 2, pp. 153-57).

19. Odoevsky's ethics seem to derive largely from Fichte's view of the nature of evil, which was seen as being caused by laxity, disloyalty of moral will, and compromise with duty, leading to cowardice and falseness. No surrender to expediency is ever justifiable. Fichte's statement 'I positively owe every man absolute frankness and truthfulness' seems to find echoes in Aristidov. See *The Encyclopaedia of Philosophy*, edited by Paul Edwards (New York and London, 1967), vol. III, p. 195, on Fichte's moral philosophy. Fichte's stress on the unique career of each person may have influenced Odoevsky's approach in 'Zhivoi mertvets', as may his emphasis on involvement and participation in the social and institutional milieu.

20. See note 18.

21. For suggestions that Odoevsky knew Schopenhauer as early as the 1830s, see Sigrid Maurer's doctoral dissertation 'Schopenhauer in Russia' (Ann Arbor, Michigan: University Microfilms, Inc , 1968), pp. 78-9, quoted in Marina Ledkovsky, pp. 26 and 159. See also note 6 above.

22. Zenkovsky, op. cit., vol. I, p. 137.

23. Schelling taught that organisms and works of art can only be properly understood teleologically, as entities in which the parts serve the whole and the whole itself is purposive. See *The Encyclopaedia of Philosophy*, cited above, vol. VII, p. 307.

24. Quoted from James H. Billington, *The Icon and the Axe* (New York 1970, p. 330).

25. The triad of *svet, pokoi,* and *liubov'* as the most desirable rewards of an afterlife seem strangely anticipatory of the values upheld in the novels of Bulgakov, where they appear (though not as a triad as such) as desiderata in *Belaia gvardiia (The White Guard)* and again as eternal rewards in *Master i Margarita.*

26. It should be remembered that Odoevsky was, among many other things, a musicologist, that he greatly admired Mozart, and assigned the highest place in aesthetics to music.

27. See Zenkovsky, op. cit. It would appear that aspects of Odoevsky's thought were at least in part responsible for propelling him into such a diversity of parallel careers throughout his life, out of a desire to embrace as far as possible the 'harmonious structure of the whole'.

28. V.G. Belinsky, *Polnoe sobranie sochinenii* (Moscow, 1953-55), vol. VIII, p. 305.

29. In his consideration of man's being in the world, Schelling was impelled to pose the question: 'Why is there anything at all? Why not nothing?' See *The Encyclopaedia of Philosophy*, vol. VII, p. 309.

30. See Arthur C. Danto, *Sartre* (London, 1975), pp. 45-6.

31. It is, however, certain that Khlebnikov knew something of Odoevsky – see references in 'Zakon pokolenii' (dated September, 1914), V.V. Khlebnikov, *Sobranie sochinenii,* 4 vols. (Munich, 1968-72), vol. III, p. 429; and R.V. Duganov, 'Kratkoe isskustvo poezii Khlebnikova', in *Izvestiia Akademii nauk SSSR. seriia literatury i iazyka,* no. 5 (1974), p. 423. This, together with the appearance of Sakulin's monumental study (see note 18) and the reprinting of *Russkie nochi* (both in 1913) makes it not unlikely that Maiakovsky had some knowledge of Odoevsky, direct or indirect.

32. F.M. Dostoevsky, *Polnoe sobranie sochinenii v tridtsati tomakh,* vol. I (Leningrad, 1972), pp. 470, 472, 480. See also Leonid Grossman, *Dostoevsky,* trans. Mary Mackler (London, 1974), p. 131. Grossman suggests that Odoevsky may have served as a prototype for Prince X of *Netochka Nezvanova* and mentions the influence of Odoevsky's 'artistic stories'. See also Cornwell (1986), pp. 260-63.

33. See the notes to *Povesti i rasskazy,* p. 487: 'It was not by chance that Dostoevsky used a quotation from Odoevsky's "The Live Corpse" as the epigraph to his first work, *Poor Folk.* Even the intonation of the protagonist's colloquial speech comes over in Dostoevsky's novella, and the epigraph takes on the appearance of being part of Makar Devushkin's letter'.

34. See, for example, Grossman, p. 131; Victor Terras, *The Young Dostoevsky (1846-1849),* (The Hague, 1969), p. 51; and G.M. Fridlender, *Realizm Dostoevskogo* (Moscow and Leningrad, 1964), p. 70.

35. Todorov considers that Dostoevsky's novels may be included in the category of the uncanny, which is limited on one side (that of the fantastic) and on the other dissolves into the general field of literature (Todorov, p. 46).

36. Some writers have taken the lines 'even if it was a dream, all this couldn't not have been', and 'all this, perhaps, was not a dream at all' (F.M Dostoevsky, *Sobranie sochinenii v desiati tomakh* [Moscow, 1956-58], vol. X, p. 436) to be intended literally, and have therefore speculated on the possible entry of the fantastic into the story (e.g. W.W. Rowe, *Dostoevsky: Child and Man in his Works* [New York and London, 1968], p. 97); or have commented on the 'dream-like quality of Dostoyevsky's realism' (Richard Peace, *Dostoyevsky* [Cambridge, 1971], p. 309).

37. Mikhail Bakhtin, *Problems of Dostoevsky's Poetics,* trans. by R.W. Rotsel [Ann Arbor, 1973] (especially pp. 122-28 for his discussion of 'Son smeshnogo cheloveka'). One can speculate that, had Bakhtin read Odoevsky, he might well have identified a number of his stories as examples of the genre, and named Odoevsky as a precursor of Dostoevsky in this respect, along with various classical and European sources, such as Hoffmann and Poe – particularly as he recognizes Menippea as 'a genre of ultimate philosophical questions'. For a discussion of the possible application of the same genre to Bulgakov's *Master i Margarita,* which may derive in some small part from Odoevsky's work (see notes 5 and 25) see Ellendea Proffer, 'The Master and Margarita', in *Major Soviet Writers,* ed. Edward J. Brown (Oxford, 1973), pp. 390-2.

38. Dostoevsky, *Sobranie sochinenii v desiati tomakh,* vol. X, p. 355 – page numbers henceforth refer to this edition. Translations from 'The Dream of a Ridiculous Man' are taken, with slight alterations, from David Magarshak's version in *Great Short Works of Fyodor Dostoevsky* (New York, 1968), pp. 717-38.

39. For an examination of the treatment of time and space, light and darkness, and other polarities and ambiguities in narrator and structure, see Roger W. Phillips, 'Dostoevsky's *Dream of a Ridiculous Man:* A Study in Ambiguity', in *Criticism,* vol. 17 (1975): 355-63.

40. Hesse wrote an essay entitled 'The Brothers Karamazov or the end of Europe' (1920), in which he identified Dostoevsky as the prophet of the European catastrophe. For references to the impact of Dostoevsky on Hesse's thought see Ernst Rose, *Faith from the Abyss: Hermann Hesse's Way from Romanticism to Modernity* (London, 1966).

41. All references are to Vladimir Maiakovsky, *Polnoe sobranie sochinenii v trinadtsati tomakh,* Moscow, 1955-1961. *Pro eto* is in vol. IV (1957), pp. 135-84.

42. Evidence for this is to be found in the works themselves, backed up by the testimony of Lilia Brik, 'Predlozhenie issledovateliam', in *Voprosy literatury,* 1966, no. 4. See also Lawrence Stahlberger, *The Symbolic System of Majakovskii* (The Hague,

1964); and I. Corten, 'The Influence of Dostoevskij on Majakovskij's Poem, *Pro eto*', in *Studies presented to Roman Jakobson by his Students* (Cambridge, Massachusetts, 1968), pp. 76-83; and Edward J. Brown (see note 43).

43. Edward J. Brown, *Mayakovsky: A Poet in the Revolution* (Princeton, 1973), pp. 248-56. This is one of the best analyses of Maiakovsky's major poetry and is also useful for its summaries of the views of a number of Soviet critics. See also Stahlberger, op. cit., and Roman Jakobson, 'On a Generation that Squandered its Poets', in *Major Soviet Writers*, pp. 7-32.

44. 'Son smeshnogo cheloveka' has also been suggested as an influence on the fantastic stories of Abram Terts (see Richard Lourie, *Letters to the Future: An Approach to Sinyavsky-Tertz* (Ithaca and London, 1975), pp. 129-30). In connection with Terts, it is also interesting to note that he considered 'the most socialist' Maiakovsky, when writing in a fantastic vein, to be the one artistically successful exponent of Socialist Realism (*Fantasticheskii mir Abrama Tertsa* [New York, 1967], pp. 442 and 446).

45. 'If as we read a text we reject all representation, considering each sentence as a pure semantic combination, the fantastic *could not appear*: for the fantastic requires a reaction to events as they appear in the world evoked. For this reason, the fantastic can subsist only within fiction; poetry cannot be fantastic (though there may be anthologies of 'fantastic poetry')' (Todorov, op. cit., p. 60). See also Cornwell (1990), pp. 4 and 230, n. 2.

46. The Russian word *nebyvalyi* means 'unprecedented' or 'imaginary' as well as 'fantastic'. Perhaps an apt translation here would be 'poetic'.

47. Brown, op. cit., p. 244, suggests that this scene is reminiscent of *Dvoinik*, and other suggestions have been made of Odoevsky's possible influence on that work (see note 34).

48. Stahlberger, op. cit., p. 63.

49. See Brown, op. cit., pp. 168-9.

50. For a discussion of the links between the thought of Fedorov, Dostoevsky, and Maiakovsky, see Brown, op. cit., pp. 253-5

# EXCURSUS:
# A NOTE ON ARISTIDOV'S MISTRESSES

At the end of V. F. Odoevsky's story 'Zhivoi mertvets' ('The Live Corpse', 1838) the protagonist, Vasilii Kuz'mich Aristidov, awakes from what has been a lengthy and frightening dream journey through his own conscience, exclaiming 'What a stupid dream!' (p. 331), and, seemingly unaffected by the harrowing psychological surgery of the dream, merely berates the authors of tales such as the one he was reading the night before for causing his sleep to be disturbed.[1] The tale then ends with Aristidov wondering which one of his mistresses to go and see.

The three references to Aristidov's mistresses during the story give rise to a rather bizarre point. His two mistresses are first named, in a conversation between the clerks overheard by Aristidov, as Karolina Karlovna and Natal'ia Kazimirovna (p. 309). The former, in Aristidov's own musings a little later in the same dream sequence, which makes up almost the entire story, has rather strangely become Karolina *Ivanovna* (p. 314). By the end of the story, however, she has reverted to the name of Karolina Karlovna. Can any explanation be offered for this inconsistent patronymic?

It has been suggested to me that the switching of patronymic (from and to the Germanic 'Karlovna') may have been intended to signal a link, or even an actual point of identification, between Aristidov and the Important Person of Gogol's 'Shinel'' ('The Overcoat').[2] The Important Person has a mistress named Karolina Ivanovna, described as 'a lady, seemingly of German extraction'.[3] The discrepancy in patronymic, if not merely a sign of Aristidov's confused mental state (or, to take the simplest explanation, either an authorial or a printing error), may thus be a deliberate ploy by Odoevsky to draw the reader's attention to the patronymic, hinting at the same national origin, and indeed doubtful origins, as the Gogolian paramour, and thereby linking in the reader's mind Aristidov and Gogol's Important Person. It may also be noted that in a variant of 'Shinel'' the Important Person's mistress went under the name of Nastas'ia Karlovna.[4]

A complete identification between Aristidov and the Important Person would appear to be unlikely, in view of a number of differences in biographical and family detail. If any such link does, however, exist between the two stories, it is not possible to be certain who borrowed from whom. 'Shinel'', written between 1839 and 1841, was published in 1842, while 'Zhivoi mertvets', dated 1838, was not published until 1844. The date of publication, however, plus other Gogolian allusions in 'Zhivoi mertvets' and Odoevsky's known penchant for borrowing characters from other writers, would suggest that Odoevsky borrowed a type, if nothing more, in this case too. A comparison between 'Shinel' and 'Zhivoi mertvets', and also Odoevsky's 'Zapiski grobovshchika' ('Notes of an Undertaker', also of 1838) has, incidentally, already been made in Gogol' criticism.[5]

There is, however, at least one further possibility. The use of the 'Karlovna' patronymic may be an intended slight at the expense of the popular contemporary writer and poetess Karolina Karlovna Pavlova (1807-1893), herself of German origin (née Jaenisch). Odoevsky is known to have made use of the figure of Pavlova in his fiction on at least one other occasion, when she served as the prototype for the character of Countess Rozenshtein in the fragmentary epistolary story 'Most' ('The Bridge'), written at the beginning of the 1840s.[6] Any such link with Pavlova would, of course, in no way account for the switch to 'Ivanovna' in the middle of the story.

The original manuscript of 'Zhivoi mertvets' appears not to have survived, but the inconsistencies in patronymic occur in both the 1844 publications of the story (*Otechestvennye zapiski*, vol. XXXII, and then *Sochineniia kniazia V. F. Odoevskogo*, part 3). More significant, perhaps, is the fact that this matter was not 'corrected' in Odoevsky's revisions of his works carried out in 1862 for a proposed second edition (which, for some reason, never went to print), despite 'Zhivoi mertvets' having been singled out for particular correction, extending to minute details of style and punctuation.[7] This would seem to confirm that the inconsistent naming of Aristidov's apparently Germanic mistress was, whatever the motivation, deliberate, for it would appear unlikely that no one, during the period from 1844 to 1862, would have brought to the author's attention such an apparently careless slip of the pen.

# Notes

1. This short note arises out of my article 'V. F. Odoyevsky's Ridiculous Dream About That?', in *Quinquereme – New Studies in Modern Languages*, Vol. 2 (1979), pp. 75-86 and 246-55. See previous chapter. My translation of the story appears in *Russian Romantic Prose: An Anthology* (Ann Arbor, 1979); revised in Vladimir Odoevsky, *The Salamander and Other Gothic Tales* (London, 1992).
2. Simon Karlinsky, private letter, dated 9 March 1977.
3. N.V. Gogol', *Shinel'*, in *Polnoe sobranie sochinenii*, vol. III (Leningrad, 1938), p . 171.
4. Ibid., p. 459.
5. See V. L. Komarovich's commentary, *Gogol'*, vol. III, p. 689.

6.  See P. N. Sakulin, *Iz istorii russkogo idealizma. Kniaz' V. F. Odoevsky*, Moscow, 1913, vol. I, part 2, pp. 122-23.

7.  A copy of Odoevsky's collected works (St. Petersburg, 1844) in three volumes, incorporating corrections, revisions, and additions for the proposed second edition, is preserved in the Odoevsky archive at the Saltykov-Shchedrin State Public Library in St. Petersburg (Fond 539, V. F. Odoevsky, opis' 1, binders 67-69).

# Chapter 3

# PERSPECTIVES ON ODOEVSKY'S ROMANTICISM

## I

Western histories of Russian literature have generally relegated V. F. Odoevsky to the sidelines as a minor figure of romantic prose, with a brief mention of *Russkie nochi (Russian Nights)* and little else. He has been accorded the occasional chapter in more specialised studies dealing with a particular theme, such as the impact on Russian literature of the German romantics, Goethe and Hoffmann.[1] John Mersereau, in his article 'The Chorus and Spear Carriers of Russian Romantic Fiction', has said that 'Prince V.F. Odoyevsky was good enough at least part of the time to take a leading role, especially when compared with Gogol in poor form (e.g. *The Portrait)';* Victor Terras has called him 'Russia's leading romantic storyteller', while Donald Fanger referred to Odoevsky as 'one of the visitors to Russian literature of the twenties, described by Marlinsky in 1825 as a "steppe, occasionally enlivened by the swift passage of journalistic Bedouins or ponderously moving caravans of translations"' and as a 'prospector in search of the philosopher's stone'.[2] An eloquent plea for Odoevsky to be treated as a major figure was made by Simon Karlinsky in an article of 1966.[3] This kind of prominence for Odoevsky has never really been acknowledged, however, in Russian and Soviet criticism of the past 150 years.

One of a number of curious circumstances arising from the creative biography of V.F. Odoevsky is the fact that, apart from his voluminous efforts in the fields of philosophy, musicology and popular education, he had three virtually self-contained and separate literary careers.[4]

The first began in the early 1820s, reached its height with the publication of the almanac *Mnemozina* in 1824-1825 and fizzled out in the aftermath of the Decembrist revolt. The tail end of this period merged indeterminately with the beginnings of the second period which really started in about 1830 and again faded after the publication in 1844 of a three-volume 'Collected Works'.[5] The third period can be said to have started in the mid-1850s and continued until Odoevsky's death in 1869. The first period made perhaps the greatest immediate impact on the advanced reading public of the day and is remembered not only as Odoevsky's formative period, but as the only stage (the heyday of the 'Liubomudry' or wisdom lovers) when his ideas could be said to have been at the very forefront of the development of Russian thought. The middle period was his most productive and successful from an artistic point of view and has naturally provided the staple diet for the bulk of Odoevsky criticism. The third period resulted in very little completed or published work and has been accorded much less attention.

Odoevsky's work of the first part of the 1820s attracted considerable attention almost from the start. *Mnemozina* quickly aroused, as had been its intention, critical controversy and a number of leading figures recorded its impact'. In the 1830s, Odoevsky began to publish his mature romantic and society tales, both singly and in cycles, and these attracted mixed critical comment with such figures as Pushkin and Gogol, for example, admiring at least some of Odoevsky's work, while the publication of *Russkie nochi* in 1844 and Belinsky's review article on the Collected Works may be said to have inaugurated Odoevsky criticism proper.[7] Critical discussion of Odoevsky's work has been largely dominated, from Belinsky to the present day, by the attitude adopted towards the romantic elements, whether identified as such or not. A full discussion of Belinsky's criticism of Odoevsky, and of their personal relations, will be presented in Chapter Five of the present study. As has been suggested earlier, it would be unjust to lay too much blame at Belinsky's door for Odoevsky's subsequent neglect; Belinsky's successors and interpreters were even more responsible and other factors were involved – not least Odoevsky's early departure from the literary scene and failure to reprint his works.

The only other serious contemporary review, by Valerian Maikov, also divided Odoevsky's works into two categories: that of the mystical (which includes nearly all of *Russkie nochi)* and that of *'povesti* of unquestionable literary worth and to which mysticism is alien'.[8] Mysticism has no place in literature (other than folk literature), which now requires 'the exposition of society and its development and of the spirit of the people' – in other words 'realism' (a term which

Maikov, like Belinsky, does not use). However, when Maikov turns to the works in which 'human life, our sufferings and our misfortunes' can be found, that is 'Kniazhna Zizi' ('Princess Zizi') and 'Kniazhna Mimi' ('Princess Mimi'), his tone immediately changes.

From 1845 until his death in 1869, Odoevsky's name appeared only fleetingly in the pages of Russian literary criticism, but one critic who paid some attention to his work was Apollon Grigor'ev. Grigor'ev, like Odoevsky, took his basic conception of art from Schelling; at the same time he considered himself, in certain senses at least, to be a follower of Belinsky.[9] In his sympathetic review of Gogol's *Selected Passages from Correspondence with Friends* (1847), Grigor'ev compares that 'apparent, for him dark, strength' pervading Odoevsky's 'Gorod bez imeni' ('Town without a Name') to Gogol's idea of evil.[10] Much more sympathetic to romantic mysticism than most of his predecessors and contemporaries, Grigor'ev nevertheless followed Belinsky and Maikov in his reading of much of Odoevsky's work: it was in his evaluation that he differed. His *Moskvitianin* articles of 1852 contain several references to Odoevsky:

> In the fine didactic stories of Odoevsky ['A Dead Man's Sneer', 'Town without a Name', 'Apartment with Heat and Lighting (*Kvartira s otopleniem i osveshcheniem)]* you will hear only a negative emotion [*pafos*], an emotion on a par with the bitter irony of Hamlet, with the sceptic's smile of sorrow, with the vague strivings of the mystic. You feel that hostility has not overpowered reality here, does not possess it in a manly way, and merely cries over it, merely promises something better in the misty boundless distance.[11]

In the character of Princess Mimi, Grigor'ev sees neither a living being nor a type but an idea, and a monstrous one at that, 'drawn out, like a mathematical computation, from exclusively melancholy and gloomy observations, a truly dialectically developed passion'.[12] He thus hints at the presence of an element of philosophical duality, divines an essential pessimism and expresses a certain dissatisfaction in the treatment of social reality.

A. Skabichevsky's 'Forty Years of Russian Criticism' *(Otechestvennye zapiski,* 1870) described Odoevsky as a 'well-known, but, unfortunately, little appreciated writer'.[13] The Populist critic took a somewhat impressionistic view of aesthetics and regarded Odoevsky as a 'second-rank' *(vtorostepennyi)* artist, but of great historical importance as a man of ideas. Skabichevsky places great emphasis on the historical importance of Schellingianism in Russia, which philosophy, with its pantheistic and intuitive elements and stress on intellectual contemplation, he saw as 'a progressive step forward' for its day, as well as 'completely corresponding to that apotheosis of feeling and fantasy in which our romantic movement manifested itself in the 1820s'. Skabichevsky pointed out the error of attempting to see Odoevsky as either a Slavophile or a Westerniser (it was possible in the 1830s to be a mixture of both and Schellingianism could serve as a base for either persuasion) and commented that Belinsky had failed to appreciate all sides of Odoevsky because of being too closely his contemporary. Yet Skabichevsky does not appear to have appreciated the extent of Odoevsky's later drift towards positivism and was also puzzled, like most of his predecessors, by the form of *Russkie nochi*.

Ch. Vetrinsky (1899) complained of the neglect of figures such as Odoevsky, drew attention to the theme of moral death in Odoevsky's work and suggested that 'Sebastian Bach' may have been based on Odoevsky's own domestic life.[14] P. Mizinov considered that the personal and biographical elements in Odoevsky's works had not yet been touched on and made an identification between the young Odoevsky and Griboedov's Chatsky (and, less plausibly perhaps, between Odoevsky and Goncharov's Aduev); Mizinov also stressed the possible influence of Odoevsky on Gogol's 'Nos' ('The Nose'*)* and 'Portret' ('The Portrait') and saw him as 'another Faust'.[15] An original, if slightly extravagant, approach by N. A. Kotliarevsky claimed Odoevsky for the Symbolist tradition: Odoevsky's goddess was always wisdom *(mudrost')* and as a writer he 'set himself the grandiose, almost unfulfillable task ... he wanted to let us see the unseeable, to speak of the inexpressible in concrete images'.[16] Kotliarevsky held *Russkie nochi* to be of immense importance, though he regarded it as simply stories 'supplied with a special philosophical commentary', and correctly stated that Odoevsky was trying to be at one and the same time 'poet, philosopher and publicist'. The reason that his stories seemed hazy *(tumannye)* to many of his contemporaries was perhaps that 'the real story was written between the lines'. *Russkie nochi,* 'permeated with romanticism and metaphysics', represented not merely 'the confession of a whole generation which has accomplished its task and is making way for new people', but also signalled 'the long sleep of metaphysical thought'.

B. A. Lezin's 1907 study, quoting from unpublished sources, stresses the autobiographical and subjective qualities in Odoevsky's work. Lezin regards *Russkie nochi* as an 'author's confession' and Arist (Odoevsky's early protagonist of the 1820s, in whom he also sees affinities with Chatsky) as a prototype of the later Faust.[17] He sees the embodiment of Odoevsky's 'practical activity' in *Segeliel' ili Don Kikhot XIX veka (Segeliel' or a Don Quixote of the 19th Century).* The supposed 'death' of Faust, subsequent to the action of *Russkie nochi,* Lezin sees as proof that Odoevsky developed beyond his Faust stage. He considers the form of *Russkie nochi* to have been borrowed from *The*

*Decameron,* stresses the dominance in it of the idea of the infinite, Odoevsky's use of antithesis and the theme of the inadequacy of language, while seeing its essential message as one of optimism and faith in the radiant future *(svetloe budushchee).*

I.I. Zamotin saw Odoevsky's view of art not as a copy of nature, but the depiction of beauty of the spirit in material form, the representation of the infinite in the finite. Life was seen as 'a synthesis of the elements of the ideal and the real'.[18] These ideas Odoevsky was attempting to demonstrate in *Russkie nochi,* which undervalued work, Zamotin felt, occupied an outstanding place in Russian literature of the 1830s. Its form Zamotin saw not so much as Hoffmannian as that of classical drama; with its dialogue and chorus figure it contained the inspiration of Plato as well as that of Schelling.[19]

R. V. Ivanov-Razumnik, stressing the impact of German philosophy on the intellectual development and literature of Russia, wrote of the 'link of continuity' between the circles of Odoevsky (in the 1820s) and Stankevich.[20] Schelling, the essence of whose philosophy is 'romanticism of genius', was regarded by Razumnik as the undisputed 'philosophical ideologue of this remarkable current of the early nineteenth century'.

P. N. Sakulin's monumental study of 1913, by far the most ambitious and detailed work on Odoevsky ever attempted, immediately became the essential reference work for all subsequent Odoevsky scholarship; therein lies its main worth, although it will also yield perceptive observations to the persistent reader. Sakulin's basic thesis is that Odoevsky's career can be divided into three periods: the period of the 'Liubomudry' and *Mnemozina* (Schellingianism); the period of 'philosophical-mystical idealism' fully expressed in *Russkie nochi;* and, dating from the second half of the 1840s, that of 'scientific realism'[21] (by which Sakulin means positivism). This labelling is now generally adjudged oversimplistic, and Sakulin's own apparent realisation of this may well have been a factor in his failure to complete his mammoth project. His traditional enough verdict on *Russkie nochi* as 'the poetic monument of philosophical-mystical idealism' has also since been questioned.[22]

The first significant response to Sakulin's study was an article by Vasilii Gippius.[23] Sakulin, in Gippius's view, 'is inclined to resolve too simply the question of Odoevsky's ideological evolution' as 'inevitable'. Odoevsky's romanticism is thereby presumed to be 'an unfortunate youthful aberration'; Sakulin thereby reveals himself to be fundamentally hostile to romanticism. Sakulin fails to compare Odoevsky with the Jena school of romanticism, and therefore the proximity he sees between Odoevsky and 'the epigone of romanticism', Hoffmann, carries less conviction. Odoevsky's romanticism should, Gippius believes, be approached 'from the point of view of romanticism', in which case it is not so much Odoevsky's 'closeness to the tenets of romanticism' that convinces us that he will later renounce these tenets, as his 'secret schism from them'. The real key is the consistent underlying presence (the story between the lines suspected by Kotliarevsky?), in Odoevsky's fiction from *Dnevnik studenta (A Student's Diary)* to *Russkie nochi*, of a pessimistic dualism, which Gippius credits Grigor'ev with having been the first to spot. He points to the influence on the 'Liubomudry' of Spinoza and regards Schelling, too, not so much as having been faithfully followed by Odoevsky as 'somehow accommodated to his dualistic disposition'. This dualism is epitomised in 'the hopeless schism of soul and flesh', the 'everyday living' *(vse zhivoe)* covered by a 'cold membrane' *(kholodnaia obolochka)* in 'Sil'fida' ('The Sylph') or the 'human clothing' *(chelovecheskaia odezhda)* in *Segeliel'*. Even the supposedly realistic 'Kniazna Mimi' is not exempt: Gippius refers to the omitted prologue in which 'devils' are shown to be living in Mimi's cellar[24] and asks what Belinsky would have made of that. A lover, potential or actual, of the female sex is presented as either a Philistine *(meshchanka)* of this world or an enchantress *(volshebnitsa)* from another one. 'Salamandra' ('The Salamander'), 'Kosmorama' ('The Cosmorama') and 'Sil'fida'. *Russkie nochi* Gippius sees as Odoevsky's romantic 'universal novel', the search to make sense of the world through studying the links between various phenomena. He sees the form as closer to Tieck's *Phantasus* than to Hoffmann. He singles out the barbs against reason and the notion that 'science must be poetic' (corresponding to the idea of Novalis that 'all knowledge must be poeticised'). In the absence of any real faith 'all romantic dreams can turn out to be illusions' and thus it was with Odoevsky, whose romanticism and Slavophilism were 'built on sand'. What started with Odoevsky as doubt, Gippius argues, developed into a new respect for 'experiment' *(opyt)* and turned less towards positivism than a 'moderate Kantianism'. An element of dualism was preserved in the division between the 'knowable' and the 'unknowable'. By the 1860s 'reason' had been restored to favour and a 'positivist phase' had been reached. Thus Gippius somewhat rearranged Sakulin's three-period chronology.

  In prerevolutionary criticism of Odoevsky we can therefore distinguish two main strains. The first, inaugurated by Belinsky and Maikov and reflected in a more elaborate form by Sakulin, separates the 'romantic' and the 'realistic' elements in Odoevsky's fiction, usually expressing a marked preference for the latter. The second, originating with Grigor'ev, was developed by Kotliarevsky and Gippius and begins from the premise that there is nothing wrong with romanticism anyway. Other commentators, from Skabichevsky onwards, occupied a more intermediate position, offering the occasional corrective insight. Views based on the Belinsky tendency were to hold almost total sway for the first fifty years of the Soviet period. O. Tsekhnovitser's introduction to an edition of Odoevsky's *Romanticheskie povesti* of 1929 *(Romantic Stories)*, chosen it might appear with Belinsky's taste in mind, followed Sakulin's periodisation of Odoevsky's evolution with no reference to Gippius. Explaining Odoevsky's shortsightedness regarding social and political change in *4338-yi god (The Year 4338)*, he writes: 'Odoevsky was still exclusively in the power of Schellingianism, of philosophical-mystical idealism, and was far from that scientific realism [Sakulin's term] which he got to only in the 50s and 60s.'[25] Without doubting Tsekhnovitser's admiration for Odoevsky, it could be said to have been unfortunate for Odoevsky scholarship that some quotations contained in Tsekhnovitser's work (and in Sakulin's study of *Russian Literature and Socialism)*[26] were subsequently used selectively to brand Odoevsky's type of romanticism as a wholly negative element in the development of Russian literature. There followed no further edition of Odoevsky's fiction until 1959, and a meagre output of literary scholarship. In most of the latter, in any case, in keeping with the times, Odoevsky's 'realistic' stories were singled out for praise and his 'fantastic' works for condemnation. B. Koz'min, in his introduction to Odoevsky's diary (1935), found it necessary to overstate Odoevsky's position as a believer in the status quo and a 'supporter of serfdom' (though admitting some modification from the late 1840s), as well as his hostility to the revolutionary movement.[27] In V. Zhirmunsky's *Goethe in Russian Literature,* just four pages are devoted to the fascinating question of Goethe's impact upon Odoevsky, whose use of epigraphs from Goethe is mentioned, but otherwise little point of contact is seen between their respective works. Odoevsky's use of the name Faust is accorded just one sentence. Zhirmunsky regarded Odoevsky as being 'in the camp of the Slavophiles' in the 1840s and that therefore any further examination of the connection appeared superfluous.[28] V. Vinogradov, in his essay 'Lermontov's Prose Style', produced a quote to establish Odoevsky as a 'conservative aristocrat' and considered his 'mystical idealism and consequent forms of fantastic depiction completely alien to Lermontov', although the latter was attracted to Odoevsky's satirical style of psychological tale, particularly his use of the Hoffmannian 'device of the doll-automaton'.[29]

Typical was B. S. Meilakh's contention that Odoevsky was 'like two distinct authors': 'the original and gifted artist' who exposed 'the world of empty, worthless society people'; but also the author of 'mystical-fantastic stories' *(*'Kosmorama', *Segeliel'*, 'Sil'fida'*)*, reflecting the heavy influence of the idealist philosophy which contaminated Odoevsky in his youth. Meilakh goes as far as to say: 'if this influence on Odoevsky's work had remained constant, then his works would hold no interest even for the literary historian'. And yet, despite these defects, there are grounds for speaking of 'ambiguities in his world view' and progressive elements are to be found in the 'strongest' of his stories – 'Kniazhna Mimi' and 'Kniazhna Zizi'. *Russkie nochi* is accorded just one paragraph, pointing to the anti-capitalist tendency of 'Gorod bez imeni'.[30]

D. Blagoi and Iu. Oksman, in 1952, placed Odoevsky 'at the head of an ever intensifying opposition' to Pushkin, planning with Kraevsky to wrest political control of *Sovremennik*. This version of events, based on a reading of one short letter from Odoevsky and Kraevsky to Pushkin, was refuted by R. B. Zaborova in 1956.[31]

By this time a rediscovery was underway of Odoevsky's role in the history of Russian music and of popular education, with large selections of his work in these areas republished.[32] The first solid sign of a restoration to literary respectability, however, was the appearance in 1959 of the volume *Povesti i rasskazy*, which included works not republished since 1844. Despite her enthusiasm for Odoevsky and her more tolerant manner, the editor, Evgeniia Khin, does not deviate far from the 1950 views of Meilakh, which, crude oversimplification though they may be, can be traced back to Belinsky.[33] No mention is made of Gippius, a 'critique of capitalism' is again a main feature of *Russkie nochi* and, true to the Belinsky-Meilakh axis, Khin maintains the split personality approach to Odoevsky's writing: 'Odoevsky the idealist, the romantic, constantly struggled with Odoevsky the realist, the sensitive artist, the humanist and enlightener'. The latter played his part in 'progressive Russian romanticism' (as opposed to the 'passive, idealist romanticism' of such as Zhukovsky, 'devotees of a feudal-monarchist order, idealizing the Middle Ages and urging withdrawal to an irrational, mystical world'). In works such as 'Kosmorama', 'Salamandra', *Segeliel'* and 'Improvizator' ('The Improvisor') (all omitted from the collection), Odoevsky trod the path of the German Romantics. 'Odoevsky in his best works took another path' – in such stories as 'Novyi god' ('New Year'), Kniazhna Mimi', 'Katia ili istoriia vospitanitsy' ('Katia or the Story of a Ward') and 'Kniazhna Zizi' (all included) – that of the 'struggle for a realistic depiction of contemporary Russian life', which Khin equates with 'Pushkin's ... definition of true romanticism as the treatment of living reality'. The only break with the Belinsky-Meilakh tradition is the appropriation of 'Sil'fida' for the 'progressive' canon, justified as 'a retreat from illusory, idealist fantasy' in its 'irony over the "mystical ravings" of its hero', whose 'ties with the other world are motivated as a psychopathic phenomenon'. The story is 'a turning point in the writer's work', which is why 'Pushkin, who was critical of Odoevsky's idealist predilections, nevertheless printed "Sil'fida" in *Sovremennik*'. In Khin's view, Odoevsky's 'true romanticism' dissolves into the new emergent realism. The overtly romantic mode, which Khin seems to believe should have been kept down by the progressive tendency, is thus depicted almost as an interloping Mr Goliadkin Junior! Writing on 'Sebastian Bach' in 1964, E.D. Chkatarashvili also viewed Odoevsky's artistic practice as 'evolving towards realism, with the artist-experimentor in 'Bach' managing to conquer the romantic theoretician-thinker in himself'.[34] Odoevsky's view of art is seen by Chkatarashvili as essentially a reflection of reality (therefore departing from the romanticism of Tieck and Schlegel), but a reality containing much that is unknown and incomprehensible. Despite remaining a Romantic, Odoevsky was not isolated from reality. He distorted it and counterposed its hostile, fantastic side but still 'breathed the juices of this reality', reproducing it in *Russkie nochi*.

It is, however, from the later 1960s that the 'modern period' of Odoevsky scholarship can be said to date. Crucial was the work of Iurii Mann, who provided the first sustained reading of *Russkie nochi* as an artistic whole, the 'basic tone' of which was one of 'total and uncompromising disappointment'.[35] Odoevsky's original idea had been 'to reduce all philosophical ideas to one denominator' and to compose 'a huge drama involving all the philosophers of the world'. Mann sees Hoffmann, Pogorel'sky, Goethe, Tieck, and Plato in the genealogy of *Russkie nochi*, but 'the principles of philosophical aesthetics and, in a wider sense, philosophical systematism of the 1820s and early 1830s as the main influence on Odoevsky's artistic design. Mann found himself less approving of the findings of Odoevsky's ambitious enquiry than of the searches and rejections, which 'are crystallised in the very structure of his work'. The material is arranged in three layers: the 'oldest' stories, originally designed for inclusion in *Dom sumasshedshikh (House of Madmen)*, investigating the lives of 'great' or 'mad' people *(bezumtsy)*, *plus* the chain of novelettes left by 'Economist'; a transitional layer of 'unplanned fragments' ('Poslednee samoubiistvo' ['The Last Suicide'] and 'Gorod bez imeni'*)* reflecting 'collective madness' and originating from the intellectual 'journey' of the two deceased friends; and thirdly the overall framework—the deliberations of Faust, Viktor, Viacheslav, and Rostislav. Interconnections exist within the parts -'each subsequent character shades in the weakness of the preceding one'; no real answers are provided, yet 'each answer in some way fills out the previous

one'. Ample use is made of 'Odoevsky's favourite device – the hand-
ing over of the narration to invented storytellers'. Thus, Mann
argues, is achieved 'an impression of multiplicity', of the passing on
of 'the spirit of the times'. Mann distinguishes 'philosophical aes-
thetics' from 'general romanticism' and sees it as a line, inspired by
German idealist philosophy, stretching from Odoevsky and
Venevitinov, through Nadezhdin, to Stankevich and Belinsky; as
such it was the 'top layer' of romantic aesthetics.[36] It carried on a dual
struggle in the 1820s: with classicism and with romanticism proper.
Aesthetically it was closer to romanticism but could nevertheless
accept elements of classicism, such as didacticism and civic feeling
*(grazhdanstvennyi pafos)* in the early Odoevsky. But inherent in its for-
mulations were 'inner difficulties and contradictions' which led it
into crisis by the late 1820s, when, in Odoevsky's testament,
'Schelling's philosophy ceased to satisfy the seekers of truth and they
dispersed in various directions'. From this crisis in philosophical aes-
thetics, Mann considers, arose 'the unique architectonics of *Russkie
nochi,* which surmounted romantic norms and carry the clear imprint
of philosophical universalism'.[37]

By the time he completed *Russkie nochi,* Odoevsky had himself
assimilated 'the idealist dialectic', by which Faust posits 'the unifica-
tion of contradictions' as 'the so-called spirit of the times'.[38] Of the
exponents of philosophical aestheticism close to Odoevsky, such as
Kireevsky and Shevyrev, Odoevsky was 'the only one who attempted
to find a way out of the crisis by artistic practice', by 'an accumulation
of new elements within old systems'. The complexity of *Russkie nochi*
was due, in Mann's view, to a combination of factors that make the
work, by 1844, seem 'out of step with the times': 'to the antiromantic
movement of the time Odoevsky reacted by means of romantic
forms, restructuring and finding new possibilities in them. The inner
stimulus of this restructuring was the philosophical task. Hence the
broadening from romantic to philosophical universalism.'[39]

Such a radical re-evaluation of *Russkie nochi* involved dissension
from previous Odoevsky criticism. The views of Belinsky, Maikov,
Sakulin, and Gippius are all faulted. *Russkie nochi,* in Mann's view,
cannot be satisfactorily accounted for in terms of the metaphysics
stressed by Kotliarevsky, the Schellingianism of Zamotin, the 'philo-
sophical mysticism' of Sakulin or the Hoffmannian ideas suggested
by Gippius. Mann is equally critical of aspects of Soviet criticism,
contending that 'the view that the representatives of Russian philo-
sophical aesthetics were political reactionaries is greatly exagger-
ated'. Social criticism may have been sublimated into 'abstract
generalised platitudes', but still, this movement was in its own way a
positive preparation for the future development of Russian thought

– 'even sociological and political thought'.[40] Just as he discerns a dialectical process in Odoevsky's fiction and in the movement whence it sprang, there can also be seen a dialectical process at work in Mann's criticism, which contains something of a synthesis of the critical approaches of Belinsky and Sakulin on the one hand, and of Grigor'ev and Gippius on the other, as well as ideas touched on earlier by Skabichevsky, Kotliarevsky, Lezin, Zamotin, and Ivanov-Razumnik and developed in more general terms by more recent Soviet commentators on the philosophy and aesthetics of the romantic period such as Z.A. Kamensky and V.V. Vanslov.[41]

E.A. Maimin follows Mann in perceiving a basic consistency throughout Odoevsky's work from the early 1820s to *Russkie nochi,* thereby rejecting the 'two Odoevskys' theory and disagreeing particularly with Khin's view that Odoevsky moved away from romanticism in the second half of the 1830s. Mysticism in stories such as 'Sil'fida', 'Salamandra' and 'Kosmorama' is seen as fulfilling the same function as the fantastic in *Pestrye skazki (Variegated Tales):* that of a device 'to switch the narration to a higher wavelength' and introduce a 'philosophical ring' – in other words 'a property related to form rather than content'.[42] On the other hand, the 'realistic' stories ('Kniazhna Mimi' and 'Kniazhna Zizi') Maimin sees as 'in no way falling outside Odoevsky's romantic system' given that 'a mercilessly truthful, critical attitude to reality' should by no means be considered the monopoly of realism. Moreover, while Odoevsky may have changed his artistic manner, 'he never changed his artistic faith'. *Russkie nochi,* Maimin claims, is perhaps closest to F. Schlegel's definition of the novel as 'a Socratic dialogue of our time' and to his view of the fragment as 'the most truthful means of artistic expression'. However, the fragmentary nature of the work 'does not detract from its wholeness in terms of inner structure'; on the contrary, it complements 'the deep *musical* unity of all its parts'. The initial idea, 'the idea of happiness', combined with a key theme of the book, that of the poet and poetry, suggests to Maimin (here he follows Lezin, rather than Gippius and Mann) 'elements of a positive solution to the problems of human knowledge and possible human happiness'.

M. I. Medovoy came close to Mann's position in regarding *Russkie nochi* as 'an idiosyncratic balance sheet' of 'the most complicated ideological processes occurring at the end of the 30s-beginning of the 40s'.[43] He questioned the traditional identification of Odoevsky with Faust: the other conversationalists are also mouthpieces for the author's ideas and, in any case, 'Odoevsky thought more broadly and more freely than his protagonists'. M.S. Shtern also pays particular attention to the composition of *Russkie nochi,* the interrelation of fragment, cycle and dialogue: 'the structure of the cycles reconstructs the

macroworld of nature, history, civilization, and the microworld of sep-
arate human existence'. This is achieved, she believes (developing
Maimin), by the 'musical-*leitmotif* character' of the composition: inner
association, variation, repetition and the interplay and development of
fundamental 'musical' themes of the book, reduced to key words or
phrases in 'the numerous individual motifs linking the various cycles
and fragments'.[44] According to B.F. Egorov, the 'saturated intellectual-
ism' of Odoevsky's stories at times approaches the 'metalanguage' of
the 'description of the process of creation itself', more normally asso-
ciated with the twentieth-century art of, say, Thomas Mann.[45]

V.I. Sakharov describes Odoevsky's so-called 'enigmatic' tales
('Sil'fida', 'Salamandra', 'Kosmorama' and 'Orlakhskaia krest'ianka'
('The Orlakh Peasant Girl') as 'masterpieces of romantic prose'.[46]
'Salamandra' had been a major target of critical disapproval since
Belinsky. The first stage in its 'rehabilitation' had been the 1971 arti-
cle by an East German scholar claiming it as the work of 'a progres-
sive romantic, the heir of civic, instructional thought' and stressing
the realistic descriptions of the Finnish landscape, folkloric elements,
the historical content and Odoevsky's preference for the methods of
the natural sciences over mysticism and cabalism.[47] Sakharov calls
'Salamandra' a 'composite' work, comprised of history, philosophy
and fiction in two parts of differing genres, and concerned with three
epochs (those of Peter the Great, the post-Petrine aftermath and
Odoevsky's own), with the fantastic elements serving merely as an
aid to this design. Sakharov emphasises the impact of Pushkin on
'Salamandra', pointing to parallels with *Arap Petra Velikogo (The Negro
of Peter the Great), Poltava, Mednyi vsadnik (The Bronze Horseman)* and
'Pikovaia dama' ('The Queen of Spades').[48] However, M. A. Tur'ian
stresses instead the prominence given to the primitive Finnish tribal
culture: 'in its way a return to the "radiant condition" of humanity at
the dawn of existence, a condition "which has now become incom-
prehensible to us"'. A distinction is made between 'rational mysti-
cism' (the pseudo-scientific 'applied alchemy' of the old Count) and
'irrational mysticism' (the 'higher' psychic powers of El'sa-Salaman-
dra) and the events of the second part are seen to arise from an
imbalance between faith in rational and in instinctive modes of cog-
nition. 'Salamandra' is thus regarded by Tur'ian as primarily a philo-
sophical tale involving the idea of *karma* and an unusually advanced
treatment of the conscious and subconscious. Odoevsky's method in
'Salamandra' is still considered as essentially romantic, but as signi-
fying 'a certain new phase in the history of Russian romanticism ...
which linked late romanticism with subsequent realist literature –
including the novels and stories of Dostoevsky and Turgenev, noted
for their keen interest in the "psychological fantastic"'.[49]

The question of Hoffmann's influence was aired again by A. B. Botnikova, who sees comparisons between 'The Retort' ('Retorta') and *The Golden Pot* and the animated dolls in *Vonegared Tales* and *The Sandman,* but regards *Pestry skazki* as essentially rationalistic and moral rather than romantic, with Odoevsky's grotesque images being used for 'allegorical' rather than 'metaphorical' purposes. Themes of madness, the predicament of the artist, and the use of musicians are common to both writers, and particularly striking are the depictions of Piranesi and Cavalier Gluck (though Botnikova sees the former rather as a reflection of the frustrations of Odoevsky's strivings for 'the systemization and generalisation of philosophical knowledge'). However, Botnikova argues that Hoffmann is never more than a point of departure for Odoevsky in the creation of 'his own aesthetic system'.[50] We will return to this, and a number of other questions, in Section III.

# II

We turn now to Odoevsky's own conception of romanticism and to a survey of the main romantic features in his works. This is intended to place Odoevsky's romanticism in a more European context, thereby to illuminate its nature more clearly, and to provide a broader perspective of Soviet views on the subject.

Although he wrote compulsively on almost every subject, including many which may be said to be related to romanticism, Odoevsky wrote very little on romanticism itself. His essays on aesthetics of the 1820s, while strongly imbued with a romantic philosophy of a mainly Schellingian hue, are at the same time primarily concerned with polemics against the hitherto dominant classical aesthetic.[51] As Mersereau has said of the journalistic criticism of the period: 'the issues themselves were far from clear, and personal animosities often were more important in determining opinions than critical attitudes'.[52] Odoevsky's published literary articles of the 1830s and 1840s are virtually devoid of theory and almost entirely polemical: this time against the dominant tendency of reactionary ignorance and bad taste propagated by the 'ruling triumvirate' of official Russian literature – Bulgarin, Grech, and Senkovsky.[53] Odoevsky's apparent reluctance to engage in theoretical discussions of romanticism is due at least in part to the confusion over the use and understanding of the term 'romantic' at that time and to the idiosyncratic nature of the literary arguments of the 1820s and 1830s in Russia.[54]

*Russkie nochi,* for example, although in content heavily, if by no means exclusively, romantic (by almost any definition of the term) uses the word only two or three times: most notably, perhaps, when Faust remarks on the apparent contradiction in Shevyrev's discovery (from Longinus) of 'romanticism in the era of ancient classicism'.[55] In 'Kniazhna Zizi', in Sakulin's view, Odoevsky is at pains to differentiate, through the characters in the story, 'true' from 'superficial' romanticism: genuine and deep idealism, as opposed to the pose of foreign imitation.[56]

The nearest thing to a consciously expressed view of romanticism is perhaps contained in Odoevsky's fragmentary and only recently published article 'Classicism and Romanticism', which appears to have been directed against the French varieties of both literary modes.[57] The distinction is nevertheless drawn between the mathematical calculation and blatant imitation of writing in the classical mode and the intuitive originality and emotional profundity achievable through the romantic approach, with Beethoven cited as the exemplary instance.[58] For Hoffmann, too, Beethoven's music evoked 'that infinite yearning which is the essence of romanticism',[59] while the view of romanticism as primarily the revolt of emotion against the rules of neoclassicism is still prevalent in modern criticism.[60] Not that Odoevsky believed, however, that there should be no restraints; in another fragment of the 1830s he wrote of the dangers of materials not being brought into: 'strict and natural order … the fruits of this chaos of ideas will manifest themselves in mistakes in philosophy, monstrosities in the world of fine arts, crimes in the world of politics'.[61] This acceptance of certain necessities and the consequent stress on method in romanticism was shared by Viazemsky.[62]

This can scarcely be considered a satisfactory exposition of the nature or extent of Odoevsky's romanticism. His real view of romanticism, therefore, has to be extrapolated from many writings of various periods, and in particular from his artistic works. While a comprehensive examination of all romantic elements in Odoevsky would obviously be beyond the scope of a single essay, we can pick out a number of the more prominent features and attempt to relate them, in particular, to Germanic models.

The impact of German *Naturphilosophie* on Odoevsky in the early 1820s has been well documented.[63] He worked on an unfinished translation of Oken[64] and attempted to explain Schelling's Transcendental Idealism and Philosophy of Identity in the pages of *Vestnik Evropy* and *Mnemozina*. His 'Aphorisms from German Philosophy', for example, argued such Schellingian points as the identity, only in dual form, of the material and the abstract, which in combination forms the absolute.[65] In *Russkie nochi* he later stressed the historical importance of Schelling as the 'Christopher Columbus of the soul'.[66] Thinkers prominent among the mentors of the German Romantics, such as Jacob Boehme and Louis Claude de Saint-Martin,[67] were to be post-Schellingian influences on Odoevsky.

India and Italy were of particular interest to the romantics[68] (especially India to Schlegel).[69] Odoevsky based a number of his apologues of the 1820s on Indian themes (mainly from the *Panchatantra*, through a French translation) and there was a mild vogue for Eastern tales in Russia at that time.[70] Odoevsky's main Italian interest was the figure of Giordano Bruno, about whom he wrote an unfinished and still unpublished novel.[71] Odoevsky saw a line of development from the sixth century B.C. Eleatic School of philosophy (precursors of the 'divine Plato'), stretching through the Neoplatonists and reappearing unexpectedly in Bruno, later giving birth to Spinoza and hence to the (German) 'new thinkers'.[72] Schelling revived Neoplatonism and derived his view of art as intellectual intuition from Bruno; echoes of Bruno and Spinoza are also present in Schelling's system of Identity, at the all-embracing 'point where all differences are reconciled'.[73] The propensity for synthesism, widespread in Odoevsky's writing (and particularly irritating to Belinsky, who took it as reconciliation with the status quo),[74] is clearly stated by Faust in the Epilogue to *Russkie nochi:* there is 'no opinion the contrary of which could not be established', the result being that 'epochs of contradiction end in what is known as syncretism'.[75] The struggle of ideas was, in Odoevsky's view, necessary; but not the triumph of one or another ⁄ rather of something in between.[76] The chief aim of Novalis was to reconcile through symbol; Roger Cardinal terms Schelling 'a born synthesizer', while 'the simultaneous validity of conflicting ideas is indeed the very systole and diastole of Romantic truth', or, in another view, the 'one salient characteristic' of the romantic movement.[77]

Odoevsky's article on the Eleatic School[78] was designed as part of a vast encyclopedic 'Dictionary of the History of Philosophy'. The scope and universality of *Russkie nochi* have been noted, as we have seen, by many critics. Even in his later more positivist years, Odoevsky was eagerly engaging in encyclopedic projects.[79] Most of Odoevsky's more ambitious projects throughout his career remained unfinished, many never getting beyond the fragmentary stage.[80] This is totally in accord with the Germanic model of romanticism, which, in the words of Glyn Tegai Hughes, 'is both fragmentary and encyclopaedic in its intentions'; Schlegel wrote of 'the textbook of universality', and the encyclopedic projects of Novalis were 'to lay a foundation for all knowledge'.[81] Cardinal speaks of 'the astonishing number of unfinished Romantic works' and Marshall Brown of 'the conception of the romantic novel as a fragment whose completion is relegated to a mythically distant future'.[82] In Brown's view, romantic art is measured by its energy rather than its achievement *(Tendenz –*

the tension and striving for perfection – being all important) and there is a tendency deliberately to set goals which can never be reached.[83] Odoevsky's single completed major project, *Russkie nochi* is, we have seen, in its basic form a collection of fragments. The fragment in itself is seen as 'a new, revolutionary and still only partly accepted form', created by Novalis and Schlegel.[84] Novalis, 'this truly interdisciplinary thinker' (or 'scientific mystic', in Maeterlinck's words), was compiling a 'scientific Bible' of notes on such topics as 'moral astronomy', 'spiritual physics', 'poetic physiology' and 'musical chemistry'.[85] Odoevsky's archive abounds in fragments and notes on a multitude of topics and combinations of topics: along with a treatise on 'Nature and Man', he was writing on such themes as 'Theosophical Physics', 'Physics – A Russian System' and 'The Science of Instinct'.[86] Thus from the philosophical basis of the identity of mind and world there arises the phenomenon of 'the Romantic scientist'.[87]

The theme of madness and obsession occurs in Odoevsky, both in conjunction with fantastic elements (as in 'Sil'fida' and 'Salamandra') and in connection with the higher forms of spiritual activity of human life (the artistic figures depicted in *Russkie nochi*). There is discussion of the thin dividing line between 'madness' and 'sanity' and of the similarity between the conditions of the madman and the poet (or any inventor of genius).[88] Schelling had written: 'people who do not carry a trace of madness in themselves are the people of empty, unproductive reason'.[89] For Hoffmann, madness had been a state of receptivity to knowledge not available to normal consciousness.[90] Faust's friends, the two seekers, ask:

> So is there not a thread passing through all the actions of the human soul and joining ordinary common sense to the derangement of concepts perceptible to madmen? On this ladder is the lofty condition of the poet, the inventor, not nearer to what is called madness than madness is to ordinary animal stupidity?[91]

'The thread', 'the ladder' and madness are, indeed, recurrent motifs for Odoevsky.

Here Odoevsky connects his investigations of 'madness' with the breakdown of communication. The theme of the deficiency of language has long been noted as prominent in *Russkie nochi*. Odoevsky, in his 'Note to *Russian Nights*', written in the early 1860s, informs us that he arrived at this idea from 'a prolonged reading of Plato'; Goethe, incidentally, was also interested in this question.[92] Such an attitude to language can be seen to fuse with certain notions of German romantic thought, such as the famous dictum of Novalis that 'the world must be romanticised ' (through the agency of the imagination and the magic utterances of the poet): 'in this way we will rediscover its original meaning'; this involves the two-way 'translation' of objects into thoughts and of thoughts into tangible form, arising once again from the concept of Identity (of mind and world) and the investigation of Nature in the spirit of 'Magic Idealism'.[93] Language is regarded as 'the prime agency in all dealings between consciousness and reality'.[94] Faust in *Russkie nochi* insists on the presence of

> a quantum of poetry in every industrial enterprise [and the other way round] ... the railways represent ... a striving to destroy time and space, a feeling of human virtue and superiority over nature; in this feeling there is, perhaps, a recollection of man's former strength and of his former slave-nature... .[95]

Odoevsky's dual stress on the inadequacy of language, yet the universal capacity of poetry, (which 'enters into every action of man'),[96] thus merges with ideas deriving from the *Naturphilosophie* of Schelling, the Magic Idealism of Novalis and the psychology of Schubert, Ritter, and Carus. At the beginning of *The Apprentices at Sais,* Novalis presents the world as a system of 'signatures' (an idea from Boehme), referring to:

> that marvellous secret writing that one finds everywhere, upon wings, egg-shells, in clouds, in snow, crystals and the structure of stones, on water when it freezes, on the inside and the outside of mountains, of plants, of animals, of human beings, in the constellations of the sky, on pieces of pitch or glass when touched or rubbed, in iron filings grouped around a magnet, and in the strange conjunctions of chance.[97]

In the introduction to 'Retorta' ('The Retort'), termed by one Soviet commentator 'a passionate defence of the romantic imagination',[98] Odoevsky (or his surrogate, the purported narrator of *Pestrye skazki,* Gomozeika) speaks warmly of the searches of medieval sages for, among other things, 'the kind of language which a stone and a bird and all the elements would heed'.[99] Of the aesthetic process in prehistory, Novalis wrote (using a 'Fichtean myth of the fission of an originally unitary art'):

> The first art is hieroglyphistics. The art of communication, reflection, or language, and the art of representation and formation, or poetry are as yet One. Only later does this raw mass divide – then arises the art of naming, language in the proper sense – philosophy, and fine art, creative art, poetry in general.[100]

*Russkie nochi* seems to posit a kind of inherited memory, preserved in legends, of a time when 'man was indeed king over nature; when every creature obeyed his voice, because he knew what to call it;

when all the powers of nature, like humble slaves, prostrated themselves at man's feet.'[101] Elsewhere, introducing a group of stories and Indian legends, Odoevsky employs similar terms of natural philosophy to describe the process of the birth of a legend; this is supposed to follow the composition and handing down of a song to future generations:

> The first epoch of the development of the basic elements is complete; the poetic flowers fade, pinned to printed pages, but they fade because the fruit is ripening; all strengths of the organism are directed to it; the life-giving juice for the fruit is being produced in mysterious vessels; for it the wind blows, for it the leaves bathe in the cold dew, for it the sun's rays parch. The flower turns into a recollection; scholars support it with commentaries; its appearance inspires new poets – and the poem continues, although under a different form; for its author is still the same – he has simply been born anew... .[102]

In his 'Psychological Notes' (1843), Odoevsky talks of ancient music as a relic of 'a primordial, natural human language', which was 'known to man instinctively'.[103] At the beginning of 'Sebastian Bach' we hear of 'a secret language, hitherto almost unknown, but common to all artists', and musical notes are referred to as 'hieroglyphics'.[104] Later in the story Albrecht recounts a potted mythic history of mankind and the birth of art, beginning at the carefree time when man had no need of *expression,* resting innocently in his cradle with an instinctive understanding of God, nature, the present, and the future:

> But ... the infant's cradle shook; the tender unfledged being, like a moth in a barely opened cocoon, was confronted by threatening and inquisitive nature: in vain the youthful Alcides strove to fetter its huge and diverse forms in his infantile babble; nature touched the world of ideas by the head and the coarse instinct of crystals by the heels, and challenged man to measure himself against it. Then were born the two constant and eternal but dangerous and perfidious allies of the soul of man: *thought* and *expression.*[105]

This provides, quite apart from anything else, the ironic spectacle of Bach, the towering genius of classical composition, being raised on romantic philosophy. The mythic imagery is analogous to that used by Hoffmann in *Meister Floh,* when Peregrinus, looking at Dörtje Elverdink through Master Flea's microscopic lens, sees through the network of nerves and silver threads beyond her thoughts: 'flowers that were being transformed into human beings, and then again human beings that flowed away into the earth to emerge glittering as jewels and minerals. And in among them moved all sorts of strange animals, which were transformed countless times and which spoke wondrous languages'.[106] Such vision is explained by Master Flea as follows:

Since the time when Chaos condensed to formative matter – the World-
Spirit has been forming all forms out of that available material, and from
it dreams proceed with their images. These configurations are sketches of
what has been or perhaps of what will be, sketches which the Mind
quickly draws at its pleasure, when the tyrant named Body releases him
from his slave's service.[107]

Odoevsky would long have been familiar with Oken's conception of
natural philosophy as 'the conjunction of empiricism and specula-
tion'.[108] The mythic elements in Hoffmann's *Märchen,* reminiscent of
Novalis, are said to derive from G. H. von Schubert, a student of the
romantic physicist J. W. Ritter, who had been greatly influenced by
Schelling's *Naturphilosophie.*[109] Schubert referred to the 'hieroglyphic
language' of dreams, connecting the inner world of the mind with
external events across time and accessible only to the 'hidden
poet'.[110] Such studies of the subconscious were carried further by the
painter and natural scientist C. G. Carus, who is now acknowledged
as a predecessor of Jung.[111] Odoevsky greatly admired the works of
Carus (one of which he reviewed in *Otechestvennye zapiski)* and once
placed him on a level with Goethe, Leibniz, and Lomonosov.[112]

Romantic literature is frequently concerned with striving or a
quest; Heinrich von Ofterdingen, in Novalis's novel of that name,
undertakes 'the quest for the Blue Flower, symbol of all man's long-
ings in this world for something that transcends it'; when he finally
plucks it he 'becomes a ringing tree, a stone'.[113] The long first sen-
tence of *Russian Nights* outlines the nature of the quest, the 'wonder-
ful task' *(chudnaia zadacha)* constantly engaged in by the human
soul.[114] The hero in Novalis is hoping to discover 'a Romantic age,
full of profundity, which underneath a simple clothing hides a
higher shape'.[115] Odoevsky goes on to speak of one layer beneath
another as the covers are removed, protecting 'the sacred secret
*(zavetnaia taina)* perhaps inaccessible to man in this life, but which
he is permitted to approach',[116] (thus prefiguring ultimate failure
from the start). Hughes says of the veiled goddess in *The Apprentices
at Sais:* 'for Novalis, the veil conceals the profoundest secrets of the
natural world'.[117] The motif of the veil in its various forms through-
out Odoevsky's writings achieves the measure of a poetic and philo-
sophical symbol. Symbols for Odoevsky are connected with ideas
on expression and the 'primordial instinctual condition of man';
when this condition returns (through the agency of the ecstatic state
of, for example, the poet), 'it seeks images for its inexpressible con-
dition; not having language (for language is a presentiment of the
epoch of reason), it uses an approximate language – i.e. symbols'.[118]
Gippius noted the significance particularly of the phrase 'human
clothing' in this respect;[119] other words used by Odoevsky include

'cover' *(pokrov)*, 'membrane' *(obolochka)*, 'veil' or 'curtain' *(zavesa* and *pokryvalo)*. These are frequently removed or peeled off to attain or reveal a further dimension of truth, essence, or perception. Beneath every feeling, we are informed in *Russkie nochi*, there hides another 'deeper and perhaps more disinterested', and behind that another and another until we reach 'the deepest recess of the human soul', where there is 'neither time nor space'.[120] This is the place of the poet: 'the state of spirit, where time and space, past present and future do not exist',[121] and of the musician. The young Sebastian's nocturnal vision in the moonlit Gothic church at Eisenach, embracing in the indescribable edifice of the organ the unity of the mysteries of architecture and harmony, is a presentiment of this state:

> Angels of melody floated on its light clouds and vanished in mysterious embraces; in graceful geometric lines rose combinations of musical instruments; above the sanctuary ascended choirs of human voices; multicoloured veils of contra-sounds coiled and uncoiled before him and the chromatic scale streamed down a cornice like a playful bas-relief... . Everything here lived a harmonious life, every iridescent motion sounded, every sound was fragrant – and an unseen voice pronounced distinctly the mysterious words of religion and art.[122]

Novalis wrote in *Blütenstaub:* 'Is not the universe within us? ... The way of mystery leads inwards. Past and future, eternity and its realms, these lie within us or nowhere'; in the words of Hughes the preoccupation here is with 'the attempt to spiritualise matter, to annihilate time and space'.[123] Schubert and Carus were also concerned with states of mind when 'boundaries between matter and spirit were blurred' and 'time and space become an indivisible unity'.[124]

Odoevsky broaches the dislocation of time and space in a number of stories, including 'Sil'fida', 'Salamandra' and 'Zhivoi mertvets'. However, the most startling treatment occurs in association with the fantastic in the long-neglected story, 'Kosmorama'. Sakulin regarded 'Kosmorama' as 'one of the best of Odoevsky's mystical stories' (detecting in it the unseen hand of the English mystic, John Pordage); a recent Western writer calls it 'a Faustian drama of divine and infernal powers struggling for the hero's soul', and notes the 'thread and links' theory of moral responsibility.[125] Midway through the story (a supposed manuscript acquired at an auction), which ends somewhat inconclusively (a proposed continuation was never written), the face of the protagonist is brushed by the hand of Count B-, the husband of his intended mistress Eliza. The count has just returned from the dead, with diabolical assistance, to take revenge on his 'faithful spouse'. The touch of the dead immediately dissolves time and space for the protagonist:

> The walls, the earth, people appeared to me as light semi-shadows, through which I could clearly distinguish another world, other objects, other people.... . Every nerve in my body received the faculty of sight; my magic gaze embraced at one and the same time both the past, the present, what had really been and what could have been.[126]

The vision includes all details of the count's past life plus the 'mysterious threads' which link these criminal events over several generations with members of the protagonist's own family; and beyond that: 'at this moment the whole history of our world from the beginning of time was clear to me' through this 'external chain of events'; his gaze gradually moved up and down 'the magic ladder' of human history:

> I realised how important every thought is, every human word, how far their influence stretches, what a heavy responsibility for them lies on the soul, and what evil for all humanity can arise from the heart of one man who has exposed himself to the influence of unclean and hostile beings ... I realised that 'man is the world' is not an empty play on words, thought up for amusement ...[127]

While not seeking to regard Odoevsky as a mere imitator of German Romanticism or to deny the role of Russian traditions in his literary production, we would suggest that the foregoing discussion does indicate that the impact of German Romanticism as a whole on the thought and fiction of Odoevsky was more considerable than has generally been acknowledged and that it extended beyond merely the theory of Schelling and the practice of Hoffmann. However, there is one further literary principle employed by those whom the early Lukács termed 'the first theoreticians of the novel, the aesthetic philosophers of early Romanticism'[128] which should not be forgotten when considering Odoevsky's romanticism: the principle of 'romantic irony', which acts in practice as a built-in defence mechanism enabling romantic fiction to combat potential criticism of its extravagances. As seen by F. Schlegel, this concept can involve 'ironic distance' or an element of self-parody: 'a stance whereby the artist becomes his own audience'; or a more complex notion of 'poetic reflection ... as though in an infinite sequence of mirrors'; 'the aesthetic principle whereby a work incorporates its own critique'.[129] This is almost literally echoed at the beginning of *Russkie nochi:* literary works of aesthetic pretensions 'must themselves be able to answer for themselves',[130] while the lengths to which Odoevsky went in so many works to distance himself from his eventual reader through pseudonyms, narrators, sub-narrators, stories within stories, and 'manuscripts' are obvious enough. The ironic treatment of romantic themes is slightly more ambiguous. Differing views exist regarding the presence of irony in 'Sil'fida', but most commentators would now agree that Odoevsky did not necessarily himself believe in the world of the sylph.[131] In the case of the *Pestrye skazki* cycle, 'Novyi Zhoko' ('The New Jocko') has been seen as a parody of the French frenetic writer Petrus Borel;[132] 'Skazka o mertvom tele ...' ('Tale of a Dead Body') could be read as a playful advance on the predicaments of Peter Schlemihl and Erasmus Spikher (in works by Chamisso and Hoffmann respectively), while in 'Retorta', which bears a slight resemblance to *The Golden Pot*, the author's intentions may be parodic as well as didactic. In fact, it is possible to read *Pestrye skazki* as a whole as a parody on various forms of currently popular literature, including those using 'excessive' forms of romanticism. There is therefore no obvious reason to take the elements of Nature Philosophy, for instance, in the introduction to 'Retorta' ,very seriously. Nature description tends, as we have seen, to be couched in the imagery of Nature Philosophy; this is all the more noticeable given the virtually total absence of 'ordinary' descriptions of nature in Odoevsky.[133]

Romantic irony has been briefly described as an awareness by the author of the principles of romantic creation, and more fully as: 'Aesthetic distance, free play of the mind, relativizing, self-criticism within the actual work of art, the teasing and mystifying of potential readers, conscious experimenting with form and modes of expression, shifting tone, multiple reflections through tale within tale'.[134]

Even the founding generation 'could never take its romanticism in deadly earnest', while Hoffmann's work is now frequently seen as filled with 'systematic irony'.[135] The elements of romantic irony listed above are clearly prominent in *Russkie nochi* and elsewhere in Odoevsky's romantic works.

Just as Odoevsky's use of the imagery of Nature Philosophy can be seen as largely contained within an ironical framework, so it could be said that in his fiction as a whole he avoids the more obscure and totally mystical excesses of the German Romantics.[136] Despite his interest in the ideas of medieval science, he never shared the romantic yearning for the Middle Ages as such. It is often well-nigh impossible to gauge an author's interest or belief in particular concepts – as opposed to his employment of them for artistic purposes – and the dimension of irony does nothing to ease the problem in the case of many romantic writers. Hoffmann, for all his apparent aspirations towards a perfect artistic world, could write: 'The ideal – it is but a deceptive, pitiful dream'.[137] As we have seen, Gippius divined an essential pessimism in Odoevsky's work and Mann has more recently stressed an overriding feeling of 'disappointment', while Maimin and Sakharov have argued for mysticism and the fantastic to be seen as essentially artistic devices. Some Western commentators, too, have seen Odoevsky as basically a rationalist; while this is certainly true of the later Odoevsky, the evidence with regard to the 1830s remains contradictory.[138] For that matter Sakulin, who is commonly accused of overstressing Odoevsky's philosophical-mystical idealism, denies that Odoevsky was ever a wholehearted Schellingian; Schelling was certainly an aesthetic influence, but it could not be said of Odoevsky that 'he subordinated the whole world to an artistic formula'.[139]

Odoevsky was in no way himself a 'romantic hero', a poet with a 'lyrical biography' in the sense in which Tomashevsky sees Byron, Pushkin, or Lermontov.[140] O. Ilyinsky sees Odoevsky as close to Goethe in the universality of his interests and the pursuit of natural knowledge, and it may well be that Goethe served as something of a model for Odoevsky's overall career.[141] Hoffmann, it should be recalled, was a musician and a lawyer as well as a writer, while Novalis was also a mining engineer. Mann sees Odoevsky as the one exponent of Russian philosophical aesthetics to attempt a way out of a philosophical crisis by artistic means. This tactic certainly conformed with Schelling's belief that 'it is art alone which can succeed with universal validity in making objective what philosophy can only portray subjectively'.[142] Sakharov in fact argues, with justification, that this practice made Odoevsky *more* of a romantic than had hitherto been the case.[143]

To conclude this survey of romanticism in the works of Odoevsky, we tentatively postulate three possible levels of romanticism in a given work. The first, which alone has been sufficient to gain for many a writer the label 'romantic', involves the presence merely of superficial romantic themes and devices: Gothic elements, exotica, historical settings, mystification, with or without a touch of the supernatural. The second level would include the presence of some or all of the above features, plus elements of technical and formal innovation, resulting in a breakdown in classical authorial restraint, thus enabling the emotions or the imagination to protrude more markedly. Most works of Russian romanticism would seem to belong in levels one or two. In the third category the presence of some or all of the elements of the first two levels would be accompanied by an identifiable underlying 'romantic' system or philosophy. Subdivisions within each level would, of course, exist: while according to this scheme Odoevsky would certainly, through many works, qualify as a 'grade three' romantic, he would probably figure lower on the scale than Hoffmann, and considerably lower than, say, Novalis.

# III

Having attempted to assess the nature of Odoevsky's romanticism, we now turn to the general evaluation of romantic works. This inevitably depends on the attitude to romanticism which is adopted and, in turn, on which conception of romanticism is accepted; the variety of conceptions on offer has been considerable. René Wellek separates the 'wider view' of romanticism (as 'a revolt against neo-classicism ... centred on the expression and communication of emotion') from a 'more narrow sense' ('a dialectical and symbolist view' comprising 'a union of opposites, a system of symbols').[144] We have already encountered the view, with which Odoevsky and Hoffmann apparently concurred, based on the primacy of emotion. That Odoevsky, for one, practised romanticism more broadly than he defined it has, it is hoped, been amply demonstrated.[145] We have also mentioned synthesism in Schelling and Odoevsky; the view of romantic literature as a synthesis of disparate elements (in particular of the sentimental and the fantastic) and a *mélange de genres* goes back to F. Schlegel. More recently a 'mixing of styles' also seems to be what Erich Auerbach understood by romanticism.[146]

The early Belinsky's essential criterion for judging poetry was a division between the 'ideal' and 'real'. Understanding classicism as 'the art of antiquity' and romanticism as 'the art of the Catholic European Middle Ages', it is scarcely surprising that he saw no meaningful debate between classicism and romanticism in Russia in the 1830s.[147] Already in the 1820s Ryleev had held that there was no such thing as 'classical' or 'romantic' poetry, only 'old' and 'new'. In an essay of 1908 the young Lukács seemed to have expressed a similar view when he agreed with Stendhal that 'everything has at some point been Romantic and everything at some time becomes classical'.[148]

By 1847, Belinsky regarded romanticism as aloofness from social problems and therefore synonymous with conservatism.[149] Victor Hugo, in contrast, had defined romanticism as 'liberalism in literature'.[150] Much Russian and Soviet criticism, as we have seen, followed the doctrine of 'two romanticisms'. This conception (implicit in his criticism of Odoevsky) seemingly originated with Belinsky and takes various forms: 'old' and 'new' (from Ryleev and Belinsky); 'active' and 'passive' (from Gorky),[151] and subsequently 'progressive' and 'reactionary'. The latter version of the dichotomy is traceable to 'Gorky and Lenin's sociologically grounded distinctions'.[152] However, it probably also owes something to the view of Lukács, some of whose works (such as *The Historical Novel*) were first published in Russian, but who was subsequently very rarely cited in Soviet scholarship. Lukács distinguishes between a 'liberal Romanticism' which 'stands for the ideology of moderate progress' and 'Romantic reaction, the apologetic glorification of the Middle Ages'. Lukács appears to hold, however, that anyone with genuinely progressive or revolutionary views cannot have been a romantic, referring to 'politically and ideologically progressive writers who frequently, though unjustly, have been treated as Romantics'.[153] Odoevsky, in the context of Tsarist Russia at least, would comfortably fit the 'liberal' category.

There is in any event a strong case for stressing the progressive side of romanticism (even in its narrower sense). While not politically engaged, even the arch-exponents of German romanticism were at first innovators in theory and practice and only in old age, in an adverse social and political climate, did those who lived long enough (or their 'epigones') embrace reaction. Kant, Fichte and Schelling all saw themselves as revolutionary philosophers (Hughes describes their movement as 'the cultural Maoism of the day') and Marx wrote of the 'honest thoughts of Schelling's youth'.[154] Novalis, himself a nobleman, criticised Goethe's *Wilhelm Meister* for its 'glorification of the hunt for the patent of nobility', complaining of its 'prosiness, Philistinism and snobbishness', while Cardinal cites the device of the mask in Jean Paul and Hoffmann as 'a revolutionary symbol of the disruption of the established order'.[155]

Hoffmann is, however, considered a special case. The hostility of the later Marx to romanticism seems to have made an exception for the writings of Hoffmann.[156] In the opinion of Lukács, only in Hoffmann and Balzac

> are the problems of the ugly new life of capitalism and the problems of the 'great world' dealt with in terms of the spirit of the new material. This new art and aesthetics thus grows out of the terrible and the grotesque, out of the distorted-sublime and the ghastly-comic.[157]

More recently James Trainer has written: '[Hoffmann's] deep interest in the occult was more scientific and methodical, and in his writings we find a great step forward in the direction of the psychological realism of the later nineteenth century'.[158] On Hoffmann's 'realism' Lukács writes: 'In Hoffmann, realism in detail goes hand in hand with a belief in the spectral quality of reality ... Hoffmann's world is ... an accurate enough reflection of conditions in the Germany of his time .'[159]

In an article of 1832 Ivan Kireevsky characterised the dominant trend in literature exemplified by Scott and Goethe as, 'the reconciling of imagination with reality, and correctness of form with freedom of content' (tendencies erroneously labelled 'classicism' and 'romanticism').[160] The primacy of the imagination over the depiction of reality (conforming with the views of Schleiermacher, Schlegel, and Novalis)[161] could almost stand as a further definition of romanticism, but never held full sway in Russia. The peculiar feature of Russian romanticism, in the view of Lidiia Ginzburg, is that 'the most abstract philosophical propositions relied on concrete facts from life and, conversely, any everyday and psychological fact was examined in the light of speculative categories'.[162] For this reason it was, as Bot-nikova points out, in the works of Hoffmann, 'the most realistic of the German romantics, that Russian aesthetics saw its natural ally'.[163]

We have already noted the image of the ladder in Odoevsky's work, but it has a somewhat wider significance in romantic literature than hitherto evident – a significance of which, it must appear, Odoevsky was well aware. Eichendorff wrote that the poet 'only raises up the ladder from earth to heaven', while Hoffmann stated: 'I believe that the base of the heavenly ladder ... must be firmly anchored in life'.[164] Odoevsky's 'Kosmorama' includes what purports to be 'an apologue by Krummacher' concerning two men, one rich and one poor, who grow up in a deep cave, from which the only way out to the light above is by 'a very steep and narrow ladder'; the poor man, aspiring to the sunlight, takes the risk, climbs out, and cannot believe the wonders of the new world; the rich man, satisfied already with his lot, remains in the cave.[165] Here the ladder thus leads from a lower world to *this* world. The unfinished novel *Segeliel'*, with its ambitious three-stage design combining the descent to earth of a Lucifer figure, society, and philosophy, was an artistic attempt 'to join heaven and earth'.[166] Furthermore it may be significant that, like Goethe's *Faust, Segeliel'* begins in heaven and descends to earth, thus reversing the Eichendorff-Hoffmann model of a ladder stretching from reality to a higher world.

Modern elements in Odoevsky's works have been noted in Soviet criticism by Mann, Egorov and Tur'ian; even Meilakh, earlier so hostile to romanticism, has compared ideas in *Russkie nochi* with 'paradoxicality' in Einstein.[167] In Western writings attention has been drawn to Odoevsky's anticipation of Jung (in his stress on the sub-conscious) and to his inclination towards existentialism.[168] A whole range of modern developments can be seen as prefigured by the German romantics.[169] Even some of what were formerly regarded as the more intuitive and eccentric speculations of the romantic thinkers can take on a new interest in the light of recent scientific the-ory.[170] We have already dealt with the awareness in Soviet criticism of a dialectical tendency in Odoevsky and the principle of synthesism in his work. Lukács too acknowledged the early nineteenth-century era of Nature Philosophy:

> It is a period in which mysticism is not merely a dead weight carried over from the theological past, but frequently, and very often in a manner dif-ficult to distinguish, an idealistic haze which veils the still unknown future methods of dialectical thinking.[171]

Returning finally to Soviet criticism, we have noted the radical reappraisal of *Russkie nochi* in the 1960s and 1970s, and a much more tolerant attitude to Odoevsky's 'enigmatic stories', formerly dismissed by most critics as mystical rubbish, or extolled by an earlier few for their overt idealism. This situation was partly attributable to a more sophisticated reading of the texts concerned in the context of their philosophical and aesthetic background by a more sensitive brand of critic, and partly to a more sympathetic and discerning attitude to the phenomenon of Russian romanticism in general, and the part it played in the development of Russian literature. Typical in many ways of this growing trend were the contributions to the volume entitled *A History of Romanticism in Russian Literature (1825-1840)*: V.Iu. Troitsky, writing on romantic prose of the 1830s, sees Odoevsky's type of universalism in relation to man and the world as preparing the ground for 'that thoroughness in relation to character and circumstances which we observe in realism'; 'the development of romantic prose', he declares, 'significantly enriched the fiction of the 30s' with its increase of pictures of everyday life and analysis and observation of society as such.[172] The fact that the contribution of romanticism is stressed in the context of natural and inexorable progress towards the emergence of realism remains, of course, significant. However, the problems attendant upon the analysis and evaluation of romantic literature were at least, during the later Soviet years, being faced more squarely than at any time since the 1920s – inescapably, because they were there to be faced – but the role of romanticism had now at least regained respectability. As the editors of *A History of Romanticism* recognised: 'Romanticism remained [in the 1830s] the only tendency which could respond to the ideological-artistic demands of its time.'[173]

## Notes

1. See André von Gronicka, *The Russian Image of Goethe* (Philadelphia, 1968), pp. 119-24; Charles E. Passage, *The Russian Hoffmannists* (The Hague, 1963), pp. 89-114; and Norman W. Ingham, *E.T.A. Hoffmann's Reception in Russia* (Würzburg, 1974,) pp. 177-93. To term Goethe a 'romantic' is, of course, to use the word in its wider sense; more will be said on this later.
2. John Mersereau Jr, 'The Chorus and Spear Carriers of Russian Romantic Fiction', in *Russian and Slavic Literature*, ed. Richard Freeborn, R.R. Milner-Gulland and Charles A. Ward (Cambridge, MA, 1976), p. 38; Victor Terras, *Belinskij and Russian Literary Criticism* (Madison, 1974), p. 160; Donald Fanger, *The Creation of Nikolai Gogol* (Cambridge and London, 1979), p. 30.

3. Simon Karlinsky, 'A Hollow Shape: The Philosophical Tales of Prince Vladimir Odoevsky', *Studies in Romanticism*, V, 3, Spring 1966, pp. 169-82.

4. 'A Man of Three Generations' was the title used by Ch. Vetrinsky ('Chelovek trekh pokolenii'), V *sorokovykh godakh: istoriko-literaturnye ocherki i kharakteristiki* (Moscow, 1899), pp. 293-330.

5. *Sochineniia kniazia V. F. Odoevskogo v trekh chastiakh* (St Petersburg, 1844).

6. For example, Pogodin and Belinsky; see P. N. Sakulin, Iz *istorii russkogo idealizma. Kniaz V. F. Odoevsky: myslitel'-pisatel'*, I, Part 1, pp. 248-9 (hereafter Sakulin, Iz *istorii).*

7. See (on Pushkin) A. S. *Pushkin-Kritik* (Moscow, 1978), p. 448; (on Gogol) Vladimir Shenrok, 'N. V. Gogol' (*Russkaia starina*, 1902, 2, pp. 264-5). V. G. Belinsky, *Polnoe sobranie sochinenii* (Moscow-Leningrad), 1953-9, I, 1953, pp. 275-6; see in particular vol.V, pp. 297-323. This essay, entitled 'Sochineniia kniazia V. F. Odoevskogo', is reprinted, with some cuts, in V.F. Odoevsky, *Poslednii kvartet Betkhovena* (Moscow, 1982), pp. 344-69.

8. (Originally in *Finskii vestnik*, I, 1845). Valerian Maikov, *Kriticheskie opyty (1845-1847)*, 2nd ed. (St Petersburg, 1891), pp. 297-312 (quotes from pp. 297, 310-11).

9. D. L. Azizov, 'Filosofsko-esteticheskaia kontseptsiia Apollona Grigor'eva', in *Romantizm v russkoi i sovetskoi literature*, vyp. 6 (Kazan, 1973), pp. 64 -91 (69); Terras, op. cit., pp. 214-22.

10. 'N. V. Gogol i ego perepiska s druz'iami', *Sobranie sochinenii Apollona Grigor'eva* (Moscow, 1916), vyp. 8, pp. 11-13.

11. 'Russkaia literatura v 1851 godu', *Sochineniia Apollona Grigor'eva* (St Petersburg, 1876), I, p. 18 (reprinted New York, 1970); also in Apollon Grigor'ev, *Literaturnaia kritika* (Moscow, 1967), p. 195.

12. *Sochineniia Apollona Grigor'eva*, op. cit., I, pp. 37-8; also in 'Russkaia literatura v seredine XIX veka', *Sobranie sochinenii Apollona Grigor'eva* (Moscow, 1916), vyp. 9, pp. 42-3.

13. *Sochineniia A. Skabichevskogo v dvukh tomakh*, 2nd ed. (St Petersburg, 1895), I, pp. 256-79 (quotations follow from pp. 258, 260 and 270-2).

14. Vetrinsky, op. cit., pp. 293-330.

15. P. Mizinov, *Istoriia i poeziia: istoriko-literaturnye etiudy* (Moscow, 1900), pp. 421-91 (esp. pp. 424, 435, 488-91).

16. N. A. Kotliarevsky, *Starinnye portrety* (St Petersburg, 1907); (reprinted in Kn. Vladimir Odoevsky, *Deviat' povestei* New York, 1954), pp. 9-28, esp. 9-11, 12, 26-7, from which quotations follow).

17. B. A. Lezin, *Ocherki iz zhizni i literaturnoi deiatel'nosti kniazia Vladimira Fedorovicha Odoevskogo* (Khar'kov, 1907), (see pp. 1, 55, 92, 103, 109, 107, 70-2, 131ff. and 67).

18. I.I. Zamotin, *Romantizm dvadtsatykh godov XIX stol. v russkoi literature* (St Petersburg, 1907), II, pp. 361-418 (410); I.I. Zamotin, 'Literaturnaia techeniia i literaturnaia kritika 30-kh godov', in *Istoriia russkoi literatury XIX v.*, ed. D. N. Ovsianiko-Kulikovsky (Moscow, 1908), I; pp. 277-330 (298-300).

19. Zamotin, *Romantizm dvadtsatykh godov*, pp. 400-1.

20. R. V. Ivanov-Razumnik, 'Obshchestvennye i umstvennye techeniia 30kh godov', in *Istoriia russkoi literatury XIX v.*, op. cit., I, pp. 247-76 (249, 254).

21. Sakulin, Iz *istorii* (I, Parts 1, 2, Moscow, 1913) I, 1, p. 7. A useful summary of Sakulin's view of Odoevsky can be found in his entry in *Entsiklopedicheskii slovar'*, 7th ed (Moscow, 1916), pp. 504-9.

22. For an exposition of Sakulin's difficulties with Volume II see M. A. Tur'ian, 'Neokonchennyi trud P. N. Sakulina o V. F. Odoevskom', *Russkaia literatura*, 1974, 2, pp. 164-71.

23. Vasilii Gippius, 'Uzkii put'. Kn. V. F. Odoevsky i romantizm', *Russkaia mysl'*, 1914, 12, pp. 1-26. The following quotations are from pp. 1-2, 9, 22, 5-6, 12, 8, 13-18, 22-3 and 25-6.

24. See Sakulin, *Iz istorii*, I, 2, pp. 103-4.

25. Orest Tsekhnovitser: 'Predislovie' (pp. 5-20) and 'Siluet: V. F. Odoevsky (vstupitel'naia stat'ia)', in V.F. Odoevsky, *Romanticheskie povesti* (Leningrad, 1929; reprinted Oxford, 1975), p. 18.

26. P. N. Sakulin, *Russkaia literatura i sotsializm* (Moscow, 1922), I, pp. 449-58.

27. "'Tekushchaia khronika i osobye proisshestviia." Dnevnik V. F. Odoevskogo 1859-1869 gg.'; B. Koz'min, introduction ('Odoevsky v 1860-e gody'), in *Literaturnoe nasledstvo* 22-4 (Moscow, 1935), p. 82.

28. V. Zhirmunsky, *Gete v russkoi literature* (Leningrad, 1937), pp. 189, 191-4; for a slightly more satisfactory discussion of the question see von Gronicka, op. cit.

29. Viktor Vinogradov, in *Literaturnoe nasledstvo* 43-4 (Moscow, 1941), pp. 517-628 (522, 541, 550-2).

30. B. S. Meilakh, 'Russkaia povest' 20-30kh godov XIX veka', in *Russkie povesti XIX veka 20kh-30kh godov,* Moscow-Leningrad, 1950, I, pp. v-xxxv (xxxi-xxxiv). By 1976, when Meilakh reviewed the 'Literaturnye pamiatniki' edition of *Russkie nochi,* his attitude was transformed: *Russkie nochi* was a 'remarkable work'; more research was needed on its ideas (which at times reminded him of 'the latest arguments of Einstein and other twentieth-century scientists') and on Odoevsky; *Russkie nochi* was 'qualitatively a new genre' which remained to be investigated; and as for Odoevsky's 'so-called mysticism, which was so exaggerated in the old studies', this was just a device, at least in his literary works – B. Meilakh, 'Pisatel' otkryvaemyi zanovo', *Voprosy literatury,* 1976, 4, pp. 282-7.

31. (Blagoi and Oksman) *Literaturnoe nasledstvo* (Moscow, 1952), LVIII, pp. 23, 289-96; R. B. Zaborova, 'Neizdannye stat' i V. F. Odoevskogo o Pushkine', in *Pushkin: issledovaniia i materialy* (Moscow-Leningrad, 1956), I, pp. 313-42.

32. V. F. Odoevsky, *Muzykal'no-literaturnoe nasledie* (Moscow, 1956), and *Izbrannye pedagogicheskiie sochineniia* (Moscow, 1955), were the main publications (with copious introductions by G. Bernandt and V. Ia. Struminsky respectively).

33. Evgeniia Khin, 'V. F. Odoevsky' in V. F. Odoevsky, *Povesti i rasskazy* (Moscow, 1959), pp. 3-38 (pp. 21, 4, 15-16, 25, 29).

34. E. D. Chkatarashvili, 'Biograficheskaia novella V. F. Odoevskogo *Sebastian Bakh'*, *Trudy Tbiliskogo gos. ped. instituta* (Tbilisi, 1964), XVIII, pp. 119-26.

35. Iurii V. Mann, *Russkaia filosofskaia estetika (1820-30-e gody)* (Moscow, 1969), Chapter 4, 'V. F. Odoevsky i ego *Russkie nochi',* pp. 104-48, and 'Conclusion', pp. 295-303; quotations are taken from this edition, see pp. 119, 113, 116-19, 122-3, 123-9, 130). A slightly shorter version of the same essay had appeared as 'Kniga iskanii (V. F. Odoevsky i ego *Russkie nochi)'* in *Problemy romantizma: sbornik statei* (Moscow, 1967), pp. 320-59.

36. Zamotin had referred simply to 'romanticism' as a single entity, while Sakulin's term 'philosophical romanticism' displays a lack of precision in his view of the various layers of romantic aesthetics (see Mann, pp. 295-6).

37. Ibid., pp. 295-300. For a further account of the 'crisis of philosophical romanticism' see V.I. Sakharov, 'V. F. Odoevsky i rannii russkiy romantizm' *(Izvestiia Akademii nauk SSSR. Seriia literatury i iazyka,* XXXII, 1973, pp. 405-18). For a detailed introduction to Russian aesthetics of the period see Z. A. Kamensky, 'Russkaia estetika pervoi treti XIX veka', in *Russkie esteticheskie traktaty pervoi treti XIX veka v dvukh tomakh* (Moscow, 1974), II, pp. 9-77 (hereafter *Traktaty); and* his book *Moskovskii kruzhok liubomudrov* (Moscow, 1980).

38. Mann, op. cit., pp. 142-3, 145.

39. Ibid., p. 146.

40. Ibid., pp. 141, 105-6, 296-7.

41. Z. A. Kamensky, 'F. Schelling v russkoi filosofii nachala 19 veka' *(Vestnik istorii mirovoi kul'tury,* 6, 1960, pp. 46-59) sees a strange opposition to this period between 'metaphysical materialism' and 'dialectical idealism'; V. V. Vanslov, *Estetika romantizma* (Moscow, 1966), is closer to traditional positivist and Soviet views in discerning two political shades of romanticism and consigning Odoevsky to the more conservative (p. 25).

42. E. A. Maimin, 'Vladimir Odoevsky i ego roman *Russkie nochi',* in V. F. Odoevsky, *Russkie nochi,* Leningrad, 1975, pp. 247-76 (this essay appears to be a revised version of a section of Maimin's book, *O russkom romantizme,* (Moscow, 1975), pp. 200-31, published a few months earlier), see pp. 257-8, 259, 262-3, 265-9.

43. M. l. Medovoy, 'Puti razvitiia filosofskoi prozy V. F. Odoevskogo v seredine 1820-1840-kh godov' (Avtoreferat dissertatsii na soiskanie uchonoi stepeni kandidata filologicheskikh nauk, L.G.P.I., (Leningrad, 1971), pp. 15-16).

44. M. S. Shtern, 'Filosofsko-khodozhestvennoe svoeobrazie prozy V. F. Odoevskogo (ot apologov k *Russkim nocham)'* (Avtoreferat dissertatsii na soiskanie uchonoi stepeni kandidata filologicheskikh nauk, L.G.P.I., (Leningrad, 1979), pp. 7-9).

45. 'Ot redaktsii', *Russkie nochi* (Leningrad, 1975), pp. 5-6 (hereafter *R.N.,* 1975).

46. V.l. Sakharov, 'Trudy i dni Vladimira Odoevskogo', in Vladimir Odoevsky, *Povesti* (Moscow, 1977), pp. 5-25 (16-17).

47. V. Feierkherd, 'Romantizm i realizm v dilogii V. F. Odoevskogo Salamandra', in *Problemy teorii i istorii literatury sbornik statei posviashchennyi pamiati professora A. N. Sokolov* (Moscow, 1971), pp. 175-87 (187).

48. Sakharov, 'Trudy i dni ...', op. cit., pp. 18-19; and V.l. Sakharov, 'Eshche o Pushkine i V. F. Odoevskom', in *Pushkin: issledovaniia i materialy* (Leningrad, 1979), IX, pp. 224-30 (227-30).

49. M. A. Tur'ian, 'Evoliutsiia romanticheskikh motivov v povesti V. F. Odoevskogo *Salamandra',* in *Russkii romantizm* (Leningrad, 1978), pp. 187-206 (195-6, 206). See also the same author's similar treatment of another neglected story: 'Igosha V. F. Odoevskogo (k probleme fol'klorizma)' *(Russkaia literatura,* 1, 1977, pp. 132-6). Some of Tur'ian's ideas expressed on these stories are similar to suggestions first made by Karlinsky ('A Hollow Shape ...', op. cit., pp. 173-4, 178-9).

50. A. B. Botnikova, *E. T. A. Gofman i russkaia literatura* (Voronezh, 1977), pp. 79, 86, 88. She is critical of the Western study by Passage, but does not appear to know the more reliable one by Ingham (see n. 1). For a full account of Russian and Soviet criticism of Odoevsky, see Chapter 11 of N. J. Cornwell, 'The Life and Works of V. F. Odoyevsky (1804-1869)' (Ph.D. thesis, Queen's University of Belfast, 1983).

51. *Traktaty,* II, p. 605, n. 24; this volume includes several essays and fragments by Odoevsky. See also Sakulin, *Iz istorii...,* I, 1, esp. pp. 270ff, 276ff.

52. John Mersereau Jr, *Baron Delvig's Northern Flowers 1825-1832: Literary Almanac of the Pushkin Pleiad,* (Carbondale and Edwardsville, 1967), p. 40.

53. See for example 'Otvet na kritiku', in *R.N.,* 1975, pp. 231-4; and the earlier 'O vrazhde k prosveshcheniiu, zamechaemoi v noveishei literature' (1836), *Sochineniia kniazia V. F. Odoevskogo,* op. cit., 1844, (n. 5), III, pp. 360-72. The latter article attacked the abuse and debasement of romantic methods, but without giving examples and without referring to romanticism as such. A number of Odoevsky's critical articles have now been reprinted: see in particular V. F. Odoevsky, *O literature i iskusstve* (Moscow, 1982).

54. For detailed discussions of this problem see Iu. Tynianov, 'Arkhaisty i Pushkin' in his *Arkhaisty i novatory* (Leningrad, 1929, reprinted Munich, 1967); and Sigrid McLaughlin, 'Russia: Romaničeskij – Romantičeskij – Romantizm' in *'Romantic' and its Cognates: The European History of a Word,* ed. Hans Eichner (Manchester, 1972).

55. *R.N.,* 1975, p. 173. For an expanded examination of this work see Chapter Four of this study.

56. See Sakulin, Iz *istorii,* I, 2, pp. 111-2.

57. *Traktaty,* II, pp. 181-2. Sakulin attributes this to the late 1830s (*Iz istorii,* I, 2, pp. 369-70).

58. It is interesting to note that the discussion of music in *Russkie nochi,* following 'Poslednii kvartet Betkhovena', does not distinguish between 'romantic' and 'classical' forms when comparing the music of Beethoven with that of Mozart and Haydn.

59. Hans Eichner, 'Germany: Romantisch – Romantik – Romantiker', in *'Romantic' and its Cognates,* op. cit., p. 127.

60. See, for example, René Wellek's 'wider' conception of the romantic movement in his *A History of Modern Criticism: 1750-1950: The Romantic Age* (London, 1955), p. 3; and, applied to Russian literature, Oleg P. Ilyinsky, 'Some Fundamental Problems of Russian Romanticism (based on V. F. Odoyevsky's prose)' (Ph.D. thesis, New York University, 1970, p. v).

61. Sakulin, Iz *istorii,* I, 1, p. 463.

62. McLaughlin, op. cit., pp. 425-6.

63. See Sakulin, *Iz istorii* (e.g. I, 1, pp. 127ff); also V. I. Sakharov, 'O bytovanii shellingianskikh idei v russkoi literature', in *Kontekst 1977. Literaturno-teoreticheskie issledovaniia* (Moscow, 1978), pp. 210-26: and the works quoted in n. 37 above.

64. Sakulin, *Iz istorii,* I, 1, pp. 135-6.

65. 'Aforizmy iz razlichnykh pisatelei, po chasti sovremennogo germanskogo liubomudriia', *Mnemozina,* 2 (Moscow, 1824), pp. 73-84 (81).

66. *R.N,* 1975, pp. 15-16.

67. Glyn Tegai Hughes, *Romantic German Literature* (London, 1979), pp. 5-6.

68. Eichner, op. cit., pp. 125-6.

69. Raymond Immerwahr, 'The Word Romantisch and its History', in *The Romantic Period in Germany,* ed. Siegbert Prawer (London, 1970), p. 50.

70. Sakulin, *Iz istorii,* I, 1, pp. 178-9 and 225.

71. For an examination of this work see M. l. Medovoi, 'Roman V. F. Odoevskogo iz epokhi ital'ianskogo vozrozhdeniia', in *Uchenye zapiski L.G.P.I.,* CDLX (Filologicheskii sbornik) (Leningrad, 1970), pp. 46-64.

72. Sakulin, *Iz istorii,* I, pp. 141-2.

73. Wellek, op. cit., p. 75; Hughes, op. cit., p. 12.

74. Belinsky, *Pol. sob.,* VIII, p. 309 is the main example.

75. *R.N.,* 1975, p. 146.

76. 'Psikhologicheskie zametki' (originally in *Sovremennik,* 1843), in *R.N.,* 1975 (p. 227).

77. Hughes, op. cit., p. 67; Roger Cardinal, *German Romantics in Context* (London, 1975), pp. 80 and 43; Immerwahr, op. cit., p. 34.

78. 'Sekta idealistiko-eleaticheskaia (otryvok iz 'Slovaria istorii filosofii')', *Mnemozina,* 4 (Moscow, 1825), pp. 160-92.

79. On Odoevsky's later writings see, for example, N. M. Mikhailovskaia, 'Vladimir Fedorovich Odoevsky-predstavitel' russkogo prosveshcheniia' *(Russkaia literatura,* 1, 1979, pp. 14-25).

64 *Vladimir Odoevsky and Romantic Poetics*

80. Unfinished projects, to name just the main examples in the genres of fiction, include: *Iordan Bruno i Petr Aretino; Segeliel'. Don Kikhot XIX stoletiia; Dom sumasshedshikh; 4338 god;* and the late *Samarianin*. Fragments of some of these were published; all were ambitious attempts at novels or cycles, upon which the author expended very considerable time and energy.
81. Hughes, op. cit., pp. 4, 53, 67.
82. Cardinal, op. cit., p. 43; Marshall Brown, *The Shape of German Romanticism* (Ithaca and London, 1979), p. 121.
83. Brown, op. cit., pp. 46 and 56.
84. Hughes, op. cit., p. 78.
85. Cardinal, op. cit., p. 65.
86. Sakulin, *Iz istorii*, I, 1, pp. 462-3, 469ff. A short piece on the last-named topic, 'Nauka instinkta: otvet Rozhalinu' (1843) is one of the appendices in *R.N*, 1975, pp. 198-203.
87. Cardinal, op. cit., p. 36.
88. *R.N.,* 1975, p. 25.
89. F. W. J. von Schelling, *Sämtliche Werke* (Stuttgart and Augsburg 1856- 61), VII, p. 470 (quoted from Botnikova, op. cit., pp. 85, 199, n. 24).
90. See Botnikova, op. cit., p. 85; Cardinal, p. 99.
91. *R.N.,* 1975, p. 26.
92. 'Primechanie k Russkim nocham', ibid., p. 191; Odoevsky does not specify any source in Plato, but the *Cratylus* would seem a likely point of departure. In Goethe see for example 'Moritz as Etymologist' from *Travels in Italy*. Elsewhere Goethe claimed that 'writing is a misuse of language': 'Goethe in Sesenheim', in J. W. von Goethe, *The Sorrows of Young Werther and Selected Writings* (trans. Catherine Hutter) ( New York, 1962), p. 175.
93. Cardinal, op. cit., pp. 36-8 (the Novalis quote is on p. 38).
94. Ibid., p. 38.
95. *R.N.,* 1975, p. 35.
96. Loc. cit.
97. Quoted from Cardinal, p. 34. In another fragment ('Poetry and Philosophy') of 1830, Odoevsky contrives to bring together a number of threads here touched upon in a single statement (the romantic – and Russian – view of the poet as prophet; the 'signature'/*signatura*; Plato; and the poeticisation of historical reality); on the function of the poet, he writes: 'At the minute of inspiration he perceives the signature of the period of that time in which he lives and indicates the goal towards which humanity must strive, in order to be on the natural path and not on a perverted one. All other people only perform; hence the elements of poetry must, despite Plato, enter the political fabric of society. In the distinction between this idea and the thought of Plato, may be seen the distinction between the old society and the new', *Traktaty*, II, p. 178.
98. A. N. Nikoliukin, 'Tipologiia zhanra romanticheskoi novelly v vostochnoslavianskikh literaturakh v sravnitel'nom otnoshenii' in *VII Mezhdunarodnyi s"ezd slavistov. Slavianskie literatury* (Moscow, 1973), pp. 319-37 (331).
99. *Pestrye skazki s krasnym slovtsom* ... (St Petersburg, 1833), p. 4.
100. Novalis, *Schriften* (Stuttgart, 1960-75), II, pp. 571-2 (quoted from Brown, op. cit., p. 82).
101. *R.N.,* 1975, p. 24 (cf. p. 35 quoted above).
102. 'Neskol'ko slov (Opyty rasskaza o drevnikh i novykh predaniiakh)', *Sochineniia*, 1844, III, pp. 43-6. Mann also draws attention to this note in a more compositional connection (Mann, op. cit., p. 130).
103. *R.N.,* 1975, p. 227.

104. Ibid., pp. 103 and 109.
105. Ibid., p. 120. The practice of mythologising the history of mankind was, of course, continued in Russian literature by Dostoevsky, particularly in *Son smeshnogo cheloveka*. For a discussion of Odoevsky's possible impact on that story (via his story *Zhivoi mertvets* in particular) see Chapter Two of the present study.
106. *Three Märchen of E. T. A. Hoffmann*, trans. Charles E. Passage (Columbia, SC), 1971, p. 331. Cf. (noted by Passage, op. cit., n. 1 above, pp. 101-2) Kipriano's newly clairvoyant perception of his 'poor Charlotte' in Odoevsky's 'Improvizator' *(R.N., 1975, p. 94)*. Minerals held a considerable significance for the romantics – viz. Odoevsky's reference to 'crystals' in the above passage from 'Sebastian Bach'; on the uses of *Kristall* in Hoffmann see Maria M. Tatar, *Spellbound: Studies on Mesmerism and Literature* (Princeton, 1978), Chapter 4.
107. *Three Märchen, p.* 350.
108. Brown, op. cit., p. 20.
109. See Hughes, pp. 118-19 and 123, Cardinal, p. 89.
110. Leonard J. Kent and Elizabeth C. Knight, Introduction to *Selected Writings of E. T. A. Hoffmann*, I: 'The Tales' (Chicago, 1969), p. 13.
111. Hughes, pp. 16-17, Cardinal, pp. 125-33.
112. *Otechestvennye zapiski*, 6, 1844; see *R.N., 1975*, pp. 74, 183, 201, 286.
113. Siegbert Prawer, Introduction to *The Romantic Period in Germany*, op. cit., p. 9; Cardinal, p. 38.
114. Cardinal, p. 38. *R.N., 1975*, p. 7.
115. Paul Roubiczek, 'Some Aspects of German Philosophy in the Romantic Period', in *The Romantic Period in Germany*, op. cit., p. 314.
116. *R..N., 1975*, p. 8.
117. Hughes, p. 68.
118. 'Nauka instinkta. Otvet Rozhalinu' (fragment), in *R.N., 1975*, p. 199.
119. Gippius, op. cit. (n. 31), p. 8. This may be compared with Hoffmann's use of the 'botanical dressing gown' in *Datura fastuosa*.
120. *R.N., 1975*, p. 34.
121. 'Nauka instinkta ...', op. cit., in ibid., pp. 199-200.
122. *R.N., 1975*, p. 113. The widespread use of synesthetic effects in romantic art is partly attributable, in Maria Tatar's view, to 'a firm belief in the existence of an internal sense that does not differentiate among the various modes of perception' (Tatar, op. cit., p. 46).
123. (Sixteenth fragment) quoted from Hughes, p. 65; Hughes, p. 66.
124. Ibid., p. 16; Cardinal, p. 132. Belief in a sixth (or 'inner') sense which allowed certain people at least 'to look into the past and future, to annul spatial limitations, and to enter into a perfect rapport with nature' was, according to Maria Tatar (op. cit., pp. 45-8, 73), common to the following thinkers: Mesmer, Baader, Ritter, Novalis, Fichte, Schelling and Schubert (the last named believed this faculty to reside in the solar plexus).
125. Sakulin, *Iz istorii ...*, I, 2, pp. 82-90 (on Pordage, pp. 83-4); Jo Ann Hopkins Linburn, 'A Would-be Faust: Vladimir Fyodorovich Odoyevsky and his prose fiction, 1830-1845' (Ph.D. thesis, Columbia University, 1970), pp. 194, 197).
126. *Otechestvennyye zapiski*, 8, 1840, pp. 34-81 (61). This story has now been reprinted and translated (see Chapter Eight).
127. Ibid., pp. 62-4. This passage can be seen as an embellishment on ideas present in 'Zhivoi mertvets' (re. an analysis of which story see Chapter Two), dated a year earlier than 'Kosmorama'.
128. Georg Lukács, *The Theory of the Novel*, trans. Anna Bostock (London, 1971), p. 74.

129. See Cardinal, pp. 48 and 51. For a more cautious view of the application of 'romantic irony' see Hughes, pp. 55-6.
130. *R.N.,* 1975, pp. 8-9.
131. For example Khin (in *Povesti i rasskazy,* op. cit., n. 41 above, p. 29) and Ingham (op. cit., n. 1 above, pp. 184-5).
132. Medovoy, 'Puti razvitiia filosofskoi prozy ...', op. cit., n. 51 above, p. 9.
133. See also the passage on 'the decline of the planet', *R.N.,* 1975, pp. 23-4. Even when the fantastic 'other realm' is involved, as in 'Sil'fida', in Ingham's view (op. cit., p. 185) 'nature has no part in it'. The Finnish scenes in 'Salamandra', which have attracted some attention, were in fact written before Odoevsky's visits to Finland. (For a list of sources available to Odoyevsky, see Feierkherd, op. cit., n. 55 above, p. 178).
134. Immerwahr (p. 35) and Prawer (p. 7), in *The Romantic Period in Germany,* op. cit..
135. Ibid. (Immerwahr), p. 59; on Hoffmann see Hughes, pp. 118-19.
136. This is not true of *all* his writings; he left scribblings of almost all imaginable kinds; suffice it to mention his 'New Mythology' of 'kardiads' and 'efirids', which Sakulin attributes to the influence of Pordage and sees as evidence of a serious interest in forms of mysticism well beyond Schelling (*Iz istorii,* I, 2, pp. 18-21).
137. *Werke,* 1871-3, V, p. 102 (quoted from Vanslov, op. cit., n. 41 above, p. 57).
138. Ilyinsky sees Odoevsky as the only follower of the line of German romanticism in Russian literature, and at the same time its sole representative of 'romantic rationalism' (op. cit., n. 60 above, pp. v and 179). Ingham (op. cit., pp. 191-2) also takes a rationalist view, based largely on the 'Letters to Countess E. P. R-i about ghosts, superstitious fears, deceptions of the senses, magic, cabbalism, alchemy and other mysterious sciences' (in *Sochineniia,* 1844, III, pp. 307-59); yet Odoevsky was also addressing letters of an intensely mystical-religious nature to the same recipient – Countess Rostopchina (see Sakulin, *Iz istorii,* I, 1, pp. 453-7) – and to a mysterious 'NN' (Leningrad, State Public Library, fond 539, Opis 1, pereplet 94): in fact, Nadezhda Nikolaevna Lanskaia (see Chapter 1).
139. Sakulin, *Iz istorii,* I, 1, pp. 150-1, 173-4.
140. 'A biography of a Romantic poet was more than a biography of an author and public figure. The Romantic poet *was* his own hero.' B. Tomashevsky, 'Literature and Biography', in *Readings in Russian Poetics,* ed. L. Matejka and K. Pomorska (Cambridge, MA and London, 1971), pp. 47-55 (49). It is, of course, possible to see *Russkie nochi* as an 'intellectual autobiography', and autobiographical elements have been perceived in certain stories.
141. Ilyinsky, op. cit., p. 4. Goethe himself seems more likely to have been a model for Odoevsky's aspirations than Goethe's Faust, who was more a figure of artistic interest (for a heavy stress on Faust in both these respects see Linburn, op. cit., passim).
142. Schelling, *Werke,* III, p. 629 (quoted in Brown, op. cit., pp. 82-3).
143. Sakharov, 'V. F. Odoevsky i rannii russkii romantizm', op. cit., n. 37 above, p. 417). For further discussion of romantic aspects and the origins of Odoevsky's thought, see Chapter 2 ('The Thinker') in Cornwell, V. *F. Odoyevsky: His Life, Times and Milieu* (London, 1986).
144. Wellek, op. cit., n. 60 above, p. 3. A somewhat vaguer view of the same distinction is given by Lukács: 'the physiognomy of Romanticism, in the proper, narrow sense, becomes blurred ... unless one wishes to extend the concepts of Romanticism to embrace all great literature of the first third of the nineteenth century', *The Historical Novel,* trans. Hannah and Stanley Mitchell (London, 1962), p. 34.

145. As early as 1825, A. A. Bestuzhev (Marlinsky) complained of the gap between theory and practice in the pages of *Mnemozina* ('Vzgliad na russkuiu slovesnost' v techenie 1824 i nachale 1825 godov', in *Literaturno-kriticheskie raboty dekabristov* (Moscow, 1978), p. 76. See also Sakharov, 'V. F. Odoevsky i rannii russkii romantizm', op. cit., pp. 408-11.

146. Immerwahr, op. cit., p. 52; Eichner, op. cit., n. 67 above, pp. 112-13; Erich Auerbach, *Mimesis: The Representation of Reality in Western Literature*, trans. Willard R. Trask (Princeton, 1968), p. 443.

147. N. Mordovchenko, *Belinsky i russkaia literatura ego vremeni*, Moscow-Leningrad, 1950, p. 53; P. Berkov, 'Belinsky i klassitsizm', in *Literaturnoe nasledstvo*, LV (Moscow, 1948), pp. 151-76 (174). See Belinsky's statement quoted above from his Odoevsky article.

148. K. F. Ryleev, 'Neskol'ko myslei o poezii: otryvok iz pis'ma k N.N.', in *Literaturno-kriticheskie raboty dekabristov*, op. cit., pp. 218-22; Lukács, *Soul and Form*, trans. Anna Bostock (London, 1974), p. 79.

149. Sigrid McLaughlin summarises Belinsky's varying views of romanticism in *'Romantic' and its Cognates*, op. cit., see n. 54 above, pp. 444-9.

150. From the introduction to *Ernani* (quoted from Vanslov, op. cit., p. 40).

151. Vanslov, p. 27.

152. McLaughlin, op. cit., pp. 456-8.

153. Lukács, *The Historical Novel*, pp. 63, 68 and 33 (he also refers on p. 68 to 'liberalish Romanticism'). At one point (pp. 33-4) he appears to be attempting to deny that Byron should be considered a romantic.

154. Hughes, op. cit., p. 9; Lukács, *Goethe and his Age*, trans. Robert Anchor (London, 1968), pp. 150 and 202.

155. See Wellek, op. cit., p. 88; Cardinal, op. cit., p. 31.

156. S. S. Prawer, *Karl Marx and World Literature* (Oxford, 1978), p. 397; Marx is known to have sent a copy of *Klein Zaches* to Engels in 1866 (ibid., p. 373).

157. Lukács, *Goethe and his Age*, op. cit., p. 243. For a fuller discussion of 'Romantic grotesque', see Mikhail Bakhtin, *Rabelais and his World*, trans. Helene Iswolsky (Cambridge, MA and London, 1968), pp. 36-45.

158. James Trainer, 'The Märchen', in *The Romantic Period in Germany*, p. 114.

159. Lukács, *The Meaning of Contemporary Realism*, trans. John and Necke Mander (London, 1963), p. 52.

160. 'Deviatnadtsatyi vek', *Polnoe sobranie sochinenii I. V. Kireevskogo v dvukh tomakh* (Moscow, 1911; reprinted Farnborough, 1970), p. 90).

161. Schleiermacher held that 'imagination is the highest and most original part of man and everything outside it only reflection upon it' (quoted by Roubiczek, op. cit., in *The Romantic Period in Germany*, pp. 314-15); F. Schlegel that 'the imagination was an important source of genuine knowledge not attainable by other means' (quoted by Eichner, op. cit., in *'Romantic' and its Cognates*, p. 122); and Novalis, too, stressed 'the one universal strength, Imagination' (Cardinal, op. cit., p. 37).

162. Quoted by Botnikova, op. cit., n. 50 above, p. 184. Cf. Faust's statement in *Russkie nochi* quoted above (see n. 95).

163. Botnikova, p. 184.

164. Brown, op. cit., p. 113; Trainer, op. cit., p. 114. On the tradition of 'steps' and 'ladders' in 'the process of psychic transformation' (from Jacob's ladder, Apuleius and the visions of Zosimos), see C. G. Jung, *Psychology and Alchemy*, trans. R. F. C. Hull, 2nd ed. (London, 1980), pp. 55-7, 62.

165. *Otechestvennye zapiski*, 8, 1840, p. 51. 'Krummacher' – presumably Friedrich Adolph Krummacher (1767-1845), author of *Parables* (1805). The ladder here,

and the use of the adjective 'narrow' *(uzkii),* is reminiscent of the phrase *uzkii put',* which recurs in Odoevsky's writing – as noted by Gippius in the text and title of his 1914 article (see n. 23).

166. Sakulin, *Iz istorii,* I, 2, p. 52.
167. Mann, op. cit., p. 148; *R.N.,* 1975, pp. 5-6; Tur'ian, op. cit., in *Russkii romantizm,* pp. 205-6; Meilakh, 'Pisatel' otkryvaemyi zanovo', op. cit., p. 285.
168. Karlinsky, op. cit., n. 3 above, pp. 173-4; see also Chapter Two.
169. See, for example, Prawer, *The Romantic Period in Germany,* pp. 5-6.
170. For example, Oken's ideas (in *Über Licht und Wärme*) on the formation of the universe ('the periphery is the centre itself – placed everywhere', quoted from Brown, op. cit., p. 105) seem strikingly similar to modern cosmological theory.
171. Lukács, *Goethe and his Age,* p. 150.
172. V. Iu. Troitsky, 'Romantizm v russkoi literature 30-kh godov XIX v. Proza' in *Istoriia romantizma v russkoi literature: romantizm v russkoi literature 20-30kh godov XIX v. (1825-1840)* (Moscow, 1979), pp. 108-72 (164, 168-9).
173. S. E. Shatalov and S. V. Turaev, introduction to ibid., p. 14.

# Chapter 4

# RUSSKIE NOCHI

Genre, Reception, and Romantic Poetics

## I

Readers of the stories of V.F. Odoevsky will have noted something of a mixture in styles, literary devices, and language: digression, philosophical disquisition, and the occasional modernistic quirk. The pages of 'Sebastian Bach' are graced with a few bars of music; the epigraph to 'Sil'fida' ('The Sylph') ends with the quotation ".? ! ?' attributed to 'the nineteenth century'; 'Zhivoi mertvets' ('The Live Corpse') uses dialogue, interior monologue, and thieves' slang; 'Kniazhna Mimi' ('Princess Mimi') has a 'foreword' in the middle; *Pestrye skazki (Variegated Tales)* adopts the Spanish use of question marks and other irregular punctuation as well as an improbable-sounding narrator. All these works date from the 1830s. Readers will also have found in abundance the standard structural devices of the period: the use of varied and multiple storytellers, subtitles ('from the notes of': 'a traveller', 'a lazy man' or 'a cautious man'); the epistolary form; and stories within stories. Much of Odoevsky's fiction is arranged in cycles, most of which are unfinished; his longer stories can appear particularly disjointed from a structural and stylistic point of view (the romantic *dilogiia*, 'Salamandra'; the science-fiction tale *4338-i god [The Year 4338]*; and the realistic society tales 'Kniazhna Mimi' and 'Kniazhna Zizi').

These oddities may be accounted for by a consideration of the structural eccentricities of other works by both major and minor writers in this transitional period of Russian literature; by Odoevsky's supposed failings as an artist – hence his over-reliance on fashionable literary devices; or by a closer look at Odoevsky's adoption of the poetics of romanticism.

It is this third approach that is the main concern of this paper, as applied to the most striking and unusual of Odoevsky's formal oddities – *Russkie nochi (Russian Nights)*.

## II

The genesis of *Russkie nochi* is a complicated one, going back at the very least to the late 1820s. A cycle to be called 'Dom sumasshedshikh' ('House of Madmen') was envisaged in the first half of the 1830s. The project then evolved into 'Russian Nights', a further cycle. The publishing history of the totality of this work is spread over thirteen years, and poses taxing problems to those wishing to take a purist textual approach.

Of the eighteen sections comprising the final text of *Russkie nochi* (an introduction, nine 'nights' – some of which have subdivisions, the 'fourth night' having no less than seven – and an epilogue), nine pieces were published separately, between 1831 ('Poslednii kvartet Betkhovena', 'Beethoven's Last Quartet') and 1839 ('Gorod bez imeni', 'City without a Name'). All the main stories included in the 'cycle', with the exception of 'Poslednee samoubiistvo', 'The Last Suicide', were published in this way. Mention was occasionally made of some of them forming part of a larger design and a 'collected works' was supposedly imminent from the mid 1830s. The stories, however, were received according to their individual merits – in many cases favourably, by such readers as Pushkin, Gogol, Belinsky, and even Herzen.

Of the two remaining 'stories', 'Mstitel' ('The Avenger') had been a part of an unfinished work called 'Iantina' (1836), under the heading 'An Apologetic for Poetry'; this was to have appeared in 1839, but did not. 'Tsetsiliya' ('Cecilia') seems to be related to another unfinished work of the same name, likewise unpublished. The section 'First Night' appeared separately as early as 1836; a continuation was promised, but never materialised.

Thus when the integral work known as *Russkie nochi* finally appeared, only in 1844 as Part I of Odoevsky's three-volumed *Sochineniia*, all that was 'new' to readers and critics of the day was one story – 'Poslednee samoubiistvo' – and the remaining portions of the frame-tale mechanism, including the weighty 'Epilogue'. It is therefore understandable that most critical reaction centred on the ideas of *Russkie nochi* and some readers felt somewhat cheated at being served what they considered to be old dishes with a new dressing. As the sense of *déjà vu* wore off, Odoevsky fell into neglect; his works were not reprinted during his lifetime (he lived another twenty-five years) and he published virtually no more fiction.

When critics (from Skabichevsky in 1870 onwards) began to consider Odoevsky's contribution to Russian literature, they tended still to concentrate on ideas rather than the fiction itself, and most remained puzzled, as we shall see, by the form of *Russkie nochi.*

Textually speaking, Odoevsky complicated matters still further in the early 1860s. Some stories had already been revised between their first appearance and the 1844 edition of *Russkie nochi;* in 1862 Odoevsky made further revisions and a number of annotations to the text for a proposed second edition and also added another preface and a 'note'. This edition, however, did not appear. Nevertheless, when *Russkie nochi* was next reprinted, half a century later still, in 1913, the 1862 revisions were taken as definitive. This action provoked a minor but extended textological polemic; it was finally defended and continued by editors of the next edition, another sixty-two years later (1975, 'Literaturnye pamiatniki').[1] This text is likely to remain the standard one; the 1981 edition reprinted the text of 1975.

## III

In an unpublished variant introduction to *Russkie nochi,* Odoevsky describes it as 'very simple' in form ('eta forma ochen' prosta ...'), suggesting that the work represents a 'higher synthesis' between the genres of drama and novel (a 'romanicheskaia drama').[2] Sakulin saw the formal structure of *Russkie nochi* more as a convenient form for the transmission of the disputes of a circle of friends.[3] Generally, critics have not tended to see it as so 'simple' or straightforward a matter, while general theorists of poetic genre tend to confuse more often than they help.

Tomashevsky writes of Pushkin's Belkin stories and Gogol's Ukrainian tales as 'framed collections of novellas', which indeed they are; however, even the most cursory reading immediately reveals that the framing device of *Russkie nochi* is of a very different order – both from these works and from Odoevsky's own earlier *Pestrye skazki*; neither does it match the systems described by Tomashevsky as 'stepped', 'circular' or 'parallel construction' (*stupenchatoe, kol'tsevoe* or *parallel'noe postroenie*).[4]

*Russkie nochi,* indeed, seems either to fall between or to combine disparate elements of almost all categories of genre-description. Its multiple forms of narration suggest it to be a work containing several points of view. Lotman traces the earliest appearance of such a phenomenon back to drama; however, *Russkie nochi* does not correspond to his examples of the subsequent development into narrative prose of systems of multiple viewpoint: the epistolary novel, such as *Les liaisons dangereuses* (with 'several personae narrating from various positions about the same thing'), or *Evgenii Onegin* (in which 'an author ... sets forth the same content from several stylistic positions').[5]

The obvious affinities of the work with drama and philosophy and the connections of both these forms with narrative fiction lead us ultimately round in a circle. As Paul Hernadi points out:

> The characters in allegorical plays and philosophical dialogues speak on behalf of ideas whose validity they have been evoked to demonstrate; for example, the rudimentary action of *Everyman* or Plato's *Symposium* suggests the inter-personal perspective of fictive characters only to subordinate it to the thematic framework of authorial vision.

This is contrasted to the 'interpersonal perspective internal to the represented action' most commonly found in normal drama; likewise, the role of the Greek chorus is seen as bringing a work closer in texture and effect to narrative fiction.[6] Vygotsky sees the presentation of authorial discourse through a contrived narrator in narrative fiction as a 'literary mask' which he equates with the moral in the fable: 'The fabulist never speaks for himself but always on behalf of a moralizing, teaching or preaching old man'.[7] This didacticism puts the fable, and by extension narrative fiction employing this device, closer once again to philosophical forms, particularly as the fable is often used therein.[8] Philosophy, of course, in its dialogic form of expression, has strong connections with drama. 'Socratic dialogues' are also, for that matter, counted by Bakhtin among the precursors of the novel; indeed, they are 'the novels of their time'.[9]

The novel form is, of course, a possible designation for *Russkie nochi*, as for almost anything else – at least, in Bakhtin's view of the novel:

> The novel, after all, has no canon of its own. It is, by its very nature, noncanonic. It is plasticity itself. It is a genre that is ever questing, ever examining itself and subjecting its established forms to review.[10]

In any case, the boundaries of literature (on one of which, at least, *Russkie nochi* must sit) are held to be constantly changing.

Another category or sub-genre to which some may be tempted to assign *Russkie nochi* is that of the 'anatomy', in the sense described by Northrop Frye (which is close to Bakhtin's conception of the Menippean satire):

ANATOMY: A form of prose fiction traditionally known as the Menippean or Varronian satire and represented by Burton's *Anatomy of Melancholy* characterized by a great variety of subject-matter and a strong interest in ideas.[11]

Frye sees one branch of this form descending from Plato through Erasmus and Voltaire. Its 'tendency to expand into an encyclopaedic farrago' and its 'intellectualized approach' provide strong grounds against dismissing out of hand any relevance of this conception of anatomy to the case of Odoevsky; indeed a number of his lesser works and unfinished projects conform very closely to it. However, the heavy stress placed on vigorous satire by Frye (and on laughter by Bakhtin) in the primary models of this genre (works by Burton, Rabelais, Swift and Sterne, not to mention Petronius, Apuleius and Voltaire) is hardly appropriate to Odoevsky.[12]

Gérard Genette quotes Lévi-Strauss's conception of mythical thought as 'a kind of intellectual *bricolage*' (a kind of do-it-yourself assemblage, made from whatever comes to hand), or the use in a new structure of the remains of previous constructions or destructions, by process of analysis and synthesis; Lévi-Strauss was dealing with myths in a 'primitive' civilization, but Genette envisages an application of this concept to literary criticism (defined by Barthes as 'discourse upon a discourse').[13] Lévi-Strauss himself had spoken of 'a poetry of *bricolage*'; furthermore the literary text can itself at times edge close to the very tissue of criticism: John Sturrock calls the stories of Borges 'as much critical as creative works'.[14] If any work of narrative fiction can justifiably be termed 'intellectual *bricolage*', then *Russkie nochi* must be close to the forefront of likely candidates.

Nevertheless, there does remain a genre (or sub-genre) to which *Russkie nochi* may be ascribed. Its narrative ploys suggest a tradition, by no means unlinked to the genres described by Frye and Bakhtin, that of the frame-tale.[15] If any further subdivision is needed, then the obvious term is the 'philosophical frame-tale'.

We shall return to the features of this tradition later, but at this stage a brief description of the structure of *Russkie nochi* itself is called for.

## IV

In the most general terms, *Russkie nochi* consists of some eighteen sections or units, including an authorial introduction (lying outside the framework device, yet in the spirit of the book as a whole and an integral part of the text in as much as it contains and foreshadows a number of motifs and themes of the work which follows), and an

Epilogue (if not exactly a conclusion to, at least a part of, the frame). Eleven of the eighteen sections are stories, interpolated or 'embedded' (Todorov's term of *enchâssement*, or Tomashevsky's *vstavnye novelly)* in the overall frame.[16] Between the authorial introduction and the frame Epilogue, the work is divided unequally into nine 'nights' on which the frame-device gatherings purport to take place. Of a total (in the 1975 edition) of some 177 pages, the stories taken together comprise just over half the whole. The frame represents an unusually high proportion in such works of the totality of the text, obviously thereby, taking on an importance greater than that of a mere device of convenience; the Epilogue in itself is well over half the length of the total frame and the longest section in the book. There is also a considerable introductory frame portion, totalling some twenty pages. The inter-story frame discussions are either short or absent altogether and the overall structure is irregular: the first story does not occur until the Third Night, while the Fourth Night includes six stories (some of which are very short).

The First Night begins, apparently with third-person narration ('The mazurka ended …'). There follows an inner monologue in the mind of Rostislav, partly a diatribe addressed to an imaginary interlocutor (just one of the variants used of the narrator-narratee situation); however, when his thoughts are described as 'fine ideas' *(prekrasnye veshchi)*, there is a possible confusion of point of view, with the narration slipping momentarily into the (authorial) first person (p. 11). 'Several people' join Rostislav and Viktor to make a visit to Faust (p. 12), but the 'discussion' of First Night ends abortively, with Faust turning the revellers away. It is carried on elsewhere but reported on only, at the beginning of the Second Night, by Rostislav.

Again a 'crowd of young people' congregates at Faust's apartment for Second Night (p. 13), but the conversationalists are Faust, Viktor, Rostislav and Vecheslav (later 'Viacheslav') only. The discussion takes place almost entirely in the form of third-person narration until Third Night, after which it is mostly set out in dramatic dialogue form. Faust dominates the early discussions, telling fables and speaking of Schelling as the Columbus of the soul (pp. 15-16), thus establishing the motif of travel as quest (or inner travel). Faust next reads from a sheet *(listok)* of paper left by two friends of his youth (really, according to Odoevsky's note, a summary of the ideas of Saint-Martin); he then reads a section called 'Desiderata', from the note-book *(tetradka)* of these two young 'seekers', interrupting himself to say that he will read only the essentials. From the *tetradka* he proceeds to the 'extracts from notes' *(otryvki iz zapisok),* in the form of varied materials – the 'Manuscript' which has passed to Faust after the death of his two friends.

Elaborate narrative ploys are clearly already at play. David Baguley, in his observations on the achieving of a variety of 'points of view' within the discourse system, remarks that:

> the only recourse is either to fragment the narrating itself as in the epistolary novel and in the collection of tales ..., or, in a less systematic way, to introduce intradiegetically other levels of narrating by means of such devices as alternative narrators, letters, documents, which provide other points of focus.[17]

Odoevsky makes some use of all these options, particularly the second and third ones, making as a result what Doležel calls 'the authentication authority of the fictional narrator' a complicated factor to assess, as many Russian critics were to find.[18] What Käte Hamburger calls the 'feint' (the 'feigned reality statement' of first-person narration) is committed to an almost grotesque degree.[19] This is particularly so in the Third and Fourth Nights, but applies also to the framing 'story' itself, and particularly to the case of the Epilogue.

The Third Night (subtitled 'Manuscript') brings the first real story – '*Opere del Cavaliere Giambattista Piranesi*', which begins as travel notes, with a visit by the two seekers to an old uncle, 'the bibliophile'. Embedded in this is the narration of the uncle, who begins by claiming to have been depicted in a well-known caricature scene of Naples; a further layer of embedding contains the core – the narration of the supposed Piranesi (the real Piranesi died in 1778, but this one styles himself the Wandering Jew, p. 32).[20] Following this story, according to Faust, the 'neatly-written pages' of the manuscript end (p. 34); he will arrange the rest. Discussion follows, including a quote by Faust from Michel Chevalier (a French 'advocate of industrialization', p. 36).

The Fourth Night consists of Faust's reading from 'a dusty sheaf' entitled 'The Economist' – fragments from the papers of a young man (one 'B') recently deceased, which were apparently sent to the two seekers, with an introductory narrative from the sender and collector (who is left unidentified). 'Brigadir' ('The Brigadier'), the first fragment from B's papers, is narrated, presumably by B, but includes an embedded narration of a life story – purportedly by a corpse. The unknown collator then links this story to the following fragments, 'Bal' ('The Ball') and 'Mstitel'' (a passage from 'The Ball', p. 46, is strikingly similar to one on p.10, on 'the cry of the infant' etc., part of Rostislav's thoughts). The unknown collator links these stories to 'Nasmeshka mertvetsa' ('The Mockery of a Corpse'), the culminating despair of B in 'Poslednee samoubiistvo' (which ends with an apparent prediction of something like a nuclear holocaust), and the perhaps redemptory fragment 'Tsetsiliia'. Faust deems the rest of this manuscript to be illegible and proceeds to a discussion of Bentham, and hence back to the travel notes of the two friends.

This brings us, under Fifth Night, to 'Gorod bez imeni'; the narrative of the seekers (or, rather, one of them) soon gives way to the embedded narration of the *neznakomets* (unknown man), or 'man in black', of the rise and fall of a Benthamite colony, dedicated to 'utility' (*pol'za*). The man in black is then explained away as an 'insane preacher' (p. 72), thus getting round the extravagant time scale of his story. Discussion by Faust and comrades follows.

Sixth Night brings a discussion of 'night' itself and the evils of cards (a pet obsession of Odoevsky's) and then a return to the Manuscript. After 'The Economist', Faust tells us, comes 'Poslednii kvartet Betkhovena', (thus even 'the numbered order' is violated in Faust's presentation, p. 79). Discussion follows.

Seventh Night goes straight into 'Improvizator' ('The Improvisor'), the next part of the Manuscript (the narrative 'I' of this being one of the friends). This story, through Kipriano's magically or diabolically induced clairvoyancy, presents a debunking of literature, history, philosophy and music in a kind of extreme *ostranenie* – everything seen strangely and known from an all-penetrating materialist and rational viewpoint – and even seems to predict the Formalist school of criticism (!): 'through the thin veil of poetic expression, he saw all the mechanical devices of its creation' (p. 94).[21] The ensuing discussion speaks of Beethoven and the Improvisor as expressing 'the one thought from "opposite sides"' in the Gogolian sense, and there is a questioning as to whether Faust is playing the game in the order in which he reads the manuscripts.

Eighth Night, the continuation of the Manuscript, provides the major story, 'Sebastian Bach' – itself an embedded narrative of a middle-aged eccentric, referred to as 'our investigator', who had been encountered by the two friends.

Discussion in Ninth Night leads to the reading of 'extra' pages of the Manuscript, as an 'epilogue', which takes the form of an allegorical judgement scene in which the earlier symbolic heroes (Piranesi, The Economist, the here personified Town Without a Name, Beethoven, The Improvisor, Bach and Segeliel, plus 'a voice from the irreconcilable abyss') all make a brief appearance in the dock.

The lengthy discussion of the Epilogue proper yields the reading of yet a further 'conclusion' to the Manuscript (pp. 145-9), in which the famous ideas of 'the rotting West' and 'the nineteenth century belongs to Russia' are first aired, to be discussed at considerable length thereafter, with the long monologues going to Faust. The frame, therefore, is rounded off by the monopolizing Ninth Night and the Epilogue, in other words, the last fifty pages of the book.

# V

Belinsky's 1844 review of Odoevsky's 'Collected Works', while repeating his earlier praise of individual stories, expressed considerable puzzlement over the 'strange form' of *Russkie nochi*, which, it was felt, might well be attributable to Hoffmann's influence, on the model of *The Serapion Brothers*. The frame-tale device Belinsky found 'unnatural and forced' – indeed, he considered that the conversational links 'weaken the impression of the stories' and would have preferred them to have been assigned to a separate article; the author had done this with the Epilogue, which had 'great merit, but bore no relation to the stories'.[22] Belinsky found himself somewhat at odds with what he considered to be Odoevsky's Slavophile positions. Odoevsky, for his part, was dismayed by Belinsky's failure to appreciate the full philosophical significance of *Russkie nochi*, though admitting that he had left 'much unsaid'; the formal criticism he felt able to face with equanimity:

> Form is a secondary matter; with me it changed in accordance wlth Pushkin's criticism that in my earlier works my personality is too visible; I am trying to be more plastic, that's all.[23]

Indeed, given Odoevsky's own apparent at least conscious disregard for form, it is scarcely surprising that Belinsky and almost all other contemporary critics should have, as Skabichevsky later said, stood too near to Odoevsky to really appreciate *Russkie nochi*, having been distracted by what they considered the ruse of resurrecting old stories under a new guise and the apparently passé nature (in 1844) of Odoevsky's romanticism.

An anonymous review in Senkovsky's *Biblioteka dlia chteniia* (*The Reader's Library*), presumably written by N.A. Polevoy, had this to say on *Russkie nochi*:

> As we don't know what it is supposed to be, we have to take *Russian Nights* as a joke, the one failing of which will consequently be that it is incredibly long, heavy and boring.[24]

The reactionary journal *Maiak* thought more highly of the literary quality of *Russkie nochi*, but found it deficient in Orthodoxy and therefore a 'Western *povest'*" while the positivist inclined critic Valerian Maikov objected to the presence of mysticism and symbols in modern literature.[25] The one strong and positive voice raised in favour of *Russkie nochi* was that of the exiled Decembrist writer and former co-editor with Odoevsky of the 'Liubomudry' journal *Mnezmozina*, Wilhelm Küchelbecker (of whom more later).

Some of the ensuing discussion, of Russian and Soviet criticism of *Russkie nochi*, has already been aired in the previous chapter (on romanticism). A small amount of repetition here may be worthwhile to ensure that a reasonably comprehensive account of the reception of this work is contained within the chapter essay exclusively devoted to it.

Skabichevsky, in 1870, while attempting something of a rehabilitation of Odoevsky, was also puzzled by the form of *Russkie nochi*, which he too felt to be Hoffmannian, and particularly by what he considered Odoevsky's reticence in conveying his thought not 'from himself' *(ot sebia)* but through the devices of 'manuscripts' and intermediaries.[26] B.A. Lezin, in 1907, regarded *Russkie nochi* as an 'author's confession', its form borrowed from *The Decameron*, and stressed the idea of the infinite and Odoevsky's use of antithesis, as well as discussing the theme of the inadequacy of language.[27] Other critics of this period preferred the biographical approach, seeing 'Sebastian Bach' as based on Odoevsky's own artistic life and Odoevsky as 'another Faust'.[28] N.A. Kotliarevsky, attempting to claim Odoyevsky for the symbolist tradition, considered *Russian Nights* to be an immensely important work (together with the philosophical letters of Chaadaev and the articles of Ivan Kireevsky), but at the same time viewed it formally as simply a collection of Odoevsky's stories, 'supplied with a special philosophical commentary'; he stressed the romantic and metaphysical aspects of the work, which account for Odoevsky's contemporaries seeing the stories as somewhat 'hazy' *(tumannye)*, and thought that perhaps 'the real story was written between the lines'.[29]

The leading scholar of romanticism of the turn of the century, I.I. Zamotin, believed that *Russkie nochi* occupied an outstanding place in Russian literature of the 1830s: its form he saw as not so much Hoffmannian as that of classical drama, in terms of its dialogue and chorus figure; it reflected the inspiration of Plato, as well as of Schelling.[30]

The outstanding Odoevsky scholar in prerevolutionary criticism, P.N. Sakulin, was, like many of his predecessors, more interested in ideas than in formal questions; therefore his verdict on *Russkie nochi* as 'the poetic monument of philosophical-mystical idealism' added nothing new, though he did suggest works by Goethe, Wieland, Tieck, and Hoffmann as antecedents.[31] The main response to Sakulin's monumental study, and to the 1913 republication of *Russkie nochi*, came from Vasilii Gippius, who, in what might be considered one of the few 'classics' of Odoevsky criticism, concentrates mainly on endeavouring to determine the exact shade of Odoevsky's romantic ideology; he stresses the general influence of Jena romanticism, perceives an underlying pessimistic dualism, and sees *Russkie nochi* as

Odoevsky's attempt at the romantic 'universal novel', with a form closer to Tieck's *Phantasus* than to Hoffmann.[32]

The Soviet period of literary scholarship contributed nothing to a consideration of the formal nature of *Russkie nochi* until as recently as 1969 when, in what is still the most significant step in the modern re-evaluation of Odoevsky's work, Iurii Mann provided the first sustained reading of the work – not as a collection of stories linked by a contrived philosophical commentary, but as an artistic whole. Mann, despite approaching the book solely from the angle of its connections with what he called 'Russian philosophical aestheticism', gives the first clear exposition of *Russkie nochi* as a literary work, providing a unified reading, a description of what was new in the work and of how it was achieved, as well as an explanation to account for the creation of such a work.[33]

Mann defines *Russkie nochi* as 'a book of searches and new timid hopes' (p.113). Its subject, 'the problems of life' (112) remains at the end unresolved, bearing witness, in Mann's view, to a break from 'the phase of mystical idealism' (so stressed by Sakulin), which is crucial to 'the impression of doubt on which *Russian Nights* is conceived' (113). At the same time, Mann sees *Russkie nochi* as 'a book about everything' (114); Odoevsky's original idea had been 'to reduce all philosophical ideas to one denominator' and to compose 'a huge drama involving all the philosophers of the world' (113); he sees Hoffmann, Pogorel'sky, Goethe, Tieck and Plato as minor participants in its genealogy, but 'the principles of philosophical aesthetics and, in a wider sense, philosophical systematism of the 1820s and early 1830s' as the main influence on Odoevsky's artistic design (116-19). In Mann's view, 'Odoevsky's searches are crystallized in the very structure of his work' (123). The material of the book is arranged in three layers: the stories originally designed for inclusion in 'The House of Madmen', which investigate the lives of 'great' or 'mad' people (the *bezumtsy*), plus the chain of novelettes purporting to be the work of The Economist – nearly all of these works were originally published before 1834 and so represent the oldest layer; a transitional (lower) layer leading towards philosophical universalism composed of the 'unplanned fragments', 'Poslednee samoubiistvo' and 'Gorod bez imeni', reflecting 'collective madness' and connected with (the upper part of the same layer) the intellectual 'journey' of the two deceased friends; and thirdly the overall framework of the deliberations of the four spokesmen – Faust, Viktor, Viachislav, and Rostislav (123-9). Apart from the structure of the whole, interconnections exist within the parts; 'each subsequent character shades in the weakness of the preceding one' and even the great musicians are not spared (124); no real answers are provided, yet 'each answer in some way fills out the previous one' (129). The ample use of 'Odoevsky's favourite device – the handing over of the narration to invented storytellers', which Mann likens to a 'round dance' (*khorovod*) of virtually characterless intermediaries – he traces to Odoevsky's conception of the transmitting of 'legends' from person to person. Through this means, he argues, Odoevsky achieves 'an impression of multiplicity', of the passing on of 'the spirit of the times' as well as extensively utilizing an authorial distancing device (129-30). Odoevsky's own designation of *Russkie nochi* as a 'drama' is seen as reinforcing, by generic definition, two of the work's main qualities: the use of the dialogue form; and the link between all the component sections and all the characters (a 'drama' in the ideal sense), reinforced by the use of the four spokesmen as chorus, which to Odoevsky means 'a personified observer', 'the representation of contemporary consciousness' (131-6).

What was new about *Russkie nochi* and how did Odoevsky achieve his effect? In Mann's view, Odoevsky provided 'a dramatic whole-ness, constructed on the autonomy of its elements and on "reticence" (*nedoskazannost*')' (132). Odoevsky's original introduction to *Russkie nochi* shows that he was in fact aware of what he was doing with its overall structure: he was both continuing old traditions ('including the tradition of the romantic cycle of stories in a dialogical frame') and at the same time introducing innovative features (133). From a position in the mainstream of Russian philosophical aesthetics, Odoevsky had now, in Mann's view, evolved to the assimilation and inculcation of 'an idealist dialectic' by which Faust posited 'the uni-fication of contradictions' as 'the so-called spirit of the times' (142-3). 'Under a veil of archaism', Mann continues, 'intensive innovatory work was accomplished': Odoevsky, as he recognized himself, did not achieve complete unification of the objective and the subjective through dramatic form – a task which Mann sees finally accom-plished only in the modern theatre of Maiakovsky, Brecht and Meierhol'd (146-8). Instead of the answer to 'the problem or life' he found 'an original form of philosophical universalism and a means of drawing the reader's reaction into the action, as well as a dialectical solution to a number of aesthetic problems' (148).

Mann points out the inadequacies of Belinsky's view of *Russkie nochi* (141), and those of Sakulin (105); Gippius's stress on the concept of *dvoemirie* is admitted as being of use in relation to a number of Odoevsky's stories, but is seen as inadequate to explain *Russkie nochi* – a work which cannot be satisfactorily accounted for in terms of the varied forms of metaphysics and romanticism stressed by Kotlia-revsky, Zamotin, Sakulin, or Gippius (106). It derives rather, in Mann's view, from Russian 'philosophical aesthetics' which, as distinct from 'romanticism' in general, he sees as a line, inspired originally by German idealist philosophy (particularly that of Schelling), stretching from Odoevsky and Venevitinov, through Nadezhdin, to Stankevich and Belinsky – the 'top layer' of romantic aesthetics. Opposed in the 1820s both to classicism and to romanticism proper, its formulations contained 'inner difficulties and contradictions' which led it into crisis by the late 1820s, the time when, in Odoevsky's testimony, 'Schelling's philosophy ceased to satisfy seekers of truth and they dispersed in various directions'. (*R.N.*, p. 15). Odoevsky transferred these problems into the artistic sphere and it was this crisis in philosophical aesthetics, Mann considers, that gave rise to 'the unique architectonics of *Russian Nights*, which surmounted the romantic norms and carries the clear imprint of philosophical universalism' (295-300).

If there is a criticism to be levelled at Mann's radical but convincing reappraisal of *Russkie nochi* it is – in contrast to Zamotin, Sakulin and Gippius – its Russo-centric tendency. *Russkie nochi* is a work which seems to cry out to be read in a European context.

Evgenii Maimin, in his essay included in the fine 1975 edition of *Russkie nochi*, sees the work as unique in many ways, perhaps closest to Friedrich Schlegel's definition of the novel as 'a Socratic dialogue of our time', and to the same authority's view of the fragment as 'the most truthful means of artistic expression'.[34] However, the fragmentary nature of the work 'does not detract from its wholeness in terms of inner structure'; on the contrary, it complements 'the deep *musical* unity of all its parts'. Musicality for Maimin is the key compositional principle of *Russkie nochi*:

> The motion of narration is determined not by the logic of a developing plot, rather by laws of inner association, variational repetition, the intensification of motivating ideas and the collision of conflicting motifs within the limits of a single theme (which in musical language is called 'counterpoint'). (263)

Although accepting a Platonic influence on the dialogues of *Russkie nochi*, Maimin sees them forming ultimately a monological rather than a polyphonic utterance, and the dialectical nature of the work residing rather in the stories, which, he says, 'are not straight analogues to the philosophical theses … but free poetic analogues of the free parable type', and particularly in the effect produced by the juxtaposition of dialogues and stories (264). Like Mann, Maimin sees *Russkie nochi* as 'a novel dedicated to the unsolved questions of life and history'; it opens with questions to which there will be no final and simple answers; but the whole plot of the novel is the search for answers (265). He also sees the novellas (270) 'in a tight ideational-plot relationship one with another' (referring to the links, for instance, between 'Bal', 'Mstitel'" and 'Nasmeshka mertvetsa'), but departs somewhat from Mann's stress on the basic tone of 'disappointment' (Mann, p. 119), declaring that 'Odoevsky's poetic consciousness can be – and at times is – tragic, but never pessimistic' (272). The problems of happiness and cognition, if not solved, are able to 'reach their highest point' in the last stories by emphasizing the medium of music – the fullest and deepest manifestation for Odoevsky of 'the poetic principle' and the form of art most capable of transmitting 'the inexpressible' (273).

B.F. Egorov, in the editorial preface to the same edition, writes that Odoevsky's 'fundamentally dialogical and ... fragmentary' method is tied up with his conception of 'the general interaction of appearances and structures'; *Russkie nochi* is, he says, a work of which 'it is impossible to give an exact generic description, and the totality of the ideas and forms of which it is impossible to describe, even within the limits of an academic monograph' (5-6). Few, one suspects, would rush to disagree with him.

V.I. Sakharov, in the introduction to his 1977 edition of Odoevsky's stories, regards Odoevsky as 'justly considered a master of the cycle of stories, in which each work shades in and explains other things and in its turn finds a new meaning'.[35] He also added Joseph de Maistre's *Les soirées de Saint-Pétersbourg* to the list of possible models for *Russkie nochi*.[36] Yet another model, or at least possible source of influence, put forward in the 1970s was Heine's *Florentine Nights*.[37]

M.I. Medovoy, in his 1971 dissertation, considered the usual identification of Odoevsky with Faust as unwarranted; the other conversationalists were also mouthpieces for the author's ideas and experiences and, in any case, 'Odoevsky thought more broadly and more freely than his protagonists'.[38]

T.N. Raspopova, in an 1977 article, attempted to demonstrate the importance of the deliberately fragmentary nature of *Russkie nochi* to its overall compositional unity by considering the 'fragment' as a genre, and then differentiating between Odoevsky's use of the terms *fragment, otryvok, zapiski* and *rukopis'*. She stresses the cumulative effect of a number of fragments arranged in a cycle – or indeed, in her view, two cycles, involving the opposition of 'spirit' to 'flesh' and representative of the Schellingian ideas of early romanticism as confronted by the more doubting late romantic stage of 'the search for truth'.[39]

Finally M.S. Shtern, in her 1979 dissertation, also stresses the interrelation of fragment, cycle and dialogue: 'The structure of the cycles reconstructs the unity of the macroworld of nature, history, civilization, and the micro-world of separate human existence.' This is achieved, she says, following Maimin's lead, by the 'musical-leit-motif character' of the composition, inner association, variation, repetition, and the interplay and development of fundamental 'musical' themes of the book, reduced to key words or phrases in 'the numerous individual motifs linking the various cycles and fragments'.[40]

Western commentators have had little enough to add, to date, to the discussion of the form of *Russkie nochi*. Karlinsky (1966) stresses the original development given by Odoevsky to ideas derived from Schelling and the 'amazingly advanced' quality of his thought, but says little about structural matters.[41] Matlaw (1965) sees a particular progression in the lives, or stories, within *Russkie nochi* but regards the Epilogue as undermining the unity and Odoevsky's inability to dramatize his dialogues sufficiently as a major shortcoming; '*Russian Nights* thus emerges as a work of grandiose intentions and formal innovation', he writes, but one whose goals were not fully realised. Nevertheless, Matlaw sees the nine unequal 'periods' comprising *Russkie nochi* as forming 'a logical and a dialectic progression':

> Each of the stories has its own independent narrative scheme and unity, but it is precisely the subordination of the stories to the larger scheme of *Russian Nights* that shows them to their best advantage.[42]

The most extensive pre-1980s published Western treatment of Odoevsky's fiction, by Claude Backvis (1968), makes only the barest passing reference to the existence of *Russkie nochi* as an entity; Charles E. Passage calls it 'an impressive if tendentious prose poem' and considers it to be non-Hoffmannian in its overall structure; while Norman W. Ingham sketches the similarities and differences between the 'frame' in Odoevsky and Hoffmann.[43] Richard Ilgner calls *Russkie nochi* 'in form a curious hybrid between drama and novel' and sees Odoevsky's earlier intention to include a further spokesman in the frame – 'Me – Russian Skepticism', as evidence of an abandoned narrator who 'was to have originally played the Mephistophelian role, which now is assigned to Faust'.[44]

Notwithstanding Mann's view of *Russkie nochi* as developing predominantly out of the Russian literary and philosophical traditions of the 1820s and 1830s, many obervations offered by Soviet and prerevolutionary Russian commentators already point towards the necessity for assessing the work in the more general context of the poetics of European, and especially German, romanticism.

# VI

It is generally agreed that the frame-tale, comprising a group or groups of stories or novellas arranged in a cycle or within a frame (*Rahmen*), and perhaps even the form of the novella itself, originated

in the literature of the East. Harald Weinrich writes of the Eastern
idea that man comes to insight and understanding not so much by
thought process as by telling and listening to stories; the novella, or
the frame-tale, usually assumes a didactic quality (the frame's function
later being taken over by the panoramic social background custom-
arily depicted in the realist novel), challenging, by the moral force
of what is narrated, the real world of power politics and absolute
despots.[45] Walter Benjamin (in a view which closely coincides with
Odoevsky's romantically expressed theory of legend – or 'epic' in its
broadest sense, to include tale and folk song) states that 'experience
which is passed from mouth to mouth is the source from which all
story-tellers have drawn'; he emphasizes the role of travellers, the
trade structure of the Middle Ages and the vital importance of mem-
ory in the furtherance of this process.[46]

Invariably cited as the most prominent early model for works of
this type of construction is *The Thousand and One Nights*, which pre-
sented a vast compendium of stories, purportedly told or retold on
that time scale by a single primary narrator under particularly con-
strained circumstances.

The first European example usually cited is *The Decameron*, Boc-
caccio's fourteenth-century book of a hundred tales, supposedly told
in ten days not just by a single narrator, but 'an assembled company
of raconteurs'.[47]

Chaucer's *The Canterbury Tales*, of course, soon followed in Eng-
land. The French *nouvelle* took *The Decameron* as its formal model, but
by the mid-sixteenth century the term had become virtually inter-
changeable with the *conte* and formal requirements inherited from
Boccaccio, such as the frame, were generally abandoned; as seven-
teenth- and eighteenth-century prose proliferated diversely in theme
and form, the terms *roman*, *nouvelle* and *conte* seem to have retained
few overtones of generic differentiation.[48] At the close of the eigh-
teenth century, however, the romantic practice, particularly in Ger-
many, of reusing old literary forms in new ways brought a new spate
of experimentation with the frame-tale genre.

During this period in particular (we quote here, and in the Appen-
dix genealogy which follows, a dozen or so examples from the half
century which separates Goethe's *Conversations with German Emi-
grants* and Odoevsky's *Russkie nochi*), considerable variations take
place: in the function of the frame; in the deployment of the narra-
tive voice (or voices); and in the arrangement of the material nar-
rated – not to mention the nature of this material and the question of
overall authorial intent.

As Martin Swales has pointed out, the frame can be used either 'as
a pointless piece of narrative sophistication', or 'it can have profound

implications for any understanding of the narrative technique of the novelle as such'; when any significant use of the frame device applies

> the work as a whole operates within two kinds of narrative direction: there is a world of which the narrator tells, and also a world within which and to which he tells his story. The central interpretative issue is the relationship between these two aspects of narrative reference.[49]

Early examples, notably *The Thousand And One Nights*, tend to operate within a structure devised to exploit the motivating principle of 'narration under pressure', or, in Todorov's phrase, 'a story or your life!'[50] The process of narration is thereby used within the text, as a matter of life or death and, beyond the text, has implications for the relationship between, as Swales points out, 'the narrator and the world that receives his art'; this applies to the listener within the frame situation and, to an extent, the readers outside it; thus 'the aim and function of narrating (and of listening) becomes part of the overall import'.[51] Hence Weinrich's comment (above) on the essentially didactic quality of the frame-tale.

The role of the listener and the possibility, indeed the dire necessity, of his/her being influenced by the narration is obviously of vital importance in *The Thousand And One Nights,* where the process of narration is used continually (for a thousand and one nights, excepting the twenty-night gap which Scherezade takes off to give birth clandestinely to twins) to put off the dreaded hour. Something of this remains in *The Decameron* in the motivation of the frame situation under the threat of plague which can be seen, in the light of the hundred stories told, to be both medical and moral. The stories themselves are presumed to be imaginary (indeed Boccaccio in the Author's Epilogue expressly denies being their inventor), and purport to adapt to the needs and nature of their particular audience (e.g. the presence within the ten of seven ladies), whose reception of each story is (generally uniformly) commented upon. The device of narration under pressure, or at a time of freak catastrophe, tends to fade somewhat in later examples, although it is still present in the background of Goethe's *Conversations of German Emigrants* (who have been displaced by the French Revolution), while it receives an ironic and perhaps parodic reversal in the motivating device of Heine's *Florentine Nights,* by which 'fantastic stuff enough' is narrated by one Maximilian for the nocturnal entertainment and edification of 'a languid girl moribund with consumption'.[52] The art of oral narrative is more commonly, however, replaced by the reading of literary works already composed (as in the examples by Tieck and Hoffmann) by the story-tellers themselves, or, in the cases of Wackenroder, Potocki, and Odoevsky, of manuscripts purportedly written by a third party, not present in the frame situation, who may well be in some way removed in time and who is often dead. Several degrees of subsidiary narrators are, in some cases, likely to be involved. In the concept of the 'night', when retained, there may be preserved something of the flavour of its oriental origins, but it is now rather more a social occasion when friends foregather.[53]

The loss of this strong compositional ingredient from what may be termed the 'novella tradition' of the frame-tale is liable to be compensated for by the introduction of a more complex, abstract and plotless discussion, which may best be seen as descending from the 'philosophical tradition' of Plato's dialogues. Goethe's *Conversations of German Emigrants*, 'a collection of novellas with a discursive dialogue framework', probably influenced by Diderot's *Jacques le Fataliste*,[54] may well have been the key work in establishing this trend. Thus the frame may take on the qualities of a symposium on art and aesthetics (in the case of Hoffmann) or a philosophical discussion of the future of Russia (in *Russkie nochi*). Alternatively, however, it may be considered to be merely 'an excuse' whose effect is to diminish the stories within it (as has been said of Tieck's *Phantasus*[55]); or be virtually non-existent, as exemplified by *The Night Watches of Bonaventura* (essentially a fictional biography in the first person, told out of chronological order,[56] but including interpolated contributions by a variety of sub-narrators) or even *The Saragossa Manuscript* (the overall framing device of which work does not extend beyond the single-page Foreword, although there is a very extensive subsidiary framework).

Of the near-contemporary works which have been suggested as possible influences upon the form of *Russkie nochi*, the first mention must be of Goethe. Although *Faust* and *Wilhelm Meister* had a considerable impact upon Odoevsky (as is evidenced by Odoevsky's adoption of the name Faust and by the second epigraph to *Russkie nochi*, quite apart from any other points of contact), it would scarcely be arguable that these works could have had more than the most tangential influence upon the structural design of *Russkie nochi* (*Faust* being in a sense a 'fragment' and *Wilhelm Meister* including interpolated novellas or narratives). *Conversations with German Emigrants* (generally considered a lesser work), as has been noted, merits much closer comparison, given both the content and the attention paid by Goethe to the frame situation which, in the words of Swales, explores 'the full thematic implications of a particular kind of narrative constellation', involving questions (not far removed from Odoevsky's interests) of interpretation and understanding.[57] This apparently unfinished work includes six stories of a previous epoch (four of them narrated by a priest); the brief dialogues between stories explore moral and aesthetic issues.

Wackenroder's *Fantasies on Art* (*Confessions and Fantasies*), com-
pleted and published posthumously by Tieck in 1799, includes the
novella of the fictional musician Joseph Berglinger and his purported
associated writings. C.M. Wieland's *The Hexameron of Rosenhaim*
(1805), a late and lesser work by a minor writer, contains three prose
fairy tales and three novellas – the first group of a wondrous nature
and the second contemporary and prosaic, reflecting Wieland's view
of the novella as taking place in the real world. The six stories issue
from six narrators, the last of whom is a woman telling what purports
to be her own story. The frame is of a contrived nature, involving
superficial salon discussions.

Tieck, himself something of a theorist of the novella, combined in
1812 some of his published stories (such as 'The Fair-Haired Eck-
bert') with some new material (such as 'The Elves'), added a Frame-
work (which he considered to be 'a novel on a small scale') and
'Boccaccio-like showed a group of friends reading and discussing
the contributions' in rather 'prolix' conversations on literary and
other aesthetic questions.[58] It was probably the compositional history
of the finished product, known as *Phantasus*, which more than any-
thing suggested the parallel with *Russkie nochi* seen by some later
Russian critics.

The most discussed work in this connection (by critics from Belin-
sky onwards, not omitting Odoevsky's own contribution dated from
the early 1860s and included in subsequent editions of *Russkie nochi*)
has been Hoffmann's *The Serapion Brothers*. This extensive work of
nearly one-thousand pages includes some twenty-eight stories,
among which are a number of Hoffmann's best-known tales. Again
the frame was constructed *a posteriori* and the form is believed to owe
something to *Phantasus*; the frame is motivated as 'a reunion of
young friends', six literati in all, who hold eight weekly evenings to
read aloud their own compositions, which are designed to illustrate
the literary, musical, aesthetic, and supernatural questions arising in
their animated and important between-story discussions, which com-
prise nearly a quarter of the whole text. A 'remarkably professional'
full translation into Russian of *The Serapion Brothers* was published (in
eight volumes) in Moscow in 1836; this fact and the rather equivocal
nature of Odoevsky's later denial of any imitation of Hoffmann in
*Russkie nochi* leave the question of the influence of this work still
open, quite apart from the extent of Hoffmann's overall impact upon
Odoevsky.[59] Nevertheless, the structural parallel is perhaps no closer
than in the cases of some of the other works mentioned and, as we
have seen, Odoevsky would not necessarily have had to be familiar
with *The Serapion Brothers* specifically in its complete form to have
been able to devise the structure of *Russkie nochi*.

In the same year which saw the Russian translation of *The Serapion Brothers*, and in the following issue of the same journal in which Odoevsky's 'First Night' was published, there appeared a translation of the 'First Night' of Heine's *Florentine Nights*. L.Iu. Romanenko perceives 'a direct contact' between Heine's work and Odoevsky's aesthetic preoccupations and even suggests that Odoevsky may have acted as Heine's translator.[60] There is, however, little structural similarity between the two works; Heine's 'novel', composed hurriedly as an uncontroversial potboiler, got no further than its second 'night' (though nevertheless it was originally to include a further portion which the author had deemed it wiser to suppress), and the closest parallel with *Russkie nochi* lies in the inclusion of romanticized depictions of musicians: in Heine's case, Bellini and Paganini.

The main Russian work occasionally cited as a predecessor to *Russkie nochi* is Pogorel'sky's *Dvoinik, ili moi vechera v Malorossii (The Double, or My Evenings in Little Russia,* 1828), a frame-story containing four tales, and also (like Hoffmann and Tieck – its likely sources) employing the device of reading one's own stories (in this case those of the narrator and his double) from manuscript.[61] Works by Vel't-man could also be considered.

It may also be relevant to mention other structural curiosities of the period which may either have had some slight impact upon, or may invite brief comparison with, *Russkie nochi.* These might include *The Night Watches of Bonaventura* and *The Saragossa Manuscript,* mentioned above (the former, the authorship of which has never been settled, was published anonymously in 1804; the first part of the latter was published, also anonymously, in St Petersburg in the same year). The extraordinary text of 'Bonaventura', although seeming to anticipate much in nineteenth-century Russian literature, seems to have been little known outside a small circle in Germany.[62] Potocki's compendious work, however, is a different matter: its original Petersburg publication, its known impact upon Pushkin and Viazemsky, and Potocki's masonic connections with Count M.Iu. Viel'gorsky[63] (a close friend of Odoevsky's) all make it unlikely that Odoevsky could have failed at least to know of *The Saragossa Manuscript.* Apart from the device of the manuscript and the motif of travel, however, there is little either formal or thematic similarity with *Russkie nochi.* The best-known structural eccentricity (or perhaps monstrosity) of the time was certainly Maturin's *Melmoth the Wanderer* (1820) which had no small impact in Russia; this work was originally planned as a frame-tale (a series of stories depicting encounters with the tempter Melmoth) or a cycle, but Maturin instead chose a system which has been described as 'Chinese-box perversity – story within story within story, a perpetual shift and distancing of narrator from reader which chills the latter's interest and belief'.[64] As it is, Maturin's 'tale' (such is the subtitle) spans nearly seven-hundred pages, a length similar to that of *The Saragossa Manuscript*.

Not to be ignored either, in a definitive study of Odoevsky's work, are various other recognized influences upon his literary development: *The Pančatantra*, the ancient Indian collection of didactic stories (containing 'five chapters' dealing with five principal topics of courtly policy); the work of Cervantes, whose narrative techniques set the pattern for European literature thereafter (quoted by Odoevsky, along with Sterne, in his later additions to *Russkie nochi*, pp. 184 and 189); La Bruyère's *Les Caractères* (1688), an important model for Odoevsky's apologues of the 1820s; and the works of Jean Paul Richter, frequently cited by Belinsky and others as antecedents of narrational techniques in particular Odoevsky tales.

In the case of *Russkie nochi*, the connection between form and content can also be traced in its philosophical precursors: Odoevsky acknowledged that his interest in Plato was by no means solely philosophical;[65] alongside the mystical ideas of John Pordage and Louis Claude de Saint-Martin may be set the dramatic dialogues of Giordano Bruno, and the poetic theosophy of Jacob Boehme or *Naturphilosophie* of Schelling. The most immediate philosophical work descended from the dialogical tradition of Plato, however, was Joseph de Maistre's *Les soirées de Saint-Pétersbourg* (1821) – a series of eleven dialogues (or *entretiens*) dealing with human government and other political and philosophical problems conducted by three 'characters' (The Count, The Knight, and The Senator). The work begins with a six-page description of St Petersburg, in the first-person narration of the Count (apparently de Maistre himself), and then breaks into a three-way dialogue; the setting device (it can scarcely be termed a frame) establishes time (July 1809) and place, then gives way to a '*symposie philosophique*'.[66] Copious notes follow each dialogue. In works of this tradition, of course, fictional tales as such are normally completely absent. Notwithstanding Odoevsky's later hostile comments on de Maistre's Catholic messianism, it seems likely that *Les soirées de Saint-Pétersbourg*, written by a pupil of Saint-Martin, at the very least impelled Odoevsky towards his earlier intention of calling his main work (which was eventually to become 'Russian Nights') 'Peterburgskie nochi'.[67]

Detailed study and further research may well reveal the degree of structural, and indeed thematic, proximity of some of the above works to *Russkie nochi* and may yet produce more prospective models.

## VII

*Russkie nochi* may thus be seen as something of a synthesis of what we have termed the novella tradition of the frame-tale, stemming from *The Thousand and One Nights*, and the philosophical tradition which comes down from Plato. The very philosophical import of *Russkie nochi*, and the view which it presents of Russia, in itself preserves more than a vestige of the didactic function of the original Eastern tales. Synthesis, as a concept in itself, embodies one of the fundamental ideas of romantic philosophy and provides in this instance a unique Russian illustration of the romantic aesthetic of the mixing of genres – the combination of innovation with archaism noted by Mann.

Indeed, we have been, throughout this discussion, moving more and more in the direction of romantic poetics; it has perhaps by now become apparent that therein may lie the compositional key to the structuring of *Russkie nochi.*

Some romantic sources of *Russkie nochi* are quite explicit: Schelling, as we have noted, is considered the Christopher Columbus of the soul and mention is made (pp. 15 and 17) of John Pordage and Saint-Martin (the latter being prominent among the mentors of German romanticism), both post-Schellingian influences on Odoevsky. Other thinkers known to have influenced Odoevsky, such as Bruno, Boehme, and Spinoza, also contributed to Schelling's system of Identity, at the all-embracing 'point where all differences are reconciled'.[68] The propensity for synthesis, so widespread in Odoevsky's writing and particularly irritating to Belinsky, is clearly stated by Faust in the Epilogue: 'there is no opinion the contrary of which could not be established', the result being that 'epochs of contradiction end in what is known as syncretism' (p.146).[69] Novalis, too, was anxious to promote the process, or philosophy, of reconciliation through symbol.

The German romantics, like Odoevsky, conceived grandiose encyclopaedic projects which often got no further than the fragmentary stage; Marshall Brown speaks of: 'the conception of the romantic novel as a fragment – whose completion is relegated to a mythically distant future', while Thomas McFarland sees the structures of romantic consciousness as favouring 'an actual incompleteness striving towards a hypothetical unity'.[70] *Russkie nochi*, Odoevsky's single completed major project, is, as we have seen, basically a collection of fragments; the fragment itself has been described as 'a new revolutionary and still only partly accepted form' created by Novalis and Schlegel.[71] According to Todorov, the romantics' favourite genres are specifically the dialogue and the fragment, the one for its unfinished character, the other for the way it stages the search for and the elaboration of ideas: both share in the same valorization of production with respect to the product.[72]

This statement could have been written as a virtual description of *Russkie nochi.*

The theme of madness in connection with the higher forms of spiritual activity, so prominent in the 'artistic' stories of *Russkie nochi*, echoes well-known views of Schelling and Hoffmann. Odoevsky's dual stress on the inadequacy of language, yet the universal capacity of poetry (which 'enters into every action of man', p. 35), compares closely to, and probably derives from, Schelling's Nature Philosophy, the 'Magic Idealism' of Novalis and the psychology of Schubert, Ritter and Carus. At the beginning of 'Sebastian Bach', we hear of 'a secret language, hitherto almost unknown but common to all artists', and musical notes are referred to as 'hieroglyphics' (pp. 103 and 109). G.H. von Schubert referred to the 'hieroglyphic language' of dreams connecting the inner mind with outside events across time, accessible only to the 'hidden poet'; Albrecht's potted mythic history of mankind (in the same story) may be compared to similar passages from Hoffmann's *Märchen*, the mythic elements of which are said to derive from Schubert (a student of the romantic physicist J.W. Ritter, who had been greatly influenced by Schelling).[73]

The long first sentence of *Russkie nochi* outlines the nature of the quest, the 'wonderful task' (*chudnaia zadacha*, p.7) constantly engaged in by the human soul. Both the quest and the layers that have to be removed to protect 'the sacred secret' (*zavetnaia taina*, p. 8) are reminiscent of quests and veils in works by Novalis. Veils in Odoevsky's work (*zavesy),* or similar articles (*pokrov* – cover, *obolochka* – membrane, *pelena, pokryvalo* etc.), are frequently removed or peeled off to attain a further dimension of truth until, as in *Russkie nochi*, we approach 'the deepest recess of the human soul …', where there is 'neither time nor space' (p. 34); this is the place of the poet and of the musician (the young Sebastian's nocturnal vision in the moonlit Gothic church). The veil and other forms of body covering, long connected with symbol and rhetoric, thus take on a special importance in Odoevsky's work.[74] Novalis, Schubert and Carus were also concerned with states of mind which blur all boundaries and in which 'time and space become an indivisible unity'.[75]

The impact of German romanticism as a whole on the thought and fiction of Odoevsky was perhaps rather more considerable than is generally acknowledged, extending beyond merely the theory of Schelling and the practice of Hoffmann. However, below these layers of theme, idea, and symbol there lies the vital substratum of romantic poetics.

The concept of 'romantic irony', which has already been discussed in the previous chapter, can be seen to feature as early as the authorial introduction to *Russkie nochi*: literary works of aesthetic pretensions 'must themselves be able to answer for themselves' (pp. 8-9), while the lengths to which Odoevsky went to distance himself from his eventual reader are obvious enough. Odoevsky's use of the imagery of, for example, nature philosophy is frequently contained within an ironical framework and his fiction as a whole avoids the more extreme obscurity and ultra-mysticism of many of the German romantics. Gippius and Mann have stressed 'pessimism' and 'disappointment' respectively in Odoevsky, while Maimin and Sakharov have argued for the mystical and fantastic elements to be seen as essentially artistic devices. Sakulin had disputed that Odoevsky was ever a wholehearted Schellingist; a strong aesthetic influence on Odoevsky, though, Schelling certainly was.[76] Schelling considered art to be 'the only true and eternal organ and document of philosophy'; art opens to the philosopher the holy of holies ...'[77] He continues:

> What we speak of as nature is a poem lying pent in a mysterious and wonderful script. Yet the riddle could reveal itself, were we to recognize in it the odyssey of the spirit.

Nature to the artist, in Schelling's view, is 'the imperfect reflection of a world existing, not outside him, but within'.[78] Schelling's vision of such an 'odyssey' or quest, as with the quest in *Russkie nochi*, is reminiscent of Todorov's view of *The Quest of the Holy Grail*: the quest for a code to decipher the divine language, 'the search for God beneath the veil of allegory' and, ultimately, 'the quest of narrative'.[79]

The connection between romantic philosophy and poetics (or, to use James Engell's term, 'transcendental poetics') cannot be more clearly stressed than in Schelling's dictum that 'only philosophy can once again open for consideration sources of art that have been largely exhausted in their creativity'.[80]

One contemporary reader at least, Wilhelm Küchelbecker, wrote of *Russkie nochi* in terms of the romantic poetics in which it was conceived:

> Odoevsky's book *Russian Nights* is one of the most ingenious books in the Russian language .... The number of questions he raises! Of course, hardly any of them are resolved, but let us give thanks for their being raised – and in a Russian book! He brings us to the threshold; the sanctum is locked; the sacrament is shut away; we are perplexed and ask: has he himself been in the sanctum? Was the sacrament exposed in front of him? Was the enigma solved for him? However, all thanks to him: he has understood that there is an enigma, and a sacrament and a sanctum.[81]

Schelling wrote, in the section on aesthetics at the end of his *System of Transcendental Idealism*:

> every true work of art ... lends itself to an infinite number of interpretations without our being able to say whether this infinity is the work of the artist himself or resides solely in the work.[82]

If, in the view of literary historians, *Russkie nochi* and Odoevsky do not totally match Schelling's ideas on art and the role of the genius, perhaps we should remember the comments by D.W. Foster on what the short stories of Borges really seek to demonstrate:

> The proper emphasis of a concern for philosophy and literature must fall not on the adequacy of the systems/texts generated, but on their diversity and the inherently curious nature of their details.[83]

# APPENDIX:

## A Tentative Genealogy of the 'Frame-Tale'

| Novella Tradition | | | Philosophical Tradition |
|---|---|---|---|
| | *Europe* | *Russia* | |
| *The East* | | | |
| Pañcatantra etc. | | | Plato's dialogues |
| *The 1001 Nights* | | | |
| | The Decameron | | |
| | The Canterbury Tales | | |
| | Cervantes | | Giordano Bruno |
| | Goethe, *Unterhaltungen deutscher Ausgewanderten* (1794) | | Diderot, *Le Neveu de Rameau* (1761) |
| | Tieck/Wackenroder, *Phantasien über de Kunst* (1799) | | *Jacques le fataliste* (1773) |
| | *Die Nachtwachen des Bonaventura* (1804) | | |
| | Potocki, *Manuscrit trouvé à Saragosse* (1804-1813) | (first part published anonymously in St Petersburg, 1804) | |
| | Wieland, *Das Hexameron von Rosenhain* (1805) | | de Maistre, *Les Soirées de Saint-Petersbourg* (1821) |
| | Tieck, *Phantasus* (1812) | | |
| | Hoffmann, *Der Serapionsbrüder* (1819-1821) | | |
| | W. Irving, *Tales of a Traveller* (1824) | Pogorel'sky, *Dvoinik, ili moi vechera v Malorossii* (1828) | |
| | *The Alhambra* (1832) | (complete Russian translation of *Der Serapionsbrüder* and partial translation of *Florentinische Nächte*, 1836) | |
| | Heine, *Florentinische Nächte* (1836) | Odoevsky, tales (from 1831) | |
| | | 'Noch' pervaia' (1836) | |
| | | *Ruskie nochi* (1844) | |

# Notes

For editions of *Russkie Nochi*, see Select Bibliography

Quotations in this paper (page numbers in the text) refer to the 1975 'Literaturnye pamiatniki' edition, under the general editorship of B.F. Egorov (referred to below as '*R.N.*').

1. See the annotations to *R.N.* 1975; on the polemic (participants in which were: P.N. Sakulin, 1913; G.O. Vinokur, 1927; N.F. Bel'chikov, 1954; and L.D. Opul'skaia, 1957) and the 1975 editors' decision to adhere to the policy of the 1913 edition, see p. 279 (n.4). Odoevsky himself (ibid., pp. 185-6), in his 1862 preface, explains the impossibility and undesirability of radically rewriting a much earlier work. For a discussion of the ideas present in *Russkie nochi*, see Cornwell (1986, Chapter Two *passim*.)

2. Quoted from P.N. Sakulin, *Iz istoriia russkogo idealizma. Kniaz' V.F. Odoevsky. Myslitel – Pisatel*, vol.I, parts 1 and 2 (Moscow, 1913), 1, 2, p. 225. See V.I. Sakharov's introductions to the 1981 edition (pp. 20, 22) and to V.F. Odoevsky, *O literature i iskusstve* (Moscow, 1982), p. 21 for further unpublished remarks by Odoevsky on the form of the novel and *Russkie nochi* in particular.

3. Sakulin, I, 2, p. 227.

4. B. Tomashevsky, *Teoriia literatury* (Leningrad, 1925; reprinted Letchworth, 1971), pp. 200, 202. Lermontov's *Geroi nashego vremeni (A Hero of Our Time)* he sees as 'on the threshold between the cycle and the unified novel' (pp. 200-01).

5. Jurij Lotman, *The Structure of the Artistic Text*, trans. by Ronald Vroon (Ann Arbor, 1977), p. 271.

6. Paul Hernadi, *Beyond Genre: New Directions in Literary Classification* (Ithaca and London, 1972), pp. 157-8, 158, 159.

7. Lev Semenovieh Vygotsky, *The Psychology of Art* (Cambridge, MA, 1971), p.112.

8. In this connection cf. Odoevsky's early practice of the apologue and later inclination towards children's literature.

9. M.M. Bakhtin, *The Dialogic Imagination: Four Essays* trans. by Caryl Emerson and Michael Holquist (Austin and London, 1981), p. 22; see also id., *Problems of Dostoevsky's Poetics*, trans. by R.W. Rotsel (Ann Arbor, 1973), pp. 88-92.

10. Bakhtin, *The Dialogic Imagination*, p. 39.

11. Northrop Frye, *Anatomy of Criticism: Four Essays* (Princeton, 1971), p. 365 (and pp. 308-12). This suggestion is put forward by Jo Ann Hopkins Linburn, 'A Would-be Faust: Vladimir Fyodorovlch Odoyevsky and his prose fiction, 1830-1845' (Columbia University Ph.D dissertation, 1970), p. 280. For Bakhtin's view of Menippean satire see *The Dialogic Imagination*, pp. 27ff; and *Problems of Dostoevsky's Poetics*, pp. 92-7. See also Bakhtin on the 'Platonic' type of biographical novel and on the 'Sophistic novel' (*The Dialogic Imagination*, pp. 130-1 and 372ff).

12. Mention of the goddess Isis, however (*R.N.* p. 8) could be seen as alluding to Apuleius's *The Golden Ass*. It would have been more immediately reminiscent, however, of *Die Lehrlinge zu Sais* by Novalis.

13. Gérard Genette, *Figures of Literary Discourse*, trans. Alan Sheridan (Oxford, 1982), pp. 3,4.

14. John Sturrock, *Paper Tigers: The Ideal Fictions of Jorge Luis Borges* (Oxford, 1977), p. 3. Cf. the romantic views that criticism, to be valid, must itself be art (quoted by Tzvetan Todorov, *Theories of the Symbol*, trans. Catherine Porter [Oxford, 1982], p. 194).

15. The term 'frame-tale' appears to derive from the German *Rahmenerzählung* and is used by Charles E. Passage in his book *The Russian Hoffmannists* (The Hague, 1963).

16.  Tzvetan Todorov, *Grammaire du Décaméron* (The Hague, 1969), pp. 68-71, 88-92; Tomashevsky, op. cit., p. 201. By 'Frame' here is meant of course something very different from Lotman's understanding of the word which, in literary terms, is simply 'the beginning and the end of the book' (Lotman, op.cit., pp. 212 and 215), corresponding with the picture frame encasing a painting or the edge of the cinema screen. Nevertheless, here it still forms a kind of inner boundary between author and reader, preceded at the beginning with the authorial introduction, an outer preliminary boundary which, given its authorial presentation and yet its forward reference to the layers enframed, contrives to blur further the distinction between 'fiction' and 'reality' and between fictional and publicistic writing.

17.  David Baguley, 'A Theory of Narrative Modes', *Essays in Poetics*, 6:2, 1981, p. 9.

18.  Lubomír Doležel, 'Truth and Authenticity in Narrative', *Poetics Today*, 1:3, 1980, pp. 11, 20.

19.  Käte Hamburger, *The Logic of Literature*, trans. Marilynn J. Rose (Bloomington, 1973), pp. 311-13 and 333-4; in the framed story, she writes, 'the character of the feint is all the more conspicuous precisely because it is the intent of this form to obstruct it' (p. 338).

20.  Historical figures in a novel, according to Hamburger (ibid., p.336), are 'as such not invented, but nevertheless *qua* figures in a novel they are fictive'; when they are used as first-person narrators, 'it depends on the nature of the narrative to what degree the author renders them feigned'. In the case of Odoevsky's Piranesi, the degree of 'feint' is a particularly grotesque one in that the 'historical' character who purportedly narrates died in 1778.

21.  Cf. Novalis's dictum that: 'The art to estrange in a pleasant manner, to make an object seem strange yet familiar and attractive, that is romantic poetics' (Lilian R. Furst, *European Romanticism: Self- Definition* [London, 1980], p. 3). See also Todorov's comments on Novalis's analysis of *Wilhelm Meister*, on the romantic aesthetic as a semiotic theory, and on romanticism and Formalism (Jakobson and Novalis, Mallarmé, and Khlebnikov,) in *Theories of the Symbol*, pp.181, 198-9 and 273-6.

22.  V.G. Belinsky, *Polnoe sobranie sochinenii*, vol.VIII (Moscow, 1955), pp. 297-323 (315).

23.  'Pis'mo A.A. Kraevskomu', *R.N.*, p. 235.

24.  *Biblioteka dlia chteniia*, 1844, t.66, otd.VI, pp. 1-9 (quoted from Sakulin, I, 2, p. 437).

25.  *Maiak*, 1844, t.XVII, kn.33, pp. 7-29 (quoted from Sakulin, I, 2, pp. 433-5); Valerian Maikov, *Kriticheskie opyty* (1845-1847) (St. Petersburg, 1891), pp. 297-312.

26.  *Sochineniia A. Skabichevskogo v dvukh tomakh*, 2nd ed. (St Petersburg, 1895), vol.I, pp. 256-79 (273).

27.  B.A. Lezin, *Ocherki iz zhizni i literaturnoi deiatel'nosti kn. V.F. Odoevskogo* (Khar'kov, 1907), pp. 1, 109, 107, 70-2 and 131ff.

28.  Ch. Vetrinsky, ('Chelovek trekh pokolenii'), *V sorokovykh godakh: istoriko-literaturnye ocherki i kharakteristiki* (Moscow, 1899); P. Mizinov, *Istoriia i poeziia. Istoriko-literaturnye etiudy* (Moscow, 1900), p. 424.

29.  N.A. Kotliarevsky, 'Kniaz' Vladimir Fedorovich Odoevsky' (1907), reprinted in Kn. Vladimir Odoevsky, *Deviat' povestei* (New York, 1954), pp. 9-28.

30.  I.I. Zamotin, *Romantizm dvadtsatykh godov XIX stol. v russkoi literature*, vol.II (St Petersburg, 1907), pp. 361-418 (400-01).

31.  Sakulin, I, 2, pp. 459 and 226; his main treatment of *Russkie nochi* is on pp. 202-78.

32.  Vasilii Gippius, 'Uzkii put'. Kn. V.F. Odoevsky i romantizm', *Russkaia mysl'*, 1914, 12, pp. 1-26 (16).

33.  Iurii V. Mann, *Russkaia filosofskaia estetika (1820-30ye gody)* (Moscow 1969), pp. 109-48 and 295-303. Page numbers are given in the text.

34.  E.A. Maimin, 'Vladimir Odoevsky i ego roman "Russkie nochi" ', in *R.N.*, pp. 247-76 (262), to which page numbers in the text refer.

35.  Vladimir Odoevsky, *Povesti* (Moscow, 1977), p. 14.

36.  V.I. Sakharov, 'V.F. Odoevsky i rannii russkii romantizm', *Izvestiia Akademii nauk SSSR*, seriia literatury i iazyka, vol. XXXII, 1975, 5, p. 408.

37.  L.Iu. Romanenko ' "Florentinskie nochi" G. Geine i "Russkie nochi" V.F. Odoevskogo', in *Sbornik trudov molodykh uchenykh*, vypusk 3 (Tomsk, 1971), pp. 63-74.

38.  M.I. Medovoy, 'Puti razvitiia filosofskoi prozy V.F. Odoevskogo v seredine 1820-40kh godov', Avtoreferat kandidatskoi dissertatsii (Leningrad, 1971), p. 16.

39.  T.N. Raspopova, 'Khudozhestvennaia funktsiia fragmenta v "Russkikh nochakh" V.F. Odoevskogo', *Izvestiia Voronezhskogo gos. ped. in-ta*, t.173, 1977, pp. 145-55.

40.  M.S.Shtern, 'Filosofsko-khudozhestvennoe svoeobrazie prozy V.F. Odoevskogo (ot apologov k "Russkim nocham")', Avtoreferat kandidatskoi dissertatsii (Leningrad, 1979).

41.  Simon Karlinsky, 'A Hollow Shape: The Philosophical Tales of Prince Vladimir Odoevsky', *Studies in Romanticism*, vol.V, 1966, no.3, pp. 169-82.

42.  Matlaw's introduction to the English translation of *Russian Nights*, p. 20.

43.  Claude Backvis, 'Trois notes sur l'oeuvre littéraire du prince Vladimir Odoevskij', *AIPS*, vol.XIX, 1968, pp. 517-97; Passage, op. cit., p. 106; Norman W. Ingham, *E.T.A. Hoffmann's Reception in Russia* (Würzburg, 1974), pp. 189-90.

44.  Richard Ilgner, 'Goethe's "Geist, der stets verneint" and its Emergence in the Faust Works of Odoevsky, Lunacharsky and Bulgakov', *Germano-Slavica*, no. 2, 1978, pp. 169-80 (175).

45.  Harald Weinrich, *Tempus*, Stuttgart, 1964 (quoted by Martin Swales, *The German 'Novelle'* [Princeton, 1977], pp. 52-3).

46.  Walter Benjamin, ('The Storyteller: Reflections on the Work of Nikolai Leskov') *Illuminations* (London, 1973), pp. 84ff. Cf. V.F. Odoevsky, *O literature i iskusstve* (Moscow, 1982), pp. 96-7.

47.  The phrase used by David Baguley, op. cit., p. 9.

48.  See J.H.E. Paine, *Theory and Criticism of the Novella* (Bonn, 1979), pp. 31-2.

49.  Swales, pp. 45-6; their interaction (p. 48) 'sets up a tension within the work as a whole'.

50.  Ibid., p. 46; Todorov, *Grammaire du Décaméron*, p. 94.

51.  Swales, p. 46.

52.  *The Works of Heinrich Heine*, translated by Charles Godfrey Leland, vol.I (London, 1891), p. l; Jeffrey L. Sammons, *Heinrich Heine: A Modern Biography* (Manchester, 1979), p. 216. See also the same author's *Heinrich Heine, The Elusive Poet* (New Haven and London, 1969), pp. 326-34.

53.  On the concept of 'night' in *Russkie nochi*, see the discussion in 'Sixth Night' and Mann's comments (Mann, pp. 137-40).

54.  Eric A. Blackall, *Goethe and the Novel* (Ithaca and London, 1976), pp. 88-90.

55.  E.K. Bennett, *A History of the German 'Novelle'*, revised by H.M. Waidson (Cambridge, 1961), pp. 56-7.

56.  See Jeffrey L. Sammons, *The Nachtwachen von Bonaventura: A Structural Interpretation* (The Hague, 1965), pp. 33ff.

57.  See Swales, pp. 49-51. Bennett (p. 36) perceives the work as an imitation of Boccaccio, plus a moralizing element.

58.  Glyn Tegai Hughes, *Romantic German Literature* (London, 1979), p. 32; Bennett, p. 57.

59. The 1836 translation, along with others of the period, is listed by Norman Ingham (p. 276). For Odoevsky's remarks, see *R.N.*, pp. 189-90. On the structural differences between *Der Serapionsbrüder* and *Russkie nochi,* see Ingham, p. 190. On this topic see also chapters in Passage, op. cit., and in A.B. Botnikova, *E.T.A. Gofman i russkaia literatura* (Voronezh, 1977).

60. *Moskovskii nabliudatel',* 1836, ch.VI, March, kn. 1 and April, kn. 2; see Romanenko, pp. 64, 65, 74. If Odoevsky *did* translate Heine, it would indeed be ironical; not long before, in the capacity of censor, Odoevsky had felt it necessary to refuse publication to Heine's *Reisebilder* (see A.V. Fedorov, 'Genrikh Geine v tsarskoi tsenzure', *Literaturnoe nasledstvo* 22-24, 1935, pp. 642-4).

61. See Ingham, Chapter II (pp. 48ff).

62. Rado Pribić's study (*Bonaventura's 'Nachtwachen' and Dostoevsky's 'Notes from the Underground': A Comparison in Nihilism* [Munich, 1974]), while seeing extensive parallels between the two works, is unable to produce any evidence that Dostoevsky even knew of Bonaventura (although the possibility is not excluded). However, a suggestion that there is 'a clear affinity' between *R.N.* and *Die Nachtwachen* has been made: see Arsenii Gulyga, *Shelling* (Moscow, 1982), pp. 290-1; this stems in part at least from Gulyga's revival of the view (p. 140-8) that Schelling was the real Bonaventura all along.

63. See I.F. Belza's article in A.S. Golema's Russian translation: Ian Pototsky, *Rukopis' naidennaia v Saragose* (Moscow, 1968), pp. 571-95. The work in question has now become available for the first time in a complete English translation: Jan Potocki, *The Manuscript Found in Saragossa,* trans. Ian McLean (London, 1995 [from the first modern edition, published in French in 1989]).

64. Alethea Hayter's introduction to Charles Robert Maturin, *Melmoth the Wanderer: A Tale* (Harmondsworth, 1977), p. 25. On Melmoth in Russia, see M.P. Alekseev, 'Ch.R. Met'iurin i ego *"Mel'mot Skitalets"'* in his edition of the Russian translation: Charlz Robert Met'iurin, *Mel'mot Skitalets* (Leningrad, 1976,) pp. 563-674 (652-74); see also Passage, pp. 147-8.

65. *R.N.,* p.191. A.W. Schlegel also drew attention to 'the dramatic nature of the dialogues of Plato' in his 'Lectures on Dramatic Literature' (see *Romanticism,* ed. John B. Halsted [London, 1969], p. 55).

66. J. de Maistre, *Les soirées de Saint-Pétersbourg ou entretiens sur le gouvernement temporel de la providence,* fifth edition, vol.I (Paris, 1845), p. 11.

67. Sakharov, op. cit., p. 408; id, 'Vstrechi s Shellingom' in *Pisatel' i zhizn'* (Moscow, 1978), p. 171.

68. Hughes, op. cit., p. 12.

69. Todorov (*Theories of the Symbol,* p. 188) differentiates between *syncretism* (by which he means the original 'amalgam of nature ... anterior to the separation of contraries') and *syntheticism* (which he understands as 'the amalgam of art ... posterior to the separation of contraries').

70. Marshall Brown, *The Shape of German Romanticism* (Ithaca and London, 1979), p. 121; see also Hughes, pp. 4, 53 and 67. Thomas McFarland, *Romanticism and the Forms of Ruin: Wordsworth, Coleridge and Modalities of Fragmentation* (Princeton, 1981), p. 47; he considers that 'incompleteness, fragmentation and ruin ... not only receive a special emphasis in Romanticism but also in a certain perspective seem actually to define that phenomenon' and are manifested in various symbols – in longing, questing, wandering etc. (p. 7).

71. Hughes, p. 78,

72. Todorov, *Theories of the Symbol,* p. 170.

73. On Schubert and Hoffmann see Leonard J. Kent and Elizabeth C. Knight, introduction to *Selected Writings of E.T.A. Hoffmann*, vol.I, 'The Tales' (Chicago, 1969), p. 13; and Hughes, pp. 118-19, 123.

74. See Todorov (*Theories of the Symbol*, pp. 74-7) on veils and clothing in the writings of Augustine; on this 'symbol' in Odoevsky, particularly the significance of *chelovecheskaia odezhda*, see Gippius, op. cit.

75. Roger Cardinal, *German Romantics in Context* (London, 1975), p. 132; see also Hughes, p. 16. For a more detailed discussion of all these and other features of Odoevsky's romanticism, see Chapter 3 of the present study.

76. See Sakulin, I, 1, pp. 150-1 and 173-4.

77. F.W.J. Schelling, *System of Transcendental Idealism (1800)*, trans. Peter Heath (Charlottesville, 1978), p. 231.

78. Ibid., p. 232.

79. Tzvetan Todorov, *The Poetics of Prose*, trans. Richard Howard (Oxford, 1977 ['The Quest of Narrative', pp. 120-42]).

80. James Engell, *The Creative Imagination: Enlightenment to Romanticism* (Cambridge, MA and London, 1981), pp. 238-41 and 324.

81. V.K. Kiukhel'beker, *Puteshestvie, dnevnik, stat'i* (Leningrad, 1979), p. 423.

82. Quoted from Todorov, *Theories of the Symbol*, p.194 (in which the translation of this passage is more readable than in Schelling, *System of Transcendental Idealism*, p. 225).

83. David William Foster, *Studies in the Contemporary Spanish-American Short Story* (Columbia and London, 1979), p. 18. For Schelling's views on genius in art, see *System of Transcendental Idealism*, pp. 222-4, 227-8 and 236.

# Chapter 5

# BELINSKY
# AND V.F. ODOEVSKY

In November of 1839, soon after transferring his residence from Moscow to St Petersburg, Belinsky wrote to V. P. Botkin:

> Despite my resolution to avoid all kinds of social contacts, I have struck up a vast number of them ... Prince Odoevsky received me and treated me in the best possible fashion. He is a kind and simple man, but worn down by the cares of life and therefore colourless *(bestsveten)* like a worn-out handkerchief. Nowadays he is mostly interested in mysticism and magnetism.[1]

At the end of this letter (XI, p. 420) Belinsky exhorts Botkin not to breathe a word of what he has said about Odoevsky. The following month Belinsky writes to Botkin of meeting foreign envoys at Odoevsky's Saturday salon and engaging with them in five-handed whist (XI, p. 428).[2] These first rather ambivalent remarks of Belinsky's, tinged with affection, respect and perhaps a modicum of derision, seem to foreshadow accurately his relations over the next decade with V. F. Odoevsky.

Belinsky and Odoevsky first met in St Petersburg in November 1839,[3] although they had been acquainted with each other's work for some time. Men from totally different social backgrounds and of ultimately conflicting ideas, they were drawn together by their respective literary activities, but also by their common philosophical origins in the Nature-Philosophy of Schelling.[4] Their paths intersected when Belinsky arrived in St Petersburg to become chief critic of *Otechestvennye zapiski*, a journal with which Odoevsky was closely connected. Their careers ran parallel, but never too close, for a few years and

then diverged as Odoevsky devoted more and more time to non-lit-
erary activities from the mid-1840s, while Belinsky left *Otechestvennye
zapiski* in 1846 to write for *Sovremennik*. For both social and intellec-
tual reasons they were never really at ease with one another.
I. I. Panaev wrote to Konstantin Aksakov in December 1839:

> Belinsky is in full flow here. Kraevsky is in ecstasies over him, Prince
> Odoevsky waits on him hand and foot ... I am taking him round and
> showing him off to everyone.[5]

Odoevsky had entertained Belinsky for dinner, together with Gogol
and Panaev.[6] Belinsky's well-founded dread of social intercourse may
be seen in Panaev's account of the disastrous outcome of Belinsky's
appearance at Odoevsky's gathering to celebrate the New Year of
1840, when the critic inadvertently leaned on a table only to end up
on the floor in a pool of blood and wine.[7] Nevertheless, 'despite such
an unsuccessful debut in high society and literary circles', Panaev
reports, this did not stop Belinsky from continuing to frequent the
same salon, 'in order to give pleasure to the cordial host, and he was
convinced that by this he really was giving him pleasure'.[8]

Indeed it appears that Belinsky was a fairly frequent visitor to
Odoevsky's salon, at least over the next few years.[9] He tells Botkin,
in February 1840, of his soul being 'stricken with longing and joy' at
Odoevsky's playing of Langer's song 'S bogom v dal'niuiu dorogu'
(XI, p. 446); and, in April, of Odoevsky's contacts with the censor-
ship being an asset in the production of *Otechestvennye zapiski*,
although he complains of the interfering attentions of one Vrasky, a
*chinovnik* and relation of Odoevsky's and 'a ferocious shareholder'
who demands money (XI, pp. 504-5). He even tried his luck again at
Odoevsky's to greet the New Year of 1841. It was at Odoevsky's that
Belinsky was able to renew his acquaintance with Lermontov during
the poet's last visit to St Petersburg in 1841, though not on the inti-
mate terms he would have wished.[10]

At the end of 1841 Gogol met Belinsky in Moscow and gave him
the manuscript of *Mertvye dushi (Dead Souls)*, which was to be handed
to Odoevsky in St Petersburg, for transmission to the Tsar; from
Odoevsky it eventually reached the censor Nikitenko, via Count
Vel'gorsky.[11] In 1842 Odoevsky was indirectly responsible, ironically
as it may seem, for one of Belinsky's first contacts with the works of
the founding fathers of Communism: Odoevsky brought back from
his visit to Germany Engels's pamphlet 'Schelling and Revelation',
which duly appeared in shortened form (and without reference to
the source) as an article entitled 'Germanskaia literatura' under the
authorship of Botkin in an 1843 issue of *Otechestvennye zapiski*.[12]

From about 1842, however, the name of Odoevsky is mentioned much more rarely in Belinsky's correspondence and in the literature on Belinsky. We may suppose that social contact between Belinsky and Odoevsky decreased as Belinsky's own Petersburg circle became established. Let us, therefore, at this stage turn our attention to the literary relations of the two, which predate the personal relationship by several years.

Following a period of relative eclipse from his position as a famous and controversial figure of pre-Decembrist literature and journalism, Odoevsky began in the 1830s to publish his more artistically mature romantic and society tales, both singly and in cycles, and these quickly attracted critical comment of a mixed nature.[13] Both Pushkin and Gogol are on record as admiring at least some of Odoevsky's work of the 1830s.[14] However, it was with the publication of *Russkie nochi* as part of the three-volume collection of 1844[15] that serious Odoevsky criticism can be said to commence and the contribution of Belinsky to this was to be immensely influential.

Before the appearance of Odoevsky's three-volume collection, Belinsky published only brief comments on Odoevsky's work, but in a generally enthusiastic tone. It can be considered unfortunate for Odoevsky's subsequent reputation that things happened this way. In his 'Literaturnye mechtaniia' of 1834, for example, Belinsky refers to Odoevsky (I, p. 97) as a 'highly notable personality of our literature', praising his talent, feeling, originality, knowledge of the human heart and of society, his erudition and observant mind; in particular he singles out Odoevsky's ability 'to measure the immeasurable emptiness and pettiness of high society' in stories such as 'Bal' ('The Ball'), 'Brigadir' ('The Brigadir') and 'Nasmeshka mertvetsa' ('The Mockery of a Corpse'). In his article on Gogol of the following year, Belinsky saw in Odoevsky's recent 'literary experiments' an unobtrusive yet tangible didacticism and a humour not so much inclined to mirth as to 'a deep feeling of displeasure at human insignificance in all its aspects, a concentrated feeling of hatred, the source of which was love' (I, p. 275). His early story 'Elladii' had, in Belinsky's view, been the first work to display 'the ideas of nineteenth-century morality', the first attack on the eighteenth century. Thereafter Odoevsky had set out on a different course, focusing in his mature work on the artist ('that marvellous riddle'), expressing lofty moments 'with amazing truthfulness ... in profound poetic symbols' in allegoric form ('Poslednii kvartet Betkhovena' and 'Sebastian Bach' were obviously in Belinsky's mind). Odoevsky then turned to poetic fantasy 'permeated with an unusual warmth of feeling, depth of thought and a kind of bitter and caustic irony', but at the same time his aim was not the *povest'* itself, 'not an essential form, but a convenient frame' (I, pp.

275-76): 'Prince Odoevsky is a poet of the ideal world and not the real world', says Belinsky, apparently not without approval (I, p. 276).[16] There is, however, in Belinsky's view of 1835, another side to Odoevsky's work: that represented by the pseudonyms 'Bezglasny' and 'Dedushka Irinei', in stories such as 'Istoriia o petukhe, koshke i liagushke' ('The Story of a Cock, a Cat and a Frog') and 'Kniazhna Mimi' – 'two true pictures of our heterogeneous society'.[17]

In the case of Belinsky's criticism, of course, an awareness of the year of authorship of his articles, and consequently the current stage of his development, is essential.[18] For the early Belinsky, the principal criteria were 'universal realism, objectivity and *narodnost'* in art and the uniqueness of the artist and his divine inspiration'; these principles were intensified in the Hegelian period (1838-1841), and 'supplemented by an increased concentration on the autonomy of the work of art as such ... conditioned by a specifically philosophical approach to literary criticism' – at this time he even 'specifically rejected the importance of the biographical and social background'.[19]

Belinsky's references to Odoevsky during this second period (usually known as that of the 'reconciliation with reality') were, if anything, even more favourable. He found 'Kniazhna Zizi', in 1839, an enjoyable story to read, even if psychologically slightly unconvincing (III, p. 188), and the published fragment of Odoevsky's never-to-be-completed Utopian novel *4338-i god (The Year 4338)* 'an excerpt rich in original thoughts' (III, p. 382). Of Odoevsky's children's stories (*Detskie skazki dedushki Irineia,* 1840), Belinsky wrote: 'in Grandad Irinei Russian children have the kind of writer whom children of all nations would envy' (IV, p. 107, a judgement which is still echoed in Russia today); in a review of the second edition of Davydov's works of the same year Odoevsky was said to have 'created for himself a special genre in which have been found neither successors nor rivals' (IV, p. 344). His tales are best described as poetical musings on life and fantastic visions; ... their hero is the inner man, ... the artist in struggle with a hostile reality'. 'Such a writer does not have merely temporary significance', we are told (loc. cit.), and regret is expressed at Odoevsky's tardiness in producing his collected works, which would certainly ensure his place in Russian literature.[20] That was not quite the way things worked out, nor quite the way in which Belinsky subsequently saw them.

The tide of his enthusiasm for Odoevsky's work was beginning to turn by 1841, as Belinsky approached his third and final phase, as 'revolutionary democrat', in which he saw the artist's essential task as the advancement of progress and the reduction of ignorance. Belinsky approved Odoevsky's rather scathing comments, in his article 'Zapiski dlia moego prapravnuka o russkoi literature', on the state of

Russian literature (IV, p. 434). In 1841 he still felt able to count the
fantastic tale 'Kosmorama' ('The Cosmorama') among 'the only
lively and interesting new works of literature of the past year' (IV, p.
441), though without further comment, and also enthused over 'Iuzh-
nyi bereg Finliandii v nachale XVIII stoletiia' (the first part of the
long story later known in its complete form as 'Salamandra', 'The
Salamander) for its depiction of Finnish life and of Charles XII and
Peter the Great 'in gigantic images of the fantastic poetry of a primi-
tive tribe' (IV, pp. 451-52). However, the continuation of this story
(later known as 'El'sa') Belinsky referred to in a letter to Botkin (XII,
p. 19) as 'pseudo-fantastic trash' *(mnimofantasticheskaia drian');* 'fan-
tastic' had by now become a term of abuse in Belinsky's vocabulary.
Henceforth Belinsky expressed enthusiasm only for Odoevsky's
publications of popular education in the four issues of *Sel 'skoe chte-
nie,* and even then not always without reservations.[21]

It was the 1844 publication of Odoevsky's *Sochineniia* in three vol-
umes which elicited Belinsky's only extensive essay on Odoevsky's lit-
erary work.[22] Odoevsky's collected works were, when they finally
appeared, by no means complete: omitted were the early works of the
1820s (which the young Belinsky had so admired) and some works of
the mature period (parts of *Pestrye skazki* and the recent 'Kosmorama',
among others). What Odoevsky did include, as Part I of his *Sochi-
neniia,* was a number of his previously published stories under a new
guise: with various additions – most notably the dialogic trappings of
the philosophical 'frame-tale' – they were now presented as a cycle
under the title *Russkie nochi.* The other two parts consisted of stories
and miscellaneous writings of the 1830s and early 1840s. The whole
was intended as the summation of Odoevsky's literary career to date.

The publication of Odoevsky's collected works in 1844 placed
Belinsky in a difficult position. Had the collection appeared four or
five years earlier, he would have certainly, as we have seen, greeted
it with considerable enthusiasm. By 1844 however, the overtly
romantic nature of much of Odoevsky's fiction, the underlying ide-
alist premises and the almost Slavophile stress in *Russkie nochi* on the
destiny of Russia, in which terms Odoevsky had chosen to sum-
marise what he saw as the vital ideas of his age, were no longer to
Belinsky's taste.[23] At the same time Belinsky had always had a high
regard for Odoevsky's contribution to the development of Russian
literature (hence his stress, both in this article and earlier, on Odoev-
sky's pioneering work of the 1820s), their personal relations had
been friendly, though never close; moreover Odoevsky was the
main figure in the background behind *Otechestvennye zapiski,* a journal
for which Belinsky was the principal critic.[24] The result may have
been, therefore, something of a compromise.

It does not need to be substantiated here that the whole Weltan-schauung of the early Belinsky was heavily imbued with German idealist philosophy, principally the nature philosophy of Schelling, though tinged from the beginning with social radicalism and the suggestion of a more reflectionist view of art.[25] This involved a necessary, though not altogether happy, acceptance of the values and forms of romanticism. Leaving aside its philosophical bases, we can provisionally adopt a recent definition of romanticism as 'a creation of new forms, often by a return to old ones – by mixing genres or recreating new ones from existing models'.[26] By 1844 Belinsky was able to pursue this theme of formal evolution, or rather dialectical synthesis, while at the same time attempting to deny that there was any such thing as romanticism in the 1820s:

> This struggle of the old and the new is known as the struggle of romanti-cism with classicism. If one is to be truthful, we had here neither classi-cism nor romanticism. There was only the struggle of intellectual movement with intellectual stagnation. (VIII, p. 297)

Subsequently he wrote: 'Young writers ... zealously chased after the new, taking it for romanticism' (VIII, p. 298).[27] He again stresses the historical importance to Russian literature of Odoevsky's early work of the first half of the 1820s and even reprints the apologue 'Stariki, ili Ostrov Pankhai' ('The Old Men – or the Island of Pan-chaea') (VIII, pp. 300-04, originally in *Mnemozina* I, Moscow, 1824). Odoevsky's apologues were remarkable in their day, Belinsky argues, for the fact that they 'resembled nothing which preceded them in Russian literature'; 'the younger generation read them avidly, and abundant were the fruits of their reading' (VIII, p. 304). In his rather different mature works (and Belinsky himself was not averse to appropriating phrases from his own earlier articles), Odoevsky was able to reach a poetic eloquence which could be com-pared to that of Jean Paul Richter ('Brigadir', 'Bal' and 'Nasmeshka mertvetsa' are once again cited as the best examples):

> Their goal is to awaken in the sleeping soul an aversion to a dead reality, the vulgar prose of life, and a sacred longing for that lofty reality, the ideal of which lies in the bold fulfilled life of the consciousness of human dignity. But, apart from that, the strong point of these pieces consists in their close, lively correlation with society. (VIII, p. 305)[28]

These stories are saved from being too fantastic, in Belinsky's view, and given a positive character by a 'restless and passionate humour' (VIII, p. 306). 'Nasmeshka mertvetsa' he goes as far as to term 'almost the best of Prince Odoevsky's works and at the same

time one of the most remarkable works of Russian literature, espe-
cially as it is the only one of its type to be found therein' (VIII, pp.
306-07) . 'In order to describe all that is best in this piece it would be
necessary to write out the whole thing' (VIII, p. 308).

Belinsky then goes on to say that Odoevsky's tales do not appeal
to everyone, and once again to regret that they had not been col-
lected in book form earlier: 'had they been, it would have been eas-
ier to judge the demands of the time according to the public
reception of each collection of stories, and to gauge in advance the
likely success of a change of direction' (VIII, p. 310). A number of
other stories are named as being of the same type as Belinsky's three
favourites, but not quite as good: 'Zhivoi mertvets' expresses the
same idea as 'Brigadir', but lacks the earlier story's 'lyrical anima-
tion'; 'Gorod bez imeni' is in the spirit of Odoevsky's best works 'but
its basic idea is somewhat one-sided' (VIII, p. 311).[29] This story, plus
a number of others, are treated less enthusiastically than had been
the case for Belinsky's earlier writings, although 'Kniazhna Mimi' is
elevated to the position of 'one of the best Russian *povesti'* (VIII, p.
313) . However, it is with the story 'Sil'fida' (which Belinsky had read
'with pleasure' in 1838: II, p. 356) that Belinsky's criticism starts to
bite: 'Sil'fida' belongs to those of Prince Odoevsky's works in which
he began to deviate decisively from his earlier direction in favour of
some kind of strange fantasy'; from this point on, in Belinsky's view,
Odoevsky's works all possess two sides (merits and demerits) – while
he remains in the realm of reality he is as impressive as before, but
as soon as he descends to the fantastic the reader does not know
what to make of him (VIII, p. 313). Anything smacking of the fan-
tastic Belinsky now sees as magical ravings which have no place in
post-Enlightenment Europe.[30] Similarly, the two stories now com-
prising 'Salamandra' are rated, the Finnish sections apart, 'incom-
prehensible' (p. 314); devices such as those used here (that is to say
the devices of romanticism) are outmoded and no longer effective.
Fantastic vagaries such as 'Neoboidennyi dom' ('The Uninhabited
House') were fruits of this trend, but there had been even earlier
offenders (such as one story 'totally incomprehensible from first
word to last': 'Igosha', from *Pestrye skazki*). The influence of Hoff-
mann (whom Belinsky had once wanted to rank alongside Shake-
speare and Goethe)[31] was seen as the probable cause of this
deviancy: Hoffmann was now regarded by Belinsky as a dangerous
model, the more so as fantasy was Hoffmann's 'weakest side' (p.
315). Belinsky was now moving towards a frontal attack on the
'strange form' of *Russkie nochi,* which he also thought might well be
attributable to Hoffmann's influence, on the model of *The Serapion
Brothers.*[32] Belinsky had enjoyed, and still enjoyed, many of the sto-

ries in their own right, but the 'frame-tale' linking device he found 'unnatural and forced' – indeed he found that the conversational links 'weaken the impression of the stories'. He admitted that the conversations contained weighty ideas, but would have preferred them to have been assigned to a separate article; the author had done this with the Epilogue, which had 'great merit, but bore no relation to the stories' (p. 315).

In the Epilogue to *Russkie nochi* Faust, whom Belinsky takes to be the author himself, talks a great deal of sense, Belinsky admits, on the subject of poverty in Europe, the desperate position of the working class and the general indifference to truth and conviction. However, as a Westernizer, he has to take strong exception to Faust's conclusion: 'there are in his words as many paradoxes as truths and in his general conclusion he completely aligns himself with the so-called "Slavophiles" ' (p. 316).[33] The West might be sick, but it is an exaggeration to talk of it 'dying'; in a dying society there are no new ideas – 'four such thinkers as Kant, Fichte, Schelling and Hegel spontaneously appear one after the other: is that really so little?' (pp. 317-18). Belinsky the progressive rationalist is also appalled by Faust's failure to see any progress in the sciences, and by Faust's view of history as a mere chaos of facts, which anyone may interpret as he will:

> He for whom the present is not higher than the past, and the future higher than the present, will see in everything stagnation, decay and death<sub>M</sub> inds li e that of aust are the true victims of science – the more they know, the less they can control their knowledge. (p. 318)

The time of scepticism is past and the time of conviction has come.

Belinsky welcomes Odoevsky's 'domestic drama', *Khoroshee zhalovan'e, prilichnaia kvartira, stol, osveshchenie i otoplenie* ('A Good Salary, A Decent Apartment, Board, Lighting and Heating'), and in particular the reprinting of his polemical article 'O vrazhde k prosveshcheniiu' ('On the Hostility to Enlightenment'), a spirited attack on the literary and journalistic practice of the repressive 'ruling triumvirate' of Russian letters – Bulgarin, Grech and Senkovsky:

> Even in the paradoxes of Prince Odoevsky there is more wit and originality than in the truths of many of our critical acrobats who, criticizing his works, take advantage of the situation to pretend they know what they are writing about and to see in him a writer of their own category. (pp. 322-23)

Belinsky concludes by again praising Odoevsky's talent and originality, even if some of his works are less successful than others, and by stressing his respect for Odoevsky as a thinker, even when disagreeing with him.

Odoevsky was less than delighted with the critical reception of his collected works. Negative reviews from journals such as *Biblioteka dlia chteniia* and *Severnaia pchela* he expected and, within reason, could take in his stride.[34] Belinsky's review was a more serious matter, and Odoevsky was provoked into writing a letter to Kraevsky, the editor of *Otechestvennye zapiski.* Belinsky's article on Odoevsky's works had appeared unsigned, so, although Odoevsky obviously knew who the author was, he began his letter: 'Tell me, who is it who loves me so ardently, but so annoyingly, so cruelly misunderstood me?'[35] Odoevsky went straight to what he saw as the main point of philosophical difference between himself and Belinsky: the latter's faith in human reason, which Odoevsky saw as a 'strange optical illusion', behind which lay nothing more than plain egoism (although Odoevsky himself is not averse to using rational arguments of logic to make his point). Formal criticism he can face with equanimity: 'Form is a secondary matter; with me it changed in accordance with Pushkin's criticism that, in my earlier works, my personality was too visible; I am trying to be more plastic, that's all.' But he does object strongly to suggestions that he is reconciled to the *poshlost'* of life (a passage on p. 309 of Belinsky's article must have been the cause of Odoevsky's pique). If his ideas were examined on their own terms, he says, many things might become clearer: 'for example, observations on the relationship of thought and expression [one of the key themes in *Russkie nochi*] belong to an area hitherto untouched and containing, perhaps, the clue to the whole of man's life.' Finally, he makes a plea for artistic freedom: 'to demand that a man should compel himself to be convinced – that is a process of psychological impossibility'.

This last observation maintains a position with which the Belinsky of 1835 had himself concurred while holding to the realistic view of art, which should express 'the idea of the general life of nature'.[36] Odoevsky, for his part, even in the 1820s had attacked the classicist aesthetic of 'reflection' (*podrazhanie*) on two grounds: firstly that it would turn the artist into an automaton (or 'chess machine'); and secondly on the philosophical grounds that the basis of aesthetic beauty (*iziashchestvo*) lay 'not in external visible nature, but in the laws of the human spirit'.[37] Belinsky, it should be said, even in his early writings had occasionally stressed the progressive and educational function of the artist and critic; and yet he was still capable, as late as 1847, of preaching 'the autonomy of Art'.[38] In his essay on Odoevsky's collected works, Belinsky does not in fact state directly his growing preference for the utilitarian ethic in art, but Odoevsky was still able to identify this as a key point in Belinsky's position, aided no doubt by his knowledge of Belinsky's criticism in general and by personal contacts with the critic.

Odoevsky was dismayed by Belinsky's failure, as he saw it, to appreciate the full philosophical significance of *Russkie nochi*, which he regarded as his culminating work, although admitting that he had left 'much unsaid'.

He did not attempt to answer Belinsky's criticisms point by point but instead proceeded, by means of what was in effect the tacit polemic of an unpublished letter, to misfire what could have been seen as the first shot in a campaign between the advocates of what Odoevsky terms 'unexpected, spontaneous' art and an art rationally committed, a campaign which was to play an immeasurably important role in Russian artistic life for the next century and beyond.[39]

And yet Belinsky's words continued to weigh on Odoevsky. He was sensitive to the criticism of figures he respected (we have seen his admission as to the effects of Pushkin's formal behests). The lasting power of Belinsky's personality over his contemporaries is well known. Not for nothing does Isaiah Berlin refer to 'the power of his invisible presence':[40] Dostoevsky, for example, was still affected by it some thirty years later. Odoevsky's own later reminiscences of Belinsky, in some respects uncharacteristically harsh, testify nevertheless to a considerable impact (see below). And the fact remains that Odoevsky wrote very little for many years after 1844. While the primary reason for this was increased involvement in other activities (notably his administration from 1846 to 1855 of the philanthropic Society for Visits to the Poor in St Petersburg), it seems highly probable that the somewhat disappointing reception of his collected works, and Belinsky's response in particular, may at least have contributed to his voluntarily fading from the literary scene. More interesting in this light, however, is Odoevsky's subsequent evolution as a thinker. While it may be difficult to substantiate fully P. N. Sakulin's view that Odoevsky passed through three distinct stages ('liubomudrie' and 'filosofsko-misticheskii idealizm' being the first two), culminating in positivistic 'nauchnyi realizm' in the 1850s and 1860s,[41] it is certainly true that he developed an increasing social consciousness, immersed himself ever more deeply in civic affairs, and read widely in areas such as political economy and even socialism. Furthermore, in the best known of his published later writings, *Nedovol'no (Not Good Enough)* of 1867, Odoevsky attacked Turgenev's disillusioned and pessimistic valedictory cry (or so it purported to be) in terms not totally dissimilar to Belinsky's 1844 attack on his own alleged scepticism: an artist had no right to take such a view at a time when so much was to be done in Russia; an artist had a duty to society.[42] Odoevsky's optimistic view of the reforms from above in Russia, which he saw as the envy of the West, would certainly not have been shared by Belinsky, had he lived, and Odoevsky distanced himself considerably from the radical intelligentsia that Belinsky represented.[43] At the same time, in later life Odoevsky did revise his view of reason, took an impeccably positive view of the progress of science, became deeply interested in history, turned his back firmly on the Slavophiles, and no longer believed in the extinction of the West and, in consequence, the automatically brilliant future of the East.

We have no evidence as to whether Belinsky ever saw Odoevsky's letter of 1844 to Kraevsky, but it is likely that he did. At any event, Belinsky alluded favourably to Odoevsky's collected works when writing his overall review of Russian literature of the year 1844:

> Now the works of Prince Odoevsky are no longer fragments, no longer separate pieces, but something whole and full, reflecting the spirit and direction of a remarkable and gifted writer. (VIII, p. 475)

Nevertheless, the relationship between the two seems to have remained cool. Such few stories as Odoevsky did publish after 1844 were not among his better efforts and could hardly have been calculated to produce great enthusiasm from the later Belinsky (see IX, p. 35 on 'Sirotinka' and IX, p. 567 on 'Martingal') . There was still some literary collaboration mooted, however. Odoevsky had contributed a story ('Martingal') to Nekrasov's *Peterburgskii sbornik* and was subsequently reported to be working on an article for Belinsky's projected almanac, *Leviafan*; he was also listed among the prospective contributors to *Sovremennik* for 1847.[44]

In a letter to Botkin of February 1847, Belinsky refers quite affectionately, if a trifle condescendingly, to Odoevsky:

> Good old Odoevsky (*dobryi Odoevsky*) once assured me, and he wasn't joking, that there is no dividing line between madness and a normal state of mind, and there isn't a single person of whom you can be positive that he isn't a madman. (XII, p. 332)

However, in a slightly later letter to the same correspondent he refers to a third party (N. A. Mel'gunov) as 'a *conciliator*, a Muscovite Odoevsky' (XII, p. 353). This term, one of virtual abuse in Belinsky's vocabulary, would appear to be the critic's last recorded comment on Odoevsky.

It was probably in the early 1860s that Odoevsky penned his posthumously published impressions of Belinsky.[45] Frequently quoted is Odoevsky's remark that 'Belinsky was one of the most superior philosophical organizations that I ever met in my life'.[46] The rest of Odoevsky's comments, however, are less well known and worth summarizing.[47] According to Odoevsky (himself widely known as one of the most educated men of his time), Belinsky took his system of philosophy from the most superficial knowledge (he could not read German), leaping from Schelling to Hegel and anticipating Comte. He was capable, on his own, of radically recasting what he received second hand ('in part from me', adds Odoevsky):

> Every time I met Belinsky (which was rarely) we argued sharply; but I could not but be surprised at the way he developed a whole organic philosophical world *sui generis* from a superficial knowledge of the principles of *Naturphilosophie*.

His trouble was that he was a victim of circumstances: 'In our day, there was nowhere for Belinsky to get an education',[48] due to the *poshlost'* of professors, bad courses and so on. In addition, however:

> Absurd persecutions for no-one knows what developed in him a certain bile *(zhelch')* which, mixed with his distinctive philosophical development, drove his fearless syllogistics to the most extreme limits.

The circumstances of his life cultivated in him the view that every man is either 'a rascal, a swindler or a fool'. The awareness of his powers in logic imparted to him such self-esteem that he was never able to admit to a mistaken conclusion. Furthermore:

> The ceaseless stripping bare *(oshchipyvanie)* of our literature, the fear of bringing into the open the most naive but new, and therefore in advance questionable, idea aroused in Belinsky such a hatred of this timidity that he saw in every extreme thought a truthful thought – only because it went against everything around him. Hence his scorn for Russian philistinism, from which he progressed to scorn for everything Russian. And so he would often say that the main vice of the Russian lay precisely in the fact of being a Russian.[49]

Belinsky was one of those people, Odoevsky felt, who was born out of time and place. In other circumstances men like Belinsky would have made their mark on European scholarship, but, as it was, 'their motor went into reverse, thereby destroying the motor'. It is a matter of regret, in Odoevsky's view, that such people did not appear at the appropriate time.

Odoevsky's almost hostile view of Belinsky had, of course, no impact on the critic's ever-increasing subsequent reputation, which may be hardly surprising given the contrast in their respective publishing histories, quite apart from other considerations. The more critical aspects of Belinsky's otherwise still favourable and even perceptive review of Odoevsky's collected works had, however, a disproportionate effect on the latter writer's subsequent reputation, both in the short and long term. After 1844-1845, for the rest of his life, Odoevsky was written about very little by Russian critics. Apollon Grigor'ev made favourable references to his works from time to time, but for Belinsky's radical successors – Chernyshevsky, Dobroliubov and Pisarev – Odoevsky might as well not have existed. In the Soviet era Belinsky's views were again rehearsed to contribute in no small measure to critical and publishing policy with regard to the writers of the 1830s and 1840s; from the 1930s, for example, Odoevsky again fell into the relative neglect from which he had only just emerged in the 1910s and 1920s. An edition of his selected stories, upon which the imprint of Belinsky could still be felt, was published in 1959,[50] and, with rare exceptions, it was well into the 1960s before Soviet literary scholarship began to take Odoevsky seriously again.

While one has to agree with Simon Karlinsky that 'Belinsky's review of *Russian Nights*, while ostensibly respectful and favourable, in fact inaugurated the tradition of minimizing or dismissing the more original and profound aspects of Odoevsky's writings in Russian criticism', it would be unjust to lay too much blame at Belinsky's door for Odoevsky's subsequent neglect.[51] In many respects, those who followed Belinsky carry the greater responsibility, whether by commission or by default.[52] It would be fairer to say, too, that what Odoevsky divined in Belinsky's criticism[53] was more genuinely attributable to his successors and interpreters.[54] There were also, as we have seen, other factors, not the least of which was Odoevsky's almost total fading from the literary scene after 1844 and his failure to reprint his works.

Skabichevsky, writing in 1870, made some attempt to redress the balance by claiming that Belinsky had stood too close to Odoevsky to appreciate his work fully.[55] This is generally true of the contemporary reception of, in particular, *Russkie nochi*; critics of the day, Belinsky included, were too easily distracted by what they considered to be the ruse of resurrecting old stories under a new guise and the apparently passé nature of Odoevsky's romanticism, consequently missing both the organic whole of the work itself and the significance and originality of many of the ideas.[56]

Finally, what of the charge obliquely hinted at by Belinsky, the one which rankled Odoevsky most – namely that he had become reconciled to the *poshlost'* of reality? A more sophisticated view of Odoevsky's overall artistic aims in *Russkie nochi* has been given by recent Soviet-Russian scholars: M. S. Shtern stresses rather that Odoevsky was striving to 'aestheticize reality'; M. I. Medovoy points out that the traditional identification of Odoevsky's views with those of his protagonist Faust is simplistic; and V. I. Sakharov contends that Odoevsky's breadth of knowledge, which impressed no less a personage than Schelling, justifiably led him to a position of doubt, but not of scepticism.[57] Criticism has come round to regarding *Russkie nochi* as a 'philosophical novel' rather than a cycle of stories – an integral whole; even 'fantastic' stories (much berated by Belinsky), such as 'Salamandra', now enjoy a fresh and sympathetic airing.[58] Belinsky's views on romanticism and its varied manifestations in Russian literature were never the least vulnerable of his critical armour; nor have they proved in practice to be the most durable.

## Notes

1. V. G. Belinsky, *Polnoe sobranie sochinenii*, 13 vols. (Moscow-Leningrad, 1953-59), hereafter *PSS*, vol. XI, p. 418. Hereafter all references will be quoted by volume and page number in the text. Translations are my own and all dates are Old Style.

2. This can be read as a parody of Khlestakov's letter to his Petersburg crony, Triapichkin, see V. A. Manuilov and G. P. Semenova, *Belinsky v Peterburge* (Leningrad, 1979), p. 33. Nevertheless the social mixture at Odoevsky's 'Saturdays' was such as not to preclude the possibility of literal truth.

3. See the commentary to *PSS*, XII, p. 491.

4. On the line of philosophical influence running from the 'Liubomudry' through Stankevich to Belinsky, see *Perepiska Nikolaia Vladimirovicha Stankevicha, 1830-1840* (Moscow, 1914), pp. 236, 276 and 292; P. N. Sakulin, *Iz istorii russkogo idealizma. Kniaz' V.F. Odoevsky: myslitel'-pisatel'*, vol.I, parts 1 and 2 (Moscow, 1913), hereafter Sakulin, I, part and page number, refers to Stankevich's admiration for Odoevsky (I, 2, p. 426) and to such common ground as did exist between Odoevsky and Belinsky in the 1840s (I, 2, p. 429). See also Z. A. Kamensky, *Moskovskii kruzhok liubomudrov* (Moscow, 1980), *passim* but especially pp. 194-217.

5. Quoted from V. S. Nechaeva, *V. G. Belinsky: zhizn' i tvorchestvo 1836-1841* (Moscow, 1961), p. 270.

6. *Literaturnoe nasledstvo*, vol. 56 (Moscow, 1950), pp. 135-36 (certain evidence is produced – p. 136, note 2 to V.S. Aksakova's letter to K.S. Aksakov – of Belinsky's discomfort at Odoevsky's gatherings); this meeting probably took place on or around 20 November 1839; see Iurii Oksman, *Letopis' zhizni i tvorchestva V. G. Belinskogo* (Moscow, 1958), p. 216.

7. I.I. Panaev, 'Vospominanie o Belinskom', in *V. G. Belinsky v vospominaniiakh sovremennikov* (Moscow, 1977), pp. 206-10. A degree of chronological uncertainty enters here, owing to Herzen's description of the same incident in *Byloe i dumy* (A.I. Gertsen, *Sobranie sochinenii v tridtsati tomakh* (Moscow, 1954-1966), vol. IX, pp. 30-31), even though Herzen was not in Petersburg for the New Year of 1840. Panaev further confuses the issue by depicting the incident as occurring on Belinsky's first visit to Odoevsky's salon, whereas we have seen that Belinsky had already made several visits there (see Oksman, op. cit., pp. 216 and 218, and Belinsky, XI, pp. 428 and 435). Furthermore, Oksman (diplomatically?) does not mention the incident; does not record Belinsky's presence at all at Odoevsky's over the New Year of 1840, but does note (p. 276) his attendance at the same venue and festival a year later (Belinsky himself wrote of that occasion: 'I saw the

New Year in at Odoevsky's – drank and because of that a terrible fever afflicted me for two days', XII, p. 10). However, if Panaev is correct in listing Lermontov among those present, then the original 'disaster' must have occurred on the New Year of 1840. It is not clear whether Herzen was himself present at this or any gathering at Odoevsky's (see M. Perkal', *Gertsen v Peterburge*, Leningrad, 1971, p. 141) or whether he was writing from general knowledge, especially in view of Panaev's assertion (p. 210) that 'Belinsky's fall from a chair became the pretext for his name to be spread by many a mouth'. Manuilov and Semenova, (op. cit., p. 32) are therefore probably justified in deciding on 1840. Manuilov and S.B. Latyshev (in *Lermontovskaia entsiklopediia* [Moscow, 1981], p. 649) seem to be in no doubt: their *Letopis'* entry for 31 December 1839 states: 'Lermontov and V.G. Belinsky at New Year's Eve party at V.F. Odoevsky's'.

8.  Panaev, op. cit., p. 210. Herzen's comments (loc. cit. in note 7 above) may therefore have been something of an exaggeration: 'he would usually fall ill then for two or three days and would curse whoever had persuaded him to go'.

9.  Manuilov and Semenova, op. cit., pp. 39 and 46. See also Iu. Arnol'd, *Vospominaniia* (Moscow, 1892), vyp. 2, pp. 202, 211.

10. Manuilov and Semenova, op. cit., p. 94; Oksman, op. cit., p. 284.

11. V. S. Nechaeva, *V.G. Belinsky: zhizn' i tvorchestvo 1842-1848* (Moscow, 1967), pp. 20-21; Manuilov and Semenova, op. cit., p. 106, and especially Belinsky's letter to Shchepkin of 14 April 1842 (XII, p. 103).

12. *Otechestvennye zapiski,* XXVI, otd. VII (St Petersburg, 1843), pp. 1-15; see *Literaturnoe nasledstvo*, vol. 56, 1950, pp. 78-80, and Nechaeva, op. cit., p. 57.

13. *Pestryye skazki* (1833), for instance, attracted a hostile review from Odoevsky's former friend N.A. Polevoy in *Moskovskii telegraf*, but a 'panegyric' from Baron Rozen in *Severnaia pchela* (see Sakulin, I, 2, pp. 32-35).

14. *A.S. Pushkin – kritik* (Moscow, 1978), p. 448; Vladimir Shenrok, 'N.V. Gogol' (*Russkaia starina*, St Petersburg, no. 2, 1902, pp. 264-65).

15. *Sochineniia kniazia V. F. Odoevskogo v trekh chastiakh* (St Petersburg, 1844).

16. The concepts of *'ideal'naia'* and *'real'naia' poeziia* provided Belinsky at this stage (1835) with set criteria for evaluating the works of the few predecessors of Gogol – see N. Mordovchenko, *Belinsky i russkaia literatura ego vremeni* (Moscow-Leningrad, 1950), p. 53. This distinction, according to René Wellek, was originally made by F. Schlegel – see Wellek's *A History of Modern Criticism: 1750-1950: The Age of Transition* (London, 1966), pp. 247-48.

17. These, in Mordovchenko's view (op. cit., p. 54), met with Belinsky's full approval. The former story Belinsky was later to identify wrongly as part of *Pestrye skazki* (1844, see VIII, p. 314).

18. For a concise account of the stages in Belinsky's development, see Joe Andrew, *Writers and Society during the Rise of Russian Realism* (London, 1980), pp. 114-50. For a full discussion of the problem of consistency in Belinsky's criticism, see Victor Terras, *Belinskij and Russian Literary Criticism* (Madison, 1974), especially pp. 32-42 and 77-91. For a view giving less weight to the stages in Belinsky's critical development, see Wellek, op. cit., pp. 244, 250.

19. Andrew, op. cit., p. 142.

20. Belinsky had been aware that this event was pending, and welcomed the news in 1838 (II, p. 387).

21. For Belinsky's comments on *Sel'skoe chtenie,* see VI, pp. 571, 681-90, VIII, pp. 139, 153-58; IX, pp. 301-05; and X, pp. 365-72. A further review of children's stories (mainly Odoevsky's) appeared in *Sovremennik*, no.4, St Petersburg, 1847 (X, pp. 147-56).

22. 'Sochineniia kniazia V. F. Odoevskogo', published in *Otechestvennye zapiski*, no. 10, 1844, pp. 37-54, unsigned (VIII, pp. 297-323) . This essay has now been reprinted, in slightly shortened form, in V. F. Odoevsky, *Poslednii kvartet Betkhovena* (Moscow, 1982), pp. 344-69.

23. Commentators generally point to the years 1842-1843 or 1843-1844 as a turning point in Belinsky's criticism: B. Egorov, *O masterstve literaturnoi kritiki: zhanry, kompozitsiia, stil'* (Leningrad, 1980), p. 106, refers to 'Belinsky's change of attitude to classical and contemporary writers' in this period; while, according to Nechaeva, (op. cit., p. 142), the demands being made on writers by Belinsky 'were forcing him to consider many writers of the 1820s and 1830s to be outmoded *(nesovremennymi)*'. Terras (op. cit., pp. 34-5) seems to go even further in regarding the year 1844 as something of a Rubicon in attitudes to Belinsky's criticism, reporting that 'the critic's right-wing followers, especially Apollon Grigor'ev, proclaimed themselves disciples of "Belinskij up to 1844", [cf. Egorov, op. cit., p. 87] while the radical left would conveniently ignore the Belinskij of the 1830s and draw their image of him from the writings of the last few years'.

24. On Odoevsky's role in the founding and running of *Otechestvennye zapiski*, see A. P. Mogiliansky, 'A.S. Pushkin i V. F. Odoevsky kak sozdateli obnovlennykh *Otechestvennykh zapisok*' (*Izvestiia Akademii nauk SSSR*, Seriia istorii i filosofii, vol. VI, no. 3, 1949, pp. 209-26 – especially pp. 224-25), and R. B. Zaborova, 'Neizdannye stat'i V. F. Odoevskogo o Pushkine', in *Pushkin: issledovaniia i materialy*, vol. I (Moscow-Leningrad, 1956), pp. 313-42. There would appear to be no real evidence that Belinsky had Odoevsky specifically in mind when he wrote to Herzen on 6 April 1846 about *Otechestvennye zapiski*: 'I have got used to sparing people who are important only in its eyes, and generally to maintaining a tone that is not always mine, but often the tone of the journal' (XII, p. 272): see V. S. Spiridonov's commentary in *PSS*, vol. VIII, p. 682. The probably gratuitous association of these remarks with Odoevsky may rather be indicative of the generally negative attitude to Odoevsky taken by Soviet critics of the 1940s and 1950s (e.g. the comments of D. Blagoi and Iu. Oksman in *Literaturnoe nasledstvo*, vol. 58, 1952, pp. 23 and 289-96 respectively) – an attitude which Mogiliansky and Zaborova, among others, are at pains to dispel. We have already noted Belinsky's acknowledgement of Odoevsky's contacts with the censorship. Furthermore, the decision to appoint Belinsky as principal critic on *Otechestvennye zapiski* caused Odoevsky to receive considerable abuse from former Moscow friends (such as N. F. Pavlov: see Oksman, op. cit., pp. 230, 244, and Sakulin, I, 2, p. 423), as did his later (1846) decision to contribute a story ('Martingal') to Nekrasov's *Petersburgskii sbornik*. See also Pavlov's letter to Odoevsky, in *Russkaia starina*, no. 4, 1904, p. 198.

25. Terras, op cit., pp. 128 and 164-65, denies that Belinsky ever actually arrived at the latter position.

26. Andrew, op.cit., p. 14. For a full discussion of definitions of romanticism as applied to Russian literature, see Robert Reid (ed.) *Problems of Russian Romanticism*, Aldershot, 1986; and Chapter 3 of the present study.

27. This attitude seems identical to that of K. F. Ryleev, twenty years earlier – see his 'Neskol'ko myslei o poezii: otryvok iz pis'ma k N.N.', in *Literaturno-kriticheskie raboty dekabristov*, Moscow, 1978, pp. 218-22. Belinsky's basic understanding of 'classicism' was as *antichnoe iskusstvo* (art of the classical period), whereas 'romanticism' he related to *iskusstvo katolicheskogo evropeiskogo srednevekov'ia* (art of the Catholic European Middle Ages): see P. Berkov 'Belinsky i klassitsizm', in *Literaturnoe nasledstvo*, vol . 55, 1948, pp. 151-76, especially p. 174. On Belinsky's varying conceptions of and attitudes to romanticism, see also Terras, op. cit., pp. 39 and 202-03.

28. Cf. Belinsky's 1841 comparison of Odoevsky with Jean Paul (V, pp. 64-65): some stories included in the 1841 comparison ('Poslednii kvartet Betkhovena', 'Operi del Cavaliere Giambattista Piranesi' and 'Improvizator') are now omitted, although two stories ('Improvizator' and 'Sebastian Bach') are included in an identical context later in this same article (VIII, p. 315).

29. In 1839 Belinsky had described this story as 'a fine work' (III, p. 124).

30. As Nechaeva, op. cit., points out (p. 143), Odoevsky's 'fantastic' stories are criticized in terms similar to those used three years later against Dostoevsky's 'Khoziaika' ('The Landlady'): 'magic in the vision of people with deranged nerves belongs under the jurisdiction of medicine and not of art' (VIII, p. 314).

31. At least according to a conversation reported by Annenkov: P. V. Annenkov, *Literaturnye vospominaniia* (Moscow, 1960), p. 147; Belinsky in 1840 certainly regarded Hoffmann as a 'marvellous and great genius' (XI, p. 507).

32. Odoevsky later (in the early 1860s) denied this in notes written for a proposed second edition of his works – see V. F. Odoevsky, *Russkie nochi* (Leningrad, 1975), pp. 189-90. On the form of *Russkie nochi* and the various 'models' which have been suggested as possible influences, see Chapter 4 of this study.

33. The word 'Slavophiles' is in inverted commas in the original, as it had only recently taken on its 'modern' meaning – having previously been used to denote the followers of A. S. Shishkov (see V. S. Spiridonov's commentary in *PSS*, VIII, p. 684). The Slavophiles themselves, however, by no means shared Belinsky's view of Odoevsky's thought – see B.F. Egorov and M. I. Medovoi, 'Perepiska kn. V. F. Odoevskogo s A. S. Khomiakovym' (*Uchenye zapiski Tartuskogo universiteta*, vyp. 251, Trudy po russkoi i slavianskoi filologii, 15, Tartu, 1970, pp. 335-49); Sakulin, I, 2, pp. 448-50; and A.N. Pypin, *Kharakteristiki literaturnykh mnenii ot dvadtsatykh do piatidesiatykh godov; istoricheskie ocherki*, 4th ed. (St Petersburg, 1909), p. 459, according to whom the Slavophiles and their allies in *Moskvitianin* could not stand what they called 'Petersburg literature' and wrote splenetically of 'the natural school, Turgenev, Odoevsky and others'.

34. See 'Otvet na kritiku', written in response to reviews in *Biblioteka dlia chteniia* and *Maiak*, published for the first time in *Russkie nochi* (Leningrad, 1975), pp. 231-34. No review in fact appeared in *Severnaia pchela*, possibly as a result of Odoevsky's letter to S. S. Uvarov, the Minister of Education, asking him to ensure that no scurrilous attacks would get through the censorship (see *Russkie nochi* [Leningrad, 1975], pp. 230-31 and 309-10). For a full summary of the rest of the contemporary reviews of Odoevsky's works, see Sakulin, I, 2, pp. 432-44.

35. 'Pis'mo A. A. Kraevskomu', in *Russkie nochi* (Leningrad, 1975), pp. 234-36. Some critics, however, presume that Odoevsky really did not know of Belinsky's authorship (e.g. Egorov and Medovoy, op. cit., p. 337, taking their lead from Sakulin, I, 2, p. 450). However, Odoevsky's knowledge of Belinsky's work and style must surely have enabled him to guess the identity of the reviewer, even had he not known it in advance.

36. See Andrew, op. cit., p. 139.

37. See Z. A. Kamensky, 'Russkaia estetika pervoi treti XIX veka' in *Russkie esteticheskie traktaty pervoi treti XIX veka v dvukh tomakh* (Moscow, 1974), vol. II, p. 27 (and Odoevsky's texts on aesthetics in this volume).

38. See Andrew, op. cit., p. 148; and Terras, op. cit., pp. 35, 75 and 186.

39. Attacks on the nineteenth-century materialist ethic had already been made by Odoevsky, notably in the story 'Gorod bez imeni' ( 1839); Simon Karlinsky, in 'A Hollow Shape: The Philosophical Tales of Prince Vladimir Odoyevsky' (*Studies in Romanticism*, vol. V, no.3, Spring 1966, pp. 169-82), sees this story as fore-

shadowing the debate of the 1860s between Dostoevsky and Chernyshevsky (p. 181). For further comment on this theme, see Chapter 2 of this study.

40. Isaiah Berlin, *Russian Thinkers* (London, 1978,) p. 182. See also Andrew, op. cit., pp. 134, 174.

41. Sakulin, I, 2, p. 457; one might, for instance, for various reasons question the following statement (loc. cit.): ' ... Odoevsky with a sure step was moving towards that ultimate goal [i.e. 'realism'] which Griboedov, Pushkin, Gogol and Belinsky had been indicating for Russian literature.'

42. Odoevsky's *Nedovol'no* has recently been republished, though with some omissions, for the first time since 1867, in V. F. Odoevsky, *Sochineniia v dvukh tomakh* (Moscow, 1981), vol. I, pp. 315-33. On Odoevsky and Turgenev, see M.A. Tur'ian, 'V. F. Odoevsky v polemike s I. S. Turgenevym (po neopublikovannym materialam)' *(Russkaia literatura* no. 1 [Leningrad, 1972], pp. 95-102); and Cornwell, *V. F. Odoyevsky*, pp. 263-5.

43. Belinsky in the 1840s, however, had some hopes of reform from above and considered himself, therefore, to some degree in alliance with liberals and reformist aristocrats (see Manuilov and Semenova, op. cit., p. 303, who cite Belinsky's 1848 review of *Sel'skoe chtenie* as evidence). Certainly the reformist aristocrats, such as Odoevsky, suffered along with Belinsky and Kraevsky in the denunciations of Bulgarin (see Sakulin, I, 2, pp. 421, 422; Oksman, op. cit., pp. 548-49). From the onset of the reaction of 1848-1855, however, the 'alliance' between reformists and revolutionary democrats split irreparably.

44. A.Ia. Panaeva, in *V.G. Belinsky v vospominaniiakh sovremennikov* (Moscow, 1977), p. 306 (Panaeva reports Belinsky's belief that Odoevsky had promised to write something for him 'ot chistogo serdtsa'). Nothing came of *Leviafan*: see Oksman, op. cit., pp. 452, 454 and 460. Odoevsky did not contribute to *Sovremennik* in 1847 or thereafter. A. N. Popov wrote to E.A. Sverbeeva, from Petersburg (mid-September 1846): 'Odoevsky sovershenno rekhnulsia, s nim prosto govorit' nel'zia, gotovit ispoved' svoikh ubezhdenii, razumeetsia protiv nas, i napechataet ee v sbornike Belinskogo' *(Literaturnoe nasledstvo,* vol. 58, p. 690).

45. 'Iz bumag kniazia V.F. Odoevskogo' *(Russkii arkhiv,* kn. 1 [Moscow, 1874], pp. 339-42), from which text ensuing quotations and summary are taken: also to be found in A. N. Pypin, *Belinsky: ego zhizn' i perepiska,* 2nd ed. (St Petersburg, 1908), pp. 466-68. Sakulin, I, 2, p. 423, dates it to the 1860s.

46. Manuilov and Semenova, for example, use it for the epigraph to one of the chapters of their book, *Belinsky v Peterburge,* p. 49.

47. Selective use of Belinsky-Odoevsky relations has been the rule; see, for example, G. Bernandt, *Stat'i i ocherki* (Moscow, 1978), pp. 27-29, while even Sakulin (op. cit, passim, but particularly I, 2, pp. 422-24, 426-29 and 444-51) is not above reproach in this respect. N. M. Mikhailovskaia's article of 1966 on Belinsky's evaluation of Odoevsky barely alludes to the negative side of Belinsky's critique; neither does it deal with Odoevsky's views on Belinsky – 'V. F. Odoevsky v otsenke V. G. Belinskogo', in *Voprosy istorii i teorii literatury,* vyp. 2 (Cheliabinsk, 1966), pp. 157-64. Disappointing too is Ivanov-Razumnik's lively but erratic commentary in *Sobranie sochinenii V.G. Belinskogo v trekh tomakh,* iubileinoe izdanie (St Petersburg, 1911), vol. II, pp. 855-60.

48. Referring to this statement, M. Poliakov comments: 'Odoevsky associated a lot with Belinsky, and his testimony probably conveys the conviction of the critic himself ' – 'Studencheskie gody Belinskogo', in *Literaturnoe nasledstvo,* vol. 56 (Moscow, 1950), p. 314. Nechaeva, op. cit., pp. 166-67, refers to Odoevsky in 1846, however, as being alone among the participants in Nekrasov's *Peterburgskii sbornik* to be 'outside the influence of Gogol and Belinsky'; the others read to,

talked to and listened to Belinsky. Odoevsky's own remark on the 'rareness' of their meetings should probably be treated with some caution.

49. On Belinsky's attitude to the Russian people, see Terras, op. cit., pp. 99-101; Dostoevsky took a similar view on this point to that of Odoevsky (ibid., p. 100).

50. V. F. Odoevsky, *Povesti i rasskazy* (Moscow, 1959), ed. with introduction and commentary by E. Khin.

51. Karlinsky, op. cit. p. 170, n. 7.

52. In a later work (*The Sexual Labyrinth of Nikolai Gogol'* [Cambridge and London, 1976]), Karlinsky places the blame squarely on the enormous impact of Chernyshevsky's 'Studies in the Gogolian period of Russian literature' of 1855-1856: 'It asserted the reputation of Belinsky as a major critic, confirmed the Belinskian view of Gogol as a critical realist, and, by insisting that Gogol and Lermontov were the first Russian prose writers of any consequence, it deleted from literary history the entire achievements of Russian Romantic prose, relegating to obscurity for almost a century such attractive and significant writers as Vladimir Odoevsky, Nikolai Pavlov and Antony Pogorelsky, among others' (p. 281).

53. V. S. Spiridonov's commentary (to *PSS*, vol. VIII, p. 683), referring to Odoevsky's 1844 letter to Kraevsky, states that Odoevsky 'wrongly' (*prevratno*) understood Belinsky's idea of 'the rapprochement of the writer with the vanguard of reality' as a demand for creative work contrary to personal convictions. It may be noted that Blok later made a similar charge against Belinsky in terms of artistic freedom (see Terras, op. cit., p. 229).

54. It is not necessary, in making such remarks, to wish to go as far as Rufus W. Mathewson, Jr, who, in *The Positive Hero in Russian Literature,* 2nd ed. (Stanford, 1975), states: 'The writer's enlistment in the service of a demanding but ultimately beneficent dialectical process, which he accelerates by reporting accurately, represents a crucial act of surrender. This definition of literature's obligatory service in the cause of human welfare needed to be changed only in particulars as it passed from the hands of one radical literary theorist to another, from Belinsky, finally to Zhdanov' (p. 30). A more balanced view of Belinsky's significance is provided, for example, by Wellek, op. cit., pp. 260-64.

55. *Sochineniia A. Skabichevskogo v dvukh tomakh,* 2nd ed. (St Petersburg 1895), vol. l, pp. 256-79, especially p. 260. Skabichevsky himself regarded Odoevsky as a second-rate artist, but an important man of ideas. A later vigorous defence of Odoevsky as a romantic was offered by Vasilii Gippius in his notable article ' "Uzkii put'". Kn V. F. Odoevsky i romantizm' (*Russkaia mysl',* 1914, no. 12, pp. 1-26).

56. Belinsky (VIII, p. 315) displayed complete ignorance of the genesis of *Russkie nochi,* which had been evolving in its author's mind since the mid-1820s. Sakulin (a great admirer of Belinsky) writes (I, 2, p. 455): 'In actual fact Odoevsky's contemporaries and even his friends did not know much of what went on in his troubled soul. Even Belinsky did not fully succeed in penetrating his inner sanctum.' Sakulin also stresses (p. 454) the baselessness of Belinsky's reproach that Odoevsky did not believe in progress.

57. M. S. Shtern, 'Filosofsko-khudozhestvennoe svoeobrazie prozy V. F. Odoevskogo (ot apologov k *Russkim nocham)'* (Candidate's dissertation, Leningrad State Pedagogical Institute, 1979), p. 13; M.I. Medovoy, 'Puti razvitiia filosofskoi prozy V. F. Odoevskogo v seredine 1820-1840-kh godov' (Candidate's dissertation, Leningrad State Pedagogical Institute, 1971), p. 16; V. I. Sakharov, 'Vozvrashchenie zamechatel'noi knigi' (*Novyi mir,* no. 4 [Moscow, I976], pp. 263-65); Sakulin, I, 2, p. 459, had referred to Faust as *'russkii skeptik'*) .

58. The key work in this process has been Iurii V. Mann's analysis, in his book *Russkaia filosofskaia estetika* (1820-30ye gody) (Moscow, 1969), pp.104-48; see also

E.A. Maimin's essay 'Vladimir Odoevsky i ego roman *Russkie nochi*', in *Russkie nochi* (Leningrad, 1975), pp. 247-76. 'Salamandra' was republished (for the first time this century) in Vladimir Odoevsky, *Povesti* (Moscow, 1977), ed., with introduction and notes by V.I. Sakharov; for a sympathetic reading of 'Salamandra', see M. A. Tur'ian, 'Evoliutsiia romanticheskikh motivov v povesti V. F. Odoevskogo *Salamandra*', in *Russkii romantizm* (Leningrad, 1978), pp. 187-206; V.I. Sakharov, 'Eshche o Pushkine i V. F. Odoevskom', in *Pushkin: issledovaniia i materialy*, vol . IX (Leningrad, 1979), pp. 224-30; and Chapter 8 of this study.

# Chapter 6

# UTOPIA AND DYSTOPIA IN RUSSIAN FICTION
The Contribution of V.F. Odoevsky

... the populace of London were scattered upon his path, and he asked himself by what wizardry they could ever be raised to high participations. there were nights when every one he met appeared to reek with gin and filth, and he found himself elbowed by figures as foul as lepers. Some of the women and girls, in particular, were appalling – staurated with alcohol and vice, brutal, bedraggled, obscene. 'What remedy but another deluge, what alchemy but annihilation?' he asked himself, as he went his way; and he wondered what fate there could be, in the great scheme of things, for a planet overgrown with such vermin, what redemption but to be hurled against a ball of consuming fire.

(Henry James, *The Princess Casamassima*, 1886, ch. 38)

U topian elements, themes, and aspirations are an obvious feature of Russian literature of the second half of the nineteenth century, in writers as disparate as Dostoevsky, Chernyshevsky and Chekhov and in thinkers as divergent as Vladimir Solov'ev and Lenin. Dostoevsky is similarly noteworthy in that the Utopian fancies of so many of his characters contrast strikingly with the dystopic (or anti-Utopian) visions included in *Zapiski iz podpol'ia (Notes from the Underground)* and *Besy (The Devils);* the two are even combined, within a single short work, in Dostoevsky's remarkable story 'Son smeshnogo cheloveka' ('The Dream of a Ridiculous Man'). The one preceding body of fiction in Russian literature to incorporate similarly opposed Utopian and dystopian elements belongs to V.F. Odoevsky. Indeed, Odoevsky may be among the first presenters of a negative Utopia in European fiction.

Even before Odoevsky, who began writing in the early 1820s, Russian literature could boast a number of now largely little known works of a Utopian nature. The Russian roots of this type of fiction lie in both folk literature and in travellers' tales – the medieval exotica of a landlocked Old Russia. Darko Suvin, in Chapter XI of his study *Metamorphoses of Science Fiction: On the Poetics and History of a Literary Genre* (New Haven and London, 1979), surveys this tradition, from early times until the 1960s, and cites Ivan Peresvetov's sixteenth-century *Skazanie o Magmete-Sultane (Legend of Sultan Mahomet)*, a plea to Ivan the Terrible for strong centralization, as the first 'exemplary political tale' (Suvin, p. 243). Eighteenth-century examples include Vasilii Levshin's *Noveishee puteshestvie, sochinennoe v gorode Beleve (The Latest Journey Written in the Town of Belev,* 1784), Mikhail Shcherbatov's unfinished *Puteshestvie v zemliu Ofirskuiu (Voyage to the Land of Ophir,* 1783-1784, published 1896), and the far better known Aleksandr Radishchev's *Puteshestvie iz Peterburga v Moskvu (Journey from Petersburg to Moscow,* 1790). More's *Utopia* was itself translated into Russian in 1789, which 'prompted a speedy suppression of the whole genre for a generation' (Suvin, p. 244).

Primitive science fiction and the fantastic frequently merged with Utopian fiction, particularly in its nineteenth-century Russian manifestations. Apart from Odoevsky, the first half of the century saw Aleksandr Ulybyshev's story 'The Dream' (1819, published 1927), which was written in French; the Decembrist Wilhelm Küchelbecker's *Evropeiskie pis'ma (European Letters,* 1820) and 'Zemlia Bezglavtsev' ('Land of the Headless', 1824); fantastic works by the Polish-born conservative publishers, Faddei Bulgarin (*Pravdopodobnye nebylitsy ili puteshestvie k sredotochiiu zemli, Plausible Fantasies or a Journey in the 29th Century,* 1824) and Osip Senkovsky (*Fantasticheskie puteshestviia barona Brambeusa, The Fantastic Adventures of Baron Brambeus,* 1833); and V. A. Sollogub's *Tarantas* (1840-1845).[1] There were also Utopian aspects of the work of Gogol and in the thought of the Slavophiles.

Russia had always been on the margins of European thought. Under Catherine II, however, there appeared a cautious promotion of the Enlightenment until its revolutionary implications became apparent in 1789. As a consequence, the rational thought of Novikov and Radishchev was suppressed and cults of the irrational – Masonic, theosophical, and other sectarian groups – began to flourish underground. In the reaction of the 1790s, and again after the first 'liberal' years of Alexander I, all philosophical trends – and, indeed, almost any thinking at all – were strenuously discouraged. The Russian advance into Europe following the events of 1812 occasioned a fresh injection of Western political and philosophical ideas, which were soon frustrated by the unbending autocracy at home. Paradoxically, the reactionary mysticism espoused by Alexander and his entourage in the years of the Holy Alliance created an atmosphere which fostered the secret 'Decembrist' societies in their pursuit of constitutional and democratic aims in the first half of the 1820s.

Such were the circumstances in which romanticism came to Russia. Weaker than in most European countries – it could scarcely be called a movement in Russia – romanticism briefly beguiled Russia's leading writer, Pushkin; it later had a certain impact on Gogol and created a major figure of its own in Lermontov.

As elsewhere in Europe, romanticism in Russia took varied forms. The slightly older generation of Ryleev and Bestuzhev-Marlinsky, centered around the journal *Poliarnaia zvezda,* combined one type of romantic aesthetic with democratic values derived from the Enlightenment and the post-1789 European situation. The 'wisdom lovers' (Liubomudry), headed by V. F. Odoevsky and D.V. Venevitinov, on the other hand, took their lead from the theories of the German romantic movement to propound a Russian philosophical idealism which tended to react against the Enlightenment. The main inspiration for this development came from the *Naturphilosophie* and 'transcendental idealism' of Schelling. Not that these two groups, up until 14 December 1825, were so very far apart, as is evident from the collaboration between Odoevsky and Küchelbecker.

After 1825 intellectual activity in Russia was again at a low ebb for some years. When the 1830s gave rise to new philosophical circles – the generation of Stankevich and Bakunin, Belinsky and Herzen – the dominant influence was still German idealism: specifically Schelling, gradually eclipsed by Hegel. French Utopian socialism, in particular that of Fourier, began to make its impact only in the 1840s, on the older Belinsky and in the Petrashevsky circle. Once again, suppression quickly followed – this time in the wake of 1848. Odoevsky, whose protagonist Faust had in *Russkie nochi (Russian Nights)* suggested that the musings of Rousseau and Voltaire were responsible for the 'rivers of blood' of the French Revolution, was himself in this period denounced as a 'communist', for his philanthropic labours!

## II

Prince Vladimir Fedorovich Odoevsky (1804-1869) – writer, music critic, thinker, educationist, philanthropist and public servant, to name only his main roles in life – was an extraordinarily versatile figure. A reputation for eccentricity, 'encyclopaedism', and dilettantism caused him to be taken less seriously during his lifetime than he deserved. Neglected for many years after his death, his reputation underwent a minor revival in the early part of this century. This was repeated in the 1950s when important collections of his educational, musical, and literary writings were published. He is now remembered mainly as a writer of fiction, more editions of his works having appeared since 1975 than in all of the previous hundred years.

In the early 1820s he attended the Raich circle and presided over the 'Society of Wisdom-lovers' – a philosophical circle, influenced mainly by Schelling and Oken, which was a principal originator of both Westernizing and Slavophile leanings in Russian thought. Together with Küchelbecker, Odoevsky founded, edited, and contributed much material to the almanac *Mnemozina* (1824-1825), which set a new standard among Russian journals and aroused considerable controversy. Following the abortive Decembrist uprising of 14 December 1825, in which he played no part, though both his cousin, Aleksandr Odoevsky, and Küchelbecker were direct participants, Odoevsky immersed himself in idealist philosophy and European romanticism, channelling his thought into creative activity which was to reach its main fruition in the 1830s. His reading was immensely wide, ranging from Greek philosophy to the German romantics and most of the links in between: gnostics and alchemists, Leibniz and Spinoza, Jacob Boehme and Saint-Martin, all claimed his interest. Of particular importance to the early Odoevsky was Giordano Bruno, whom he saw as a tragic figure caught between faith and science. He also read French moralists, English social thinkers, Swiss and Italian educationists and the latest developments in the natural sciences.

Experimentation in fiction led to uneven artistic success. Nevertheless, the range of stories written by Odoevsky in the decade or so from the late 1820s is remarkable for its breadth: artistic 'biographies' of Beethoven and Bach, caustic satirical tales, society tales, Gogolian whimsy and tales based on romantic mysticism, as well as the futuristic works of relevance to the present essay. Two of the latter, 'Gorod bez imeni' ('City Without a Name') and 'Poslednee samoubiistvo' ('The Last Suicide'), are included in his ambitious and substantial philosophical frame-tale, *Russkie nochi* (1844), designed to combine the genres of novel and drama. This work included a number of stories published separately during the 1830s, enclosed by a framing device which takes the form of a dramatic philosophical dialogue reflecting intellectual strands of the 1820s and 1830s in a manner unique in Russian fiction.[2]

His literary works have traditionally been divided, by Russian and Soviet critics, into the romantic and the realistic; however, the division is by no means hard and fast and the chronological mix of these supposed genres is quite striking. While conforming to most definitions of a romantic writer – in terms of the superficial trappings, the mixture of styles and the underlying idealist philosophical system – Odoevsky remains a complicated figure, far closer to the German romantics than to the English or the French. While his thought developed, even in the 1830s, beyond pure Schellingism, Odoevsky, in many of his literary works, retains the artistic theory of Schelling and the practice of Hoffmann – together with discernible traces of other German romantic writers and thinkers.

A more unusual romantic current, particularly notable in Odoevsky's dystopian stories, is a debt to the tradition of Mary Shelley. While patently sharing her interest in the consequences which can arise from the blind and irresponsible pursuit of even the most idealistic aims, as expressed in *Frankenstein*, Odoevsky paid particular attention to the English novelist's rambling and, until recently, neglected novel, *The Last Man*. Having published a review of that novel in *Moskovskii vestnik* in 1827, he later returned to sketch, on a vastly reduced scale, its theme of 'the narration of misery and woeful change' in his powerful short work, 'Poslednee samoubiistvo' (see below). We witness, then, a writer who is deeply involved in and concerned with narrative theory and the problems of authorial and narratorial voice. Such an interest is hardly surprising in a teller of Utopian or dystopic tales, for there always remains the problem of who is telling the story, be he a surviving witness of catastrophe and apocalypse or an indifferent or partisan observer of a new age. The author strives to conceal his own identity behind the persona of the narrator or narrators. Odoevsky's complex of tales within tales makes his storytelling at once sophisticated and, for its time, subtle.

### III

Odoevsky's most striking experimental story of the 1820s, and his first of any note with a science fiction or futuristic theme, is the short work 'Dva dni v zhizni zemnogo shara' ('Two Days in the Life of the Terrestrial Globe' 1825, published 1828).[3] The story speculates upon the possible results of a comet's impending collision with earth, a topical theme in Europe in the mid-1820s, with the expected arrival of a comet in 1832, and one to which Odoesky was later to return in *4338-i god (The Year 4338)*. This work of just five pages is unusual in that it begins as a society tale, takes on an air of science fiction, and concludes in a Schellingian aura of benign apocalypse, in which 'the heavenly became the earthly, the earthly the heavenly, the Sun became the Earth and the Earth the Sun' (*Vzgliad skvoz' stoletiia*, p. 222). A romantic writer of the period close to Odoevsky, Dmitrii

Venevitinov (1805-1827), had written a dialogue called 'Anaxagoras', in which Plato speaks of an ancient Egyptian prophecy of the sun swallowing the earth, thus achieving harmony in the universe.[4] This story may be seen to reflect, in the mid-1820s and in fictional form, Odoevsky's most genuinely Schellingian phase, as expressed in his more confident and optimistic philosophical writings of that period, in marked contrast to the somewhat starker and gloomier outlook which pervades a number of his later stories.

In *4338-i god,* Odoevsky envisages the world lasting for at least two and a half millenia beyond his own time. The year 4338 is chosen as the year before 4339 when, it was computed in the 1820s, Biela's comet would collide with the Earth; in fact the comet in question, which had an orbital period of only 6.6 years, burned up later in the century.

This work was originally conceived as the third part of a trilogy which was also to have featured depictions of Russia in the era of Peter the Great and in the contemporary period (the 1830s); the first part was never written and the second and futuristic third parts remained unfinished: fragments were published in 1835 and 1840 and the fullest version, of just the Utopian part, only (as a book) in 1926. The 'contemporary' fragment was published as 'Petersburgskie pis'ma' ('Petersburg Letters'), which seems to have been intended as the overall title. Then came the futuristic fragment, 'The Year 4338: Petersburg Letters'. The English translation in *Pre-Revolutionary Russian Science Fiction: An Anthology* (Ann Arbor, 1982) for some reason omits the first letter and the end 'fragments'.

Knowledge of this distant epoch is obtained by the supposed ability of the anonymous donor of the letters which make up the work to time travel at will, using an advanced form of Mesmerism (an early nineteenth-century equivalent of modern theories of science fiction). Along with Odoevsky's attentions to alchemy, the occult and spiritualism, it should be stressed, went an intense and extensive engagement with the natural sciences; indeed, such interests seemed far less divorced from each other in the early part of the nineteenth century than in the twentieth. The world described in *4338-i god* is in certain respects not totally unlike the twentieth century (or perhaps the twenty-first?); in other ways it is very different. Many technological advances familiar to us are present: air travel (though it can take eight days by balloon from Peking [or Beijing] to Petersburg), space travel (to the moon – it is not clear how), the telephone, photocopying. Hallucinogenic and truth drugs (in the form of gaseous drinks and 'magnetic baths') remove all hypocrisy from social life. However, Russia and China are now the centres of world power (Russia covers half the globe and Moscow is a part of Petersburg); China is very much the junior, backward partner (something like Russia in relation to Europe in the nineteenth century).[5] Europe seems to be of no account; the English appear to be privatizing the British Isles, with Russia the purchaser! There is a marked absence of strife, suffering and misery, and various grandiose feats of engineering and climatic control have been accomplished. 'Elastic glass' seems to be a basic, multipurpose material. The question of the comet's imminent arrival seems to be of minor importance. Odoevsky provides little indication, however, of how all these developments came about. Progress in science, together with a certain natural social evolution, is likely to have interacted, from what we may conjecture from Odoevsky's other writings, with an essential degree of spiritual regeneration from within, aided at crucial times, perhaps, by the paternalistic hand of a benevolent *dirigisme*.

Interest inevitably centres on the social features of Odoevsky's Utopia, though the ironic presentation of this and the other works here discussed should signal a certain caution against any overly serious interpretation. Due mainly to the lack of durability of books and texts, which is emphasized a number of times, knowledge of such distant epochs as the nineteenth century is extremely hazy (historians, for example, cannot agree on the changing names of Petersburg: Petropol', Petrograd[!] and Piter are conjured with). It is perhaps not so very surprising, therefore, that institutions such as the monarchy and the church appear to have disappeared without trace somewhere along the way. Technology and art are the dominant values and a republic (albeit of an aristocratic nature) seems to constitute the extremely stable status quo. Education is highly elitist; poets, historians, and philosophers occupy high ministerial positions. An important (and strikingly Odoevskian, not to say Schellingian) feature of this system (which smacks more of enlightened technocracy than of democracy) is the presence of a 'Minister of Concilations', one of whose main duties is the settling of scientific and literary disputes. The lower orders remain essentially outside the civilized scholarly establishment (their literary life appears to have reached that level of factions and squabbles with which Odoevsky was familiar; the work has topical allusions too, and was intended in part as a riposte to Faddei Bulgarin, with whom Odoevsky had many a journalistic altercation).

A Soviet critic has recently pointed out the similarity between the pleasure-filled, suffering-free Utopia of *4338-i god* and the ideal realm to which the sylph of Odoevsky's romantic story 'Sil'fida' wishes to lure her consort (and contrasts Odoevsky's apparent rejection of suffering with the opposite view taken by Dostoevsky).[6] A recent German study of Odoevsky's Utopianism emphasizes the prophetic relevance of Odoevsky's vision to the modern world.[7] In any event, there is no denying the achievement of imagination present in *4338-i god,* despite its fragmentary nature. Darko Suvin has written that 'Odoevsky remains one of the more interesting SF writers of the pre-Wellsian age of Europe' (Suvin, p. 247), while a recent Russian commentator considers that Odoevsky's 'Cosmic worldview' (the interdependence of everything in the universe and 'the responsibility before the whole of humanity of each for his every action') is 'only now beginning to be adopted by humanity'.[8]

These two comments combine the two major features of Odoevsky's literary personality: Odoevsky the experimenter in narrative technique (especially with regard to narratorial voice) and Odoevsky the idealist still in the thrall of Schelling's theory of universal spiritual forces. We might also note the presence of an elitist mentality and a belief in the superiority of the artist-intellectual which, while not uncommon in the period, achieves its most resounding expression in writers and thinkers of the later part of the nineteenth century: Carlyle, Pater, Wells, Anatole France and – in the present century – Huxley and Orwell.

## IV

'Poslednee samoubiistvo' and 'Gorod bez imeni' belong to the Fourth and Fifth Nights respectively of *Russkie nochi.*[9] The Fourth Night consists of the reading, by the protagonist Faust, from a dusty sheaf of papers entitled 'The Economist' – fragments from the writings of a young man (one 'B'), recently deceased, which were purportedly lent to the two intermediate narrators known as the two seekers (friends of Faust). 'Poslednee samoubiistvo', the fifth of six embedded stories in this section (or Night), represents the culminating despair of B and is the one substantial *Russkie nochi* story not to have been published earlier and independently of the frame-tale cycle. 'Gorod bez imeni', (first published as a separate story in 1839), is part of the narrative of the two seekers and comprises the Fifth Night, together with five pages of frame-tale discussion, conducted by Faust and his colleagues, pursuing some of the issues which arise.

While the complex narrative devices adopted by Odoevsky in *Russkie nochi* and elsewhere may tend to assist his storytelling – for example, on occasion his futuristic visions – it should be borne in mind that they are equally applicable to the creation of scenes set in the present or the past. Utopian or dystopian stories constitute a relatively small proportion of Odoevsky's fictional output and an explanation for his employment of such techniques may be sought in the

realm of romantic poetics, rather than in direct links with the subject
matter treated (although, in true romantic fashion, the relationship
between form and content may often be close).

The range of ideas treated by Odoevsky in *Russkie nochi,* and
elsewhere in his writings, fictional and nonfictional, is vast. *Russkie
nochi* has indeed been widely seen as a summation of Odoevsky's
philosophical development up to the 1840s and of the ideas which
moved his generation. Various philosophical ideas and concepts are
important throughout the stories which make up the overtly fictional
side of the work – especially in the clearly tendentious stories under
consideration here. However, notwithstanding the artistic signifi-
cance of the whole as an interlinked network of fiction and philoso-
phy, the main ideational thrust of the work is to be found in the
discussional sections of the frame-tale device, particularly in the
dominating monologues of Faust.

*Russkie nochi* is largely concerned with such romantic philosophi-
cal pursuits as the quest for ultimate knowledge, the nature of the
symbols which reveal both material and inner life, an understanding
of causation, and the problem – not to say impossibility – of com-
municating 'truth'. This problem is, of course, effectively pointed up
in another sense by Odoevsky's use of multiple narrators. The theme
of the inadequacy of human language as a means of communication,
which anticipates by many decades the philosophies of Wittgenstein
and others, was a constant preoccupation in Odoevsky's own quest
for 'truth'. That quest took him, over many years, back to the roots
of romanticism; to Plato and the pre-Socratics. In the social realm,
lies and hypocrisy were his constant *bêtes noires.* Also prominent are
the questioning of the attainments of civilization (medicine, mathe-
matics, physics, chemistry, the law, poetry); 'the happiness of *all* and
*everyone'*; a critique of the ideas of Adam Smith, Malthus, and Ben-
tham, among others; and a consideration of the nature of madness.
The concept of 'the dying West', which Russia is poised, at least spir-
itually, to regenerate, is introduced in the conclusion of the manu-
script of the two seekers. Here we touch again on the theme of the
guiding artist-intellectual, the nineteenth-century sage and prophet.
Although this idea has generally been taken as Odoevsky's own
view, which would place him squarely in a tradition, stretching from
the Slavophiles to Solzhenitsyn, of a Holy Russia offering spiritual
redemption to the world, it should be pointed out that in *Russkie
nochi* this concept is disputed by the other spokesmen and even
admitted by Faust to have been 'exaggerated' by the two seekers
(p. 150/p. 213). Odoevsky's own largely Western-oriented cultural
background would also suggest that the overemphasis here was
deliberate – both for dramatic effect and to reflect a particular cur-

rent in Russian thought of the period. Nevertheless, the idea of an enlightening mission and a catalytic role for the Russian intelligentsia does approximate to historiosophical notions which occur elsewhere in Odoevsky's writings and which may best be seen as Russian adaptations of facets of German romantic philosophy. Odoevsky's debunking of the faith of many of his contemporaries in inevitable progress, however, should be seen as warning of the dangers of a blind, exclusive faith in any particular concept or ideal (such as, elsewhere, the worship of 'reason'), rather than as displaying an unmitigated hostility to the concept itself or a dogmatic insistence on the superiority of the spiritual. Balance and synthesis are the essence of Odoevsky's thought.

It is therefore in such a framework that the attacks on the 'philosophers of logic', Malthus and Bentham, belong. They are assailed in the philosophical discussions of the frame-tale, but particularly vigorously in anti-Utopian fictional form in 'Poslednee samoubiistvo' and 'Gorod bez imeni', which are powerful parables designed to lay bare the folly of following the ideas of these luminaries to their logical conclusion. An element of tongue-in-cheek distortion in Odoevsky's representation of their ideas, however, cannot be excluded. The latter story, in which the description of the economic activities of the Benthamites resembles, in the view of Andrzej Walicki, 'an exaggerated version of Weber's "spirit of capitalism"',[10] gives rise to a damning appraisal of the economic theories of Adam Smith (read by Odoevsky in the French edition of 1802), who is seen delighting, from his professorial chair, the English shopkeepers and merchants by bestowing on them a divine right to exercise the free-market economy as they please (pp. 118-19/75-76).

The exact relationship between Odoevsky as author and Faust as protagonist, let alone the subsidiary spokesmen at even further structural removes from the author (the two seekers and the Economist, B), cannot be elucidated here. There is in any case always room for the exercise of a certain degree of caution before ascribing ideational concepts extrapolated from works of fiction to a system of beliefs allegedly held by their author. In the most general terms, however, it would be fair to say that Odoevsky consistently criticised the philosophy and excesses of Western mercantile capitalism from a liberal aristocratic position; a believer in reform from above, he was to be, in the 1860s, an avid supporter of the reform legislation of Alexander II.

Our remaining concern here, however, is with 'Poslednee samoubiistvo' and 'Gorod bez imeni' as stories in their own right. 'Poslednee samoubiistvo' relates a situation in which drastic overpopulation and misery lead to despair and a final manic mass suicide in a gigantic (one would now assume nuclear) explosion. The story, of just six pages, is presented as the product of a mind in the last stages of despair, inspired by 'the absurd reasoning of the English economist' (Malthus) (p. 91/p. 53). The story begins:

> The time predicted by the philosophers of the nineteenth century arrived: the human race had multiplied; the balance between nature's production and the needs of mankind was lost. Slowly but incessantly it had been approaching this catastrophe. Driven by destitution, the city dwellers ran to the fields, the fields turned into villages, villages into towns, and the towns imperceptibly expanded their limits. (p. 91/p. 54)

This had taken place over a period of centuries, despite a technology which had reclaimed the deserts and the icecaps. The entire planet had nevertheless become a single teeming city, with its attendant catalogue of disasters – destitution, starvation, disease, depravity, iconoclastic destruction and a reversal of normal civilized values:

> Everyone saw in his fellowman an enemy ready to deprive him of the last means of his destitute life: a father would cry when learning that a son had been born; daughters would dance around their mother's death bed; but most frequently a mother would strangle her child at birth, while the father would applaud her. Suicides ranked as heroes. Charity became an act of freethinking, scorn at life became a usual greeting, love became a crime. (pp. 92-3/p. 55)

Escape from the horrors of life into love, poetry and philosophy was no longer adequate. Atrocities became the norm. Eventually a feeling spread of the impossibility of the human situation and there grew an antilife cult which attached to 'violent Life' the emotions normally associated with death. Finally 'the Messiah of despair' pronounced the word; all the devices of destruction known to humanity were assembled in the vaults of the earth. A ceremonial holocaust was enacted:

> At a fixed solemn hour, people finally fulfilled the dreams of ancient philosophers about a common family and general agreement of mankind. Wild with joy they joined hands. Thundering reproach was in their eyes.

A single dissenting couple in love implored humanity to change its mind, but:

> ... terrible laughter came as an answer; it was a prearranged signal – the next moment fire flashed high, the roar of the disintegrating earth shook the solar system, torn masses of Alps and Chimborazo flew up into the air, groans were heard ... then ... again ... ashes returned to ashes ... everything became quiet ... and eternal Life repented for the first time!
> (p. 97/p. 58)

Such a scene may be compared with the apocalyptic visions familiar to us from romantic painting of the period.

'Gorod bez imeni' begins as a narrative of the two seekers (or, rather, one of them), but this soon gives way to a further level of embedded narration conducted by a 'stranger' (*neznakomets*), or 'man in black'. The following narrational removes thus now stand between the reader and the supposed events related: the author, Faust, one of the seekers; the man in black. The last named's narrative is given over to recounting, in a spirited manner characteristic of Odoevsky, the triumphant mercantile expansion of a Benthamite colony dedicated to utility. However, gradual self-destruction through the strife of sectional interests (virtually class warfare) then ensues. In the end the man in black is explained away as an 'insane preacher' (p. 114/p. 72); thus the extravagant time scale of his story is effectively obviated.

The eloquent eccentric, or madman, is a phenomenon frequently encountered in Odoevsky's fiction and his proximity here to the author is betrayed early on in his observation that the location is a graveyard 'of many thoughts, many feelings and memories' (p. 102/p. 62 – an image which Odoevsky was fond of applying to libraries). The location, his fatherland, no longer has a name but is the site of a former colony founded by European followers of Bentham. 'Utility' ('benefit' – *pol'za*) was the ubiquitous slogan. The epigraph, from Humboldt, signals the setting as North America. Success was total at first. Anything not immediately utilitarian was questioned (a church, a theatre), but permitted. Trade was established with a neighbouring agricultural community and a successful policy of exploitation pursued. War was resorted to when other means failed. A familiar story of statehood ensued:

> On the other hand, inhabitants of our internal cities, limited in space, sought an expansion of the state borders and found it rather profitable to start quarrelling with neighbours, if only for the purpose of getting rid of their own surplus population. The vote was divided. Both sides had one thing, the common benefit, in mind without noticing that each side used this word only to mean its own good. There were still others who thought of preventing this argument by starting to talk about self-sacrifice, about natural concessions, about the necessity of sacrificing something now for the good of future generations. (pp.107-8/p. 66)

Need and competition, first to maintain, then to restore the former standard of living, gross mismanagement and the activities of predatory financial interests led to the law of the mercantile jungle. Ruin, discord, wars and natural disasters contributed to the decline in well-being and standard of living, which gave rise to a rampant anti-intellectualism:

Man's strength was dwindling. Ambitious plans, which could have increased trade activity in the future, but were at present dissipating the merchant-administrators' profits, were called prejudice. Deceit, forgery, intentional bankruptcies, total disdain of human dignity, idolatory of gold, satisfaction of the crudest bodily needs became an obvious, permissible and indispensable matter. Religion became a completely foreign subject; morality was reduced to the proper balancing of accounts; intellectual occupations, to searching for means of deceit without any loss of credit; poetry, to the balancing of an account book; music, to the monotonous rattling of machines; painting, to the drawing of plans. (p. 111/p. 69)

The one dissenting voice, 'a pale man, his hair in disorder, wearing a funereal cloak' (p. 111/p. 69) was carried off to an asylum. This 'pale man' fleetingly prefigures the man in black himself; they may be seen as romantic 'mad prophet' figures, further variations upon the types of inspired maniacs (*bezumtsy*) who populate *Russkie nochi* (reflecting its origins in an unrealised earlier project, to have been called 'The House of Madmen'). This idea extends to the narrators as well: the economist B went mad in his pursuit of truth, the two seekers separately came to a premature end, while Faust, the author himself and even the reader would seem by no means immune. As in Byron, truth in Odoevsky is a temptation. The pursuit of absolute knowledge, though irresistible to some, seems not to bring the happiness of each and everyone. This thought may explain the choice of Faust as narrator. The reader of *Russian Nights* may well concur with Byron's Manfred (a latter-day Faust) that:

> Sorrow is knowledge: they who know the most
> Must mourn the deepest o'er the fatal truth,
> The Tree of Knowledge is not that of Life.

In this Benthamite city-state, merchants vied with craftsmen and farmers to usurp the administration. Defeated factions turned to banditry. Starvation, internecine strife and earthquakes completed the task, until: 'Only one square stone remained to sustain old memories, the stone on which in olden days the statue of Bentham stood' (p. 114/p. 71). This stone became a shrine and a sacrificial spot for prisoners, until the stranger in black alone was left to weep over it and curse it.

Thus, notwithstanding the declared origins of Benthamism in the eighteenth century, we are treated, in the space of fourteen pages, to the rise and fall of a civilization that purports to span centuries. The disastrous fall of these civilizations, as well as illustrating the philosophical point of Odoevsky's opposition to a narrow and one-sided application of even idealistic values, is indicative of what has been widely perceived as a deterioration in his idealist beliefs during the

1830s in the direction of disillusion and philosophical pessimism. A number of his works of the period, indeed, display features anticipatory of a more modern existentialism. At the same time, Odoevsky's interests in science, technology and popular education grew: he was a fervent proponent, for example, of the installation of a railway system in Russia. These contradictions in Odoevsky's views, however, may be seen as fuelling, or fuelled by, the old romantic ideal of the reconciliation of opposites: material progress with individual spirituality, reason with instinct. Odoevsky's subsequent development, ironically it may seem, led him in the 1850s and 60s to a position much closer to positivism than would have been thought possible in the author of *Russkie nochi*. His views on art and music remained romanticist, but a burgeoning eclecticism enabled him to essay in practice the genre of the realist novel and to generate, in the decade of 'great reforms', a naive optimism with regard to the future of Russia.

# V

The two stories discussed in the last section are early examples of dystopian parables, designed to polemicize with particular ideas of their time. They are particularly noteworthy, perhaps, for the way in which they comprise the kind of concise potted histories of a planet, or a civilization, familiar to us in works such as Dostoevsky's 'Son smeshnogo cheloveka' (itself unusual for its time in 1877) and in the twentieth-century science fiction of writers such as Olaf Stapledon and, more recently, Stanislaw Lem. Odoevsky's forays against reason and logical systems in these and other works had an impact on Dostoevsky and have been seen as anticipating the Dostoevsky-Chernyshevsky confrontation of the 1860s. Odoevsky's fantastic prophecies in 'Gorod bez imeni', indeed, foreshadow Raskolnikov's dream in the epilogue of *Prestuplenie i nakazanie (Crime and Punishment)*. There would also appear to be a direct line of descent from that same Odoevsky story to Briusov's 'The Republic of the Southern Cross' (1907), in which a Utopian, futuristic republic in the Antarctic, based on benevolent dictatorship and state capitalism, is brought to its knees by a psychic disorder called *mania contradicens*, a form of compulsive contradictory behaviour with extreme antisocial consequences. Stories by Odoevsky and Bulgarin form the starting point of Leland Fetzer's interesting collection in English translation, cited above, entitled in full *Pre-Revolutionary Russian Science Fiction: An Anthology (Seven Utopias and a Dream)*. The 'Dream' belongs to Chernyshevsky's Utopian novel, *Chto delat'? (What is to be done?)*

(1863), while Fetzer moves into the twentieth century to include two Briusov stories (including 'Respublika iuzhnogo kresta', 'The Republic of the Southern Cross'), two by Kuprin and Aleksandr Bogdanov's 'Martian novel' of socialism achieved: *Krasnaia zvezda: utopiia, Red Star: A Utopia* (1908), long neglected by the Soviets for its author's ideological unorthodoxy.

These works by Odoevsky, and the other writers mentioned, together with the strikingly unusual ideas of thinkers such as N. F. Fedorov (author of *The Philosophy of the Common Cause,* posthumously published in 1913) and Konstantin Tsiolkovsky (the pioneering theorist of space travel), fuelled the strong experimental and fantastical tradition in Soviet literature of the 1920s, which gave us the enormously varied Utopian, dystopian, and science fiction works of such writers, as Bulgakov, Chaianov, Platonov, Aleksei Tolstoy and Zamiatin, to name only the most prominent.[12]

## Notes

1. Most of the works mentioned (from Levshin to Sollogub, but not that by Bulgarin) have been collected in an anthology entitled *Vzgliad skvoz' stoletiia: russkaia fantastika XVIII i pervoi poloviny XIX veka* (Moscow, 1977).

2. *Russkie nochi* was translated into English by Olga Olienikov and Ralph E. Matlaw (New York, 1965), reprinted Evanston, IL, 1997. Translations of three further Odoevsky stories are to be found in *Russian Romantic Prose: An Anthology,* ed. Carl R. Proffer (Ann Arbor, 1979). On *The Year 4338,* see below. A detailed formal description of *Russkie nochi* and its antecedents has been attempted in Chapter 4.

3. 'Dva dni [sic] v zhizni zemnogo shara' is reprinted for the first time in *Vzgliad skvoz' stoletiia* (see note 1) pp. 217-22. The Russian of the title would normally be expected to be 'Dva dnia ...'.

4. This dialogue has been translated (by Larry Andrews): D. V. Venevitinov, 'Anaxagoras: A Platonic Dialogue', *Russian Literature Triquarterly,* XI, 1975, pp. 182-5.

5. For comments on, and possible explanations of this see Olga Lang, 'Two Visions of the Future: Russia and China as Pictured in Two Nineteenth-Century Russian Tales', in *Perspectives on a Changing China. Essays in Honor of Professor C. Martin Wilbur ...,* ed. Joshua A. Fozel and William T. Rowe (Boulder, Colorado, 1979), pp. 7-31. The second story discussed is 'Life One Hundred Years After', from the collection *Christmas Evenings (Sviatochnye vechera,* written 1878-1879) by G. P. Danilevsky.

6. N. K. Mikhailovskaia. 'Utopicheskie povesti V. F. Odoevskogo', *Russkaia literatura,* 4, 1980, pp. 135-40; she also points to the similarity between the endings of 'Poslednee samoubiistvo' and Saltykov-Shchedrin's *Istoriia odnogo goroda (The*

*History of a Town)*, and makes comparisons with other Utopian works contemporary to Odoevsky, especially Küchelbecker's *Evropeiskie pis'ma.*

7. Winfried Baumann, *Die Zukunftsperspektiven des Fürsten V. F. Odoevskij* (Frankfurt and Bern, 1980).

8. Vl. Muravev, 'Russkii Faust', in V. F. Odoevsky, *Poslednii kvartet Betkhovena* (Moscow, 1982), p. 4.

9. Quotations here will be given from the English translation by Olienikov and Matlaw (see note 2 above), with appropriate page numbers in the text; secondary page numbering will refer to the standard Russian edition, V.F. Odoevsky, *Russkie nochi,* 'Literaturnye pamiatniki' (Leningrad, 1975).

10. Andrzej Walicki, *The Slavophile Controversy: History of a Conservative Utopia in Nineteenth-Century Russian Thought,* translated by Hilda Andrews-Rusiecka (Oxford, 1975), p. 77.

11. Bogdanov's sequel to *Red Star, Engineer Menni* is included in a single volume in another translation: Alexander Bogdanov, *Red Star: The First Bolshevik Utopia,* ed. L. Graham and R. Stites, trans. C. Rougle (Indiana, 1984). A Russian reprint of the two works was produced by an émigré publishing house: A.A. Bogdanov, *Krasnaia zvezda. Inzhener Menni* (Hamburg, 1979).

12. Some of these authors are discussed in an essay by Jurij Striedter, 'Three Postrevolutionary Russian Utopian Novels', in *The Russian Novel from Pushkin to Pasternak,* ed. John Garrard (New Haven and London, 1983). An issue of *Revue des Etudes Slaves* (vol. 56, 1984) is devoted to the theme of Slavic Utopianism and contains a short article on Odoevsky and some interesting research on his contemporaries as well as more modern Utopian writers.

Chapter 7

# V. F. ODOEVSKY AND HIS *PESTRYE SKAZKI*

You will be surprised to learn that I wrote my harlequinesque fairy tales in the most bitter moments of my life.

V. F. Odoevsky

## I

Throughout an intellectual career lasting half a century, Odoevsky never ceased to conceive grandiose philosophical, encyclopaedic educational and literary projects. Few of these achieved more than a fragmentary existence. The two literary projects which were completed, *Pestrye skazki* (1833) and *Russkie nochi* (1844), (*Variegated Tales* and *Russian Nights* respectively) were both conceived in the 1820s, and yet combine to mark the onset and the climax, respectively, of Odoevsky's 'mature' period as a writer.

Odoevsky's fiction of the 1820s can be broadly described as didactic – whether social satire in the manner of Griboedov (but in prose, in works such as 'Dni dosad' ['Days of Vexation'] and 'Elladii') or the terse allegory of the apologues – such as 'Novyi demon' ('A New Demon') and 'Stariki, ili Ostrov Pankhai' ('The Old Men – or the Island of Panchaea'). By the end of the decade, Odoevsky had become well versed in the poetics as well as the philosophy of romanticism – both the 'high' German romanticism of E. T. A. Hoffmann, Wackenroder, Novalis and Jean Paul, and the 'lower' varieties of the French *école frénétique*. He also continued to experiment in form, using both European and Russian models.

Experimentation went hand in hand with uneven artistic success. Nevertheless, the range of the stories written in the decade or so from the late 1820s is remarkable for its breadth. *Pestrye skazki* as a cycle provides an early demonstration of this, as do the artistic 'biographies', 'Poslednii kvartet Betkhovena' ('Beethoven's Last Quartet', 1830) and 'Sebastian Bach' (1835). These two stories which, along with 'Opere del Cavaliere Giambattista Piranesi' (1831) and 'Improvizator' ('The Improvisor', 1833) were originally intended for a cycle to be called 'Dom sumasshedshikh' (or 'House of Madmen'), are to be numbered among Odoevsky's best and were eventually incorporated into *Russkie nochi*. Caustic satirical tales such as 'Brigadir' ('The Brigadir', 1833) and 'Nasmeshka mertvetsa' ('The Mockery of a Corpse', 1834), frequently with supernatural or fantastic elements, led to full blown society tales ('svetskie povesti') such as 'Kniazhna Mimi' (1834) and 'Kniazhna Zizi' (1839), ('Princess Mimi' and 'Princess Zizi') in which social portraiture predominates, and to stories of mixed genre such as 'Zhivoi mertvets' ('The Live Corpse', dated 1838) – a mélange of didactic satire and romantic philosophy in fantastic trappings (see Chapter 2). Odoevsky was also capable of Gogolian whimsy – in parts of *Pestrye skazki* and in the humorous 'Istoriia o petukhe, koshke i liagushke' ('The Story of a Cock, a Cat and a Frog', 1834) – and author of the anti-Utopian satires 'Gorod bez imeni' ('City Without a Name', 1839) and 'Poslednee samoubiistvo' ('The Last Suicide', 1844) and one of the first Russian works of science fiction, '4338-i god. Petersburgskie pis'ma' ('The Year 4338. Petersburg Letters', 1840). Mystical and alchemical studies contributed to his most interesting romantic stories: 'Sil'fida' ('The Sylph', 1837), the until recently neglected 'Kosmorama' ('The Cosmorama'), and the substantial 'dilogy', 'Salamandra' ('The Salamander', 1841).

While his voluminous archive abounds with unfinished novels, cycles, and plays on all manner of themes, many of which did not get far beyond the planning stage, Odoevsky did manage to bring to fruition one of his most ambitious literary projects, the philosophical frame-tale *Russkie nochi*, designed to combine the genres of novel and drama. This included a number of stories published separately during the 1830s, enclosed by a substantial framing device which develops into dramatic dialogue of a largely philosophical nature, reflecting the intellectual themes of the 1820s and 1830s in a manner unique in Russian fiction. It also remains a formal curiosity which has no real counterpart in either Russian or European literature (see Chapter Four).

After 1844, in which year he published his three-volume collected *Sochineniia* (*Russkie nochi* appearing for the first time as Part

One of this), Odoevsky wrote and published very little fiction, becoming more and more occupied by other activities. He resurfaced in the 1860s with a few publicistic pieces – notably *Nedovol'no* (*Not Good Enough*, 1867), a spirited riposte to Turgenev's purportedly valedictory *Dovol'no* (*Enough*), but a late attempt at a realistic novel, to be called 'Samarianin' ('The Samaritan'), remained at his death largely unwritten.

## II

The cycle of stories with one of the longest titles in Russian literature – *Pestrye skazki s krasnym slovtsom, sobrannye Irineem Modestovichem Gomozeikoiu, magistrom filosofii i chlenom raznykh uchenykh obshchestv, izdannye V. Bezglasnym* – was published as a de-luxe small format volume, appropriately adorned with variegated designs and illustrations, in St. Petersburg in 1833. The collection, as an entity, was republished for the first time in Britain in 1988, with a facsimile of the original edition appearing in Russia in 1991.[1]

Odoevsky published many of his works over several decades under a variety of pseudonyms. 'Bezglasny' (the supposed publisher of *Pestrye skazki*) was one of his favourite sobriquets of that period. Gomozeiko, however, (or 'Gomozeika') was more than just another pen name; he was a persona over whom Odoevsky took considerable trouble. 'Master of Philosophy and member of various learned societies', an afficionado of occult sciences who 'knows all possible languages: living, dead and half-dead' and just about everything else, Gomozeiko is a poverty-stricken encyclopaedist; as such he assumes the role of a whimsical alter ego: a middle-aged eccentric, an exaggerated self-projection. The fact that Odoevsky had further plans for the figure of Gomozeiko adds a dimension that goes beyond Pushkin's treatment of Ivan Belkin, or Gogol's of Rudyi Pan'ko, with whom Gomozeiko is frequently compared (indeed, Odoevsky went so far as to propose combining these three 'collectors' of tales in a single volume). Gomozeiko was conceived as the first resident of the unrealized 'house of madmen'; his 'autobiography' and 'historical researches' are alluded to in Bezglasny's introduction to *Pestrye skazki*. Of the historical researches there is no trace, but the autobiography was started, covering Gomozeiko's provincial upbringing, education, and government service (in which he struggled in vain to bring improvement to the urban district sanitary services, only to be accused of practising 'Carbonari-type ideas'). Connected with this project, or extracted from it, is 'Istoriia o petukhe, koshke i liagushke', subtitled 'a provincial story' and set in Rezhensk (the scene of Ivan Sevast'ianych's traumatic experiences with the body which belonged to no one). Odoevsky's knowledge of provincial life and officialdom only displayed in these two stories, probably derives from visits to his mother and stepfather. There was to have been much more of Gomozeiko – a whole cycle of adventures (*pokhozh-deniia*) in the provinces and the capital which might have formed an interesting counterpart to Gogol's later *Mertvye dushi* (*Dead Souls*). The only completed tale, however, in which Gomozeiko makes a return appearance, as a garrulous storyteller, is 'Prividenie' ('The Apparition', 1838).

*Pestrye skazki* can be seen as in many ways a transitional work between Odoevsky's fictional output of the 1820s and that of the 1830s. It is also a text which has never produced any real critical consensus; this fact seemingly applies equally to the author as critic; when appropriating 'Otryvki iz *Pestrykh skazok* (1833)' as a section for Part Three of his 1844 *Sochineniia*, Odoevsky omitted a good deal of the original cycle and rearranged the rest. Only stories number IV, II, VII and VIII were included; 'Igosha' (V) was placed in a different section.

As early as January 1829, Odoevsky referred to *Pestrye skazki* in a letter to M.P. Pogodin:

> Having withdrawn from literature for a time in readiness to bring out a work [*bol'shoi trud*], I certainly don't want to remind the public of myself by the commission of old sins.[2]

The 'old sins' remained, however – at least as far as some readers were concerned. N.A. Polevoy, in *Moskovskii telegraf*, criticised *Pestrye skazki* as too much allegory and too little thought, seeing in them cold imitations of Hoffmann and evidence of Odoevsky's aristocratic aloofness; Baron E.F. Rozen, on the other hand, greeted the cycle as original tales of the miraculous at various levels, reminiscent of 'the one and only Hoffmann'.[3] P.A. Viazemsky did not agree with either of these assessments; in a letter to Zhukovsky, he wrote:

> Odoevsky has published his *Pestrye skazki*, the fantastic ones. I haven't seen it yet but they say the edition is a very fine one, fetching and fantastic. I think that Odoevsky's genre is not the fantastic, at least in the Hoffmannian sense. He has a more observant and reflective mind and his imagination is not at all whimsical and playful.[4]

Odoevsky's friends and associates (including Gogol, who probably had a hand in the book's design) responded fairly enthusiastically to the collection; I.I. Davydov went further than Viazemsky in calling *Pestrye skazki* the first attempt in Russian literature at the philosophical tale; however, a little later, A.I. Koshelev wrote to Odoevsky concerning his tales:

> In general they have not made any great impression: there are very few people who understand them and still fewer who would genuinely appreciate their quality.[5]

This confusion can perhaps be attributed to the presence in *Pestrye skazki* of 'old sins' (didactic and allegorical satirical apologues) alongside more innovatory works. However, even a brief examination of *Pestrye skazki* will reveal a diversity and complexity which has led the original critical doubts and differences to persist.

Between the two prefaces at the beginning (from the 'publisher' and the 'author', or rather collector) and the epilogue (itself merely a restating of the epigraph to the last story) we are given stories numbered I to VIII; there is in fact a total of seven stories, as VIII is a sequel, or rather a 'reverse' of VII.

The first story, 'Retorta' ('The Retort'), opens its four short chapters with an 'Introduction' which reads like a veritable credo of romanticism on the part of the narrator, or supposed author. Chapter Two of the story finds the somewhat eccentric narrator at the usual venue for the opening of an Odoevsky tale, a society ball; annoyed when the conspiratorial ritual of the card table asserts its supremacy over the hot air of narratorial digression, our storyteller retreats to cool himself by a *fortochka*, only to find the air there just as hot, despite the twenty degrees of frost outside; the entire house and its occupants prove to be enclosed 'in a glass retort with a curved nose'. The narrator pokes his nose out of the retort and is immediately, in Chapter Four, cast by a young devil (*satanenok*) into a Latin dictionary; on his travels from page to page through the dictionary he meets 'a spider, a dead body, a night-cap, Igosha and other amiable young people whom the accursed young devil had gathered from all sides of the world and forced to share my fate'. Some of these denizens of the dictionary are so steeped in words that they are turning into fairy tales; the narrator himself begins to undergo this transformation:

> my eyes turned into an epigraph, from my head a few chapters sprouted, my torso became a text, and my nails and hair took up the space for linguistic mistakes and misprints, an unavoidable appurtenance to any book .... (p. 26)

At this point the ball ends and the exodus from it breaks the retort; the young imp takes off in alarm, his dictionary thrust under his arm – dropping a few pages in his haste along with some of its fictional captives, the narrator ('Your humble servant') included. The narrator has the presence of mind to grab his erstwhile comrades from the dropped pages, rolling them into a ball and stuffing them into his pocket in order subsequently 'to present them for the inspection of the esteemed reader ...' (p. 27).

Thus it is by this whimsical interaction of society tale and fairy tale and play on the relationship between narrator and reader, integral text and its component parts (characters and devices, words, and punctuation), that Odoevsky motivates his discourse to present, at various removes, the succession of unlikely (*pestrye* – 'variegated' or 'motley') stories (II-VIII) which follow. The concept of 'fairy tales for old children' was utilized on more than one occasion by Odoevsky in the 1830s. Discourse, both in written form and as incongruous dialogue, is a strong sub-theme, too, of 'Skazka o mertvom tele ...' ('Tale of a Dead Body Belonging to No One Knows Whom') (II); indeed the stress on written articulation in this story almost matches Gogol's emphasis in 'Shinel'' ('The Overcoat') on incoherence in speech. 'Novyi Zhoko' ('The New Jocko') (III), a spider's viewpoint on the universe, which is ironically subtitled 'a classical tale', is primarily a burlesque of 'frenetic' French romantic forms; this polemical parodic thrust has been long since lost, but a quality of the bizarre lingers. 'Skazka o tom po kakomu sluchaiu ...' ('The Tale of How it Happened ...') (IV) offers a pre-Gogolian look inside a Petersburg chancellery and culminates in a demonic card game (cards, along with society balls, were a pet hate of Odoevsky's). 'Igosha' (V) builds on to a Russian folkloric base a study in child psychology, while 'Prosto skazka' ('Just a Fairy Tale') (VI) is more or less what its title suggests: that is to say, some sort of a fairy tale and little more.

'Skazka, o tom, kak opasno devushkam ...' ('The Tale of How it is Dangerous for Girls to Walk in a Crowd along Nevsky Prospect') is an allegorical cautionary tale of the rape of Russian beauty. Together with its 'opposite', 'Ta zhe skazka, tol'ko na izvorot' ('The Same Tale, only in Reverse') (VIII) – a narratorial digression and Gomozeiko's parting shot, balancing his introduction at the beginning, this story leads into '... Gospodin Kivakel', and represents a censure of the absurdities of female upbringing in Petersburg society, motivated perhaps more by concerns of artistic taste than with crude preoccupations of proto-Slavophilism. The repetition of the epigraph reinforces the theme of *kukol'nost'* ('mannequinism', 'automatonism', or who manipulates whom?).

The tales are individually slight, but diverse in their use of inventive whimsy, satire, and the grotesque; not for the only time in Odoevsky's oeuvre one has the suspicion that the whole may exceed the sum of the parts. Soviet criticism of this generally neglected cycle tended to emphasize the angle of social satire; *Pestrye skazki* was said to anticipate Gogol's Petersburg tales and to prefigure Odoevsky's own 'Improvizator' and 'Zhivoi mertvets', which continue a similar grotesque-satirical line.

*Pestrye skazki* is not to be pinned down, however, as easily as that. While seeing in the cycle a near approach to the subsequent 'satirical-realist Gogol' in its 'realistic analysis of contemporary Russian reality', shrewder critics also point to the constantly undercutting effects obtained by the employment of romantic irony. The importance of Gomozeiko and some of the quirks of narration in the cycle have been touched on above and the work is clearly best read, once again, in the light of both the theory and practice of the poetics of romanticism. V.I. Sakharov, a contemporary specialist on Odoevsky, sees the tales as allegories, 'complicated by such Hoffmannian romantic motifs as puppetry, automatonism and the spectrality of bureaucratic life', directed towards social satire; however, he argues that Odoevsky was attempting 'to unite pre-romantic prose with the recently-learned rules of romantic poetics' and that it was 'the forthright didacticism and the somewhat archaic quality of the satirical prose' which brought forth the critical reaction of certain contemporaries.[6] Furthermore, as the same commentator has also pointed out, the composition and reception of *Pestrye skazki* must also be considered in light of the literary polemics of the day, in which the brand of romanticism with which Odoevsky was experimenting ran contrary to the more robust variety (à la Victor Hugo) favoured by writers such as Polevoy and Marlinsky.[7]

Nevertheless, despite their transitional position in Odoevsky's development, these *Pestrye skazki* are not quite as transitory in their significance as their author modestly indicated a decade later, when, introducing the truncated selection deemed worthy of inclusion in his 1844 works, Odoevsky referred to the cycle as 'a joke, the main aim of which was to demonstrate the possibilities for luxury editions in Russia and to launch woodcuts and other forms of illustration'.[8] Earlier, he had written of *Pestrye skazki* to his friend Koshelev: 'You will be surprised to learn that I wrote my harlequinesque fairy tales in the most bitter moments of my life' (see epigraph to this chapter): humour and distress often go hand in hand.[9] While *Pestrye skazki* can be seen both as a series of tongue-in-cheek exercises, parodying various forms of romantic excess (in tune with Odoevsky's critical articles of the 1830s), and as a preliminary rehearsal for a number of the themes and ideas which inform *Russkie nochi*, the cycle still retains its own idiosyncratic and enigmatic qualities.

Following a century and a half of oblivion, however, Odoevsky's *Pestrye skazki* have now undergone four reprintings since 1988.[10] In her supplement to the 1991 facsimile edition, M.A. Tur'ian remarks that criticism has accorded little attention to *Pestrye skazki*, either in general terms or as an entity (or cycle). She attempts to rectify this in a pamphlet running to forty-seven pages, providing what is the most detailed account yet of its compositional history, the background influences, and the critical reception accorded it by Odoevsky's contemporaries.[11]

Concluding his introduction to the (1993) edition, V.N. Grekov writes:

> Just like Odoevsky's protagonists, we are surrounded by mirages. They do not confront us at another pole of reality but interweave with life, sometimes taking its place. And how hard it is to distinguish authentic values from the false, truth from imitations thereof, mirages from life... . However, we can profit from the spiritual experience of the protagonists of *Pestrye skazki* ...; enduring along with them, we learn not to yield to deception.[12]

We are thus returned full circle to the didactic intention which originally informed Odoevsky's cycle of tales, as it had much of his work of the 1820s, but with the suggestion that *Pestrye skazki*, like so much else among Odoevsky's writings, has a certain, perhaps even a newly-found, relevance for the modern world.

## Notes

1. *Variegated Tales with a verbal frill, collected by Irinei Modestovich Gomozeika, master of philosophy and member of various learned societies, published by V. Bezglasny* (St. Petersburg, 1833). Reprints: V.F. Odoevsky, *Pyostryye skazki* [sic], ed. Neil Cornwell (University of Durham, 1988); *Pestrye skazki s krasnym slovtsom ...* (Moscow, 1991). Page references here are to the original edition (matched, of course, by the 1991 facsimile). Odoevsky's name did not appear in the original book (cf. Pushkin's shadowy appearance in the first edition of his *Tales of Belkin* as the publisher 'A.P.', 1831). The cycle was originally to have been entitled 'Makhrovye skazki' (meaning 'double' tales, probably in the botanical sense of possessing more than the usual flower petals.)
2. Quoted from V.I. Sakharov, 'Evoliutsiia tvorcheskogo oblika V.F. Odoevskogo', in his *Vremia i sub'by russkikh pisatelei* (Moscow, 1981), p. 26.
3. Quoted by P.N. Sakulin, *Iz istoriia russkogo idealizma: Kniaz' V.F. Odoevsky. Myslitel' – Pisatel'* (Moscow, 1913), vol. I, part 2, pp. 32-4 and 34-5; Sakulin gives an account of contemporary reactions (including those of Odoevsky's mother) to *Pestrye skazki* on pp. 32-7.
4. P.A. Viazemsky, 'Iz pisem kniazia Viazemskogo k Zhukovskomu', *Russkii arkhiv*, 3, 1900, p. 373.

5.  See Sakulin, I, 2, pp. 36-7.
6.  V.I. Sakharov, 'E.T.A. Gofman i V.F. Odoevsky', in the collection *Khudozhestven-nyi mir E.T.A. Gofmana* (Moscow, 1982), p. 175.
7.  Sakharov, 'Evoliutsiia tvorcheskogo oblika ...', pp. 27-8.
8.  *Sochineniia kniazia V.F. Odoevskogo*, vol. III (St. Petersburg, 1844), pp. 169-70.
9.  For an account of Odoevsky's personal difficulties over these years, based on new research, see M.A. Tur'ian, '*Strannaia moia sud'ba* ...'. *O zhizni Vladimira Fedorovicha Odoevskogo* (Moscow, 1991).
10. See note 1 above; two further editions (published in Russia *and* in the new orthography) have now appeared: V.F. Odoevsky, *Pestrye skazki/Skazki Dedushki Irineia* (Moscow, 1993), in the series 'Zabytaia kniga' ('forgotten book'). This also incudes fourteen of Odoevsky's fairy tales (*Pestrye skazki* apart), as well as the first modern reprinting of an extract from the unfinished novel *Segeliel', ili Don-Kikhot XIX stoletiia* (for more on which see Neil Cornwell, *V.F. Odoevsky: His Life, Times and Milieu* (London, 1986), pp. 63-4). The most recent edition is that edited by M.A. Tur'ian, in the 'Literaturnye pamiatniki' series (St Petersburg, 1996).
11. M.A. Tur'ian, *Skazki Irineia Modestovicha Gomozeiki: primechaniia k faksimil'noi chasti*, supplement to facsimile edition of *Pestrye skazki* ... (Moscow, 1991).
12. N.V. Grekov, introduction to V.F. Odoevsky, *Pestrye skazki/Skazki Dedushki Irineia* (Moscow, 1993), p. 22.

Chapter 8

# VLADIMIR ODOEVSKY AND RUSSIAN GOTHIC

## I

Few literary forms have returned to popularity so sweepingly and so rapidly as the 'Gothic'. This has been achieved, over the past decade or two, under a variety of labels: the 'literature (or "tale") of terror', the 'horror story', the 'fantastic', 'fantasy' and 'suspense', as well as the Gothic ('gothic', or occasionally 'Gothick'). Still further comparable studies have issued forth, especially on Russian literature, under the banners of romanticism and latterly gender studies. Many have stretched their attentions into the twentieth century, some engaging with the revival of their theme up to and under postmodernism. Such criticism has encouraged the reprinting of classic and neglected texts, Gothic or fantastic, while recent fiction has continued to include its fair share of rambling mansions, sinsister guardians and vampirical proclivities.

'Russian Gothic' is not a term that has enjoyed a great deal of currency to date in critical studies of Russian literature. The word 'Gothic' is commonly used in connection with Dostoevsky: in the case of the early works, such as *Dvoinik (The Double)* and 'Khoziaika' ('The Landlady'), which may be said to *be* Gothic; or of the later novels, which may include Gothic elements or traces. Otherwise, what might have been termed Gothic in Russian literature has tended, with rare exceptions, to be submerged under the blanket heading of 'Russian romanticism', or alternative generic terms such as 'the supernatural' or 'the fantastic'; at least one recent Russian essay, though, by V.E. Vatsuro, promises a possible redressing of the bal-

ance.[1] There is, for example, no entry under 'Gothic' in Victor Ter-
ras's *Handbook of Russian Literature*, (New Haven, 1985), while even
the *Kratkaia literaturnaia entsiklopediia* (vol. 2, Moscow, 1964) runs to
only a very brief entry under 'Goticheskii roman' ('Gothic Novel,
The'); likewise, *The Modern Encyclopedia of Russian and Soviet Litera-
tures* (vol. 9, Gulf Breeze, 1989) has a mere half-page on the subject.

Even an anthology (Moscow, Raduga) entitled *Russian 19th-century
Gothic Tales* appeared to acquire that title for its English translation by
chance (the Russian title is given as *Fantasticheskii mir russkoi povesti*).[2]
This particular volume includes a range of stories extending from
Pogorel'sky and Somov in the 1820s to Odoevsky's 'Zhivoi mertverts'
('The Live Corpse', published 1844, but dated 1838) and A. K. Tol-
stoy's early vampire story 'Upyr' ('Vampire') of 1841. Early Dosto-
evsky apart, this period may be said approximately to represent the
heyday of this style in Russia. Lermontov and Gogol are featured
('Nos' ['The Nose'] may be problematic, residing more plausibly
within the realm of pure psychological fantasy, but 'Portret' ['The
Portrait'] clearly belongs). Included too is Russia's one undisputed
masterpiece in the genre, Pushkin's 'Pikovaia dama' ('The Queen of
Spades'), as well as works by a number of minor writers.

The dust jacket of this collection (it contains no general introduc-
tion) refers to 'enchanting flights of imagination, vivid imagery bor-
rowed from folk tale and legend, grotesque fantasy and utopian
dreams of a distant, happy future'. While this may have something in
common with Western definitions of the Gothic, we tend to think
rather of dark castles or crumbling mansions, wicked uncles and
helpless maidens, ghostly manifestations, or the living dead (see
below). Apart from a folkloric input, Russian Gothic derives from an
amalgam of European influences: the English Gothic novel, certain
tales of E. T. A. Hoffmann and the French *fantastique* tradition
(together with the more contemporaneous *école frénétique*). Various
common nonliterary Russian and Western sources can also be pin-
pointed. A particularly Russian element, though drawn from Ger-
man romanticism, is the concept of *dvoemirie* (or philosophical
dualism, later to be taken up again and developed by the Symbol-
ists). Parallels can be drawn with Edgar Allan Poe, while Russian lit-
erature, like its Western counterparts, went on to include fin de siècle
Gothic elements within the Russian Symbolist movement and a
twentieth-century revival emerged, even within the context of Soviet
literature, in the writing of Mikhail Bulgakov.

However, if we return to the period referred to above, from 1825
to 1844, we find that these dates almost exactly span the creative
career of a writer from whose pen issued what is arguably the most
impressive body of something like genuine Russian Gothic writing.

However, Odoevsky's reputation in this area is only now beginning to receive due attention, both in the West and in Russia.

## II

Prince Vladimir Fyodorovich Odoevsky (1804-1869) was one of the most extraordinarily versatile figures in nineteenth-century Russia. Despite a full career as a public servant, which lasted from 1826 until his death, he managed to enjoy fame as a romantic writer, children's writer, thinker, musicologist, educationalist, philanthropist, amateur scientist and general 'Renaissance man'.[3] A man of many pseudonyms, he even published gastronomic pieces under the name of 'Mister Puff'. He has frequently been dubbed 'the Russian Hoffmann' or 'the Russian Faust': in some ways (though he did not write poetry and the comparison doubtless flatters) 'the Russian Goethe' would be nearer the mark. A reputation for eccentricity, 'encyclopaedism', and dilettantism led to his being taken less seriously than was his due for much of his lifetime. Following many years of neglect, his reputation enjoyed one minor revival in the early part of this century and another in the 1950s, when important collections of his literary, musical, and educational writings were published. A few of his children's stories remain highly popular, but it is as a leading representative of high Russian romanticism that he now finds his niche: a recent Moscow paperback selection of his 'Tales and Stories' enjoyed a print run of no less than two million, seven hundred thousand copies.[4]

The last in the line of one of Russia's oldest families (as a *kniaz'* he traced his lineage back to Rurik), and in later life officially Russia's 'premier nobleman', Odoevsky nevertheless always had to work for a living. The family fortune had been dissipated during the eighteenth century and Odoevsky's father had married beneath him – virtually into the peasantry. These factors, together with being raised largely by Moscow relatives (his father had died in 1808 and his mother remarried), made Odoevsky something of an aristocratic outsider who, despite years of loyal government service, regained little political trust in the wake of his tenuous links with the Decembrist revolt which at the end of 1825 inaugurated and determined the reactionary reign of Nicholas I.

Odoevsky's first flush of literary success (alludeded to in the story 'Novyi god' ['New Year'], dated 1831) occurred in the first half of the 1820s, when he presided over the Society of Wisdom Lovers, a philosophical circle influenced mainly by Schelling, which included among its adherents some of the principal originators of both Westernising and Slavophile thought. He also co-edited the almanac

*Mnemozina* (1824-5) which, in its four issues, was as culturally vital as it was financially hopeless.

Following the Decembrist upheaval, Odoevsky married, entered governmental service, moved to St. Petersburg and immersed himself ever deeper in the esoteric and occult philosophy which lay at the roots of European romanticism, channelling his thought into creative activity which was to reach fruition only in the 1830s – to which decade we shall shortly return.

He lived in St. Petersburg until 1862 and during this period his literary career again blossomed and then declined. He held a number of important administrative posts, became in the 1840s strenuously involved in educational and philanthropic projects, and was always a leading personality in Russian musical life. In this field he actively promoted both the home product (particularly the music of Glinka) and the pick of the West: Bach, Mozart, Beethoven – and subsequently the 'moderns', Berlioz and Wagner. He played an important backstage part too in the continued development of Russian literary journalism, as co-founder of Pushkin's *Sovremennik* and principal backer of *Otechestvennye zapiski* (in which thick journals many of his own tales made their first appearance).

Not least, Odoevsky hosted one of the main literary and musical salons of St. Petersburg and later Moscow. His circle remained, for over forty years, a meeting place for artistic celebrities from home and abroad. The Russian literary scene was nothing if not incestuous and Odoevsky was involved with everyone who was anyone, from Griboedov and Pushkin to Turgenev and Tolstoy; he befriended and encouraged the brooding Lermontov, the prickly young Dostoevsky and later the aspiring Tchaikovsky. Back in the 1830s, in the heyday of his salon, it was remarked that 'on Odoevsky's divan sits the whole of Russian literature'.

Always to be counted among the more progressive elements of the nobility, though wary of radicalism and revolution, Odoevsky was, as his later diaries show, an enthusiastic supporter of the reforms of Alexander II. At the same time, he wearied of the social and financial strains of Petersburg life and in 1862 took up an appointment to the Moscow Senate. At the time of his death, in 1869, he was up to his ears in more projects than ever: musical, historical, scientific and, once again, literary.

## III

If Odoevsky is to be credited with a particular forté in his literary production, it lies in his unusual creations of cycles of stories. The 'cycle', as opposed to the mere collection, requires at least oblique thematic and stylistic connections, or threads, between its member stories. Several of these attempts remain uncompleted – still others were never more than pie in the sky. However, two which did achieve completion are now to be counted among the fundamental works of Russian romantic prose. *Pestrye skazki* (1833), the first real fruit of Odoevsky's 'mature' literary period, is a delicate collection of parodies on aspects of Russian and European romantic themes. The remarkable *Russkie nochi* (completed in 1844), which includes some fine individual stories (ranging from the Gothic, to the musical and the anti-Utopian), is surrounded by a substantial philosophical frame-tale, addressing many of the preoccupations of Russian intellectual circles of the 1830s.[5] A discussion of Gothic elements within *Russkie nochi* would require a separate essay in itself; some, however, do receive a certain coverage in other chapters of this volume.

The decade and a half, from about 1829 until the issuing of his three-volume *Sochineniia* in 1844 and his subsequent virtual retirement from literature, saw the flowering of Odoevsky's literary achievement. The selection of stories recently chosen for a volume in translation is drawn from this period and includes just one story from *Pestrye skazki* ('Skazka o mertvom tele, neizvstno komu prinadlezhashchem' ['The Tale of a Dead Body belonging to No One Knows Whom']), and none from *Russkie nochi*, given that this work was translated in toto in 1965.[6] Also not included were two other sides of Odoevsky's versatile fictional output: the society tale (of which 'Kniazhna Mimi' ['Princess Mimi'] and 'Kniazhna Zizi' ['Princess Zizi'] are the best examples) and his science fiction (see the unfinished futuristic novel *4338-i god* [*The Year 4338*]).[7]

Instead the emphasis fell largely on Odoevsky's more overtly Gothic fiction, which includes some of his most stimulating writing, and yet had long been particularly neglected. Of the eight tales featured, my translation of 'Zhivoi mertvets' ('The Live Corpse') had been published in an earlier anthology (and was revised for the later collection); 'Sil'fida' had appeared in two earlier translations (but was retranslated for the new volume).[8] The other six stories appeared in English for the first time. Even in Russian, several works had only in recent years made their first reappearance in print this century; indeed one story (Odoevsky's 'Letter IV' to Countess Rostopchina) received its first printed airing in any form since 1844.

'Novyi god' ('New Year') represents a backward glance at the literary circles of the early 1820s and is, in its own way, a mini society tale, expressing poignant nostalgia over the decline of good fellowship and intellectual idealism, in the form here of male camaraderie. 'Skazka o mertvom tele, neizvestno komu prinadlezhashchem' and

'Istoriia o petukhe, koshke i liagushke' ('The Tale of a Cock, a Cat and a Frog'), both set in the fictitious provincial area of Rezhensk, are examples of Odoevsky's ready wit and a Gogolian tendency towards whimsical black comedy: the former story is an early instance of Odoevsky's use of the fantastic, while the latter tale elaborates on the Gogolian Mirgorod model of grotesque provincial life.

'Letter IV' [to Countess E. P. R ... .] is one of a series of letters to Evdokiia ('Dodo') Petrovna Rostopchina, herself a writer and society hostess, 'on apparitions, superstitious fears, sensual deceptions, magic, cabbalism, alchemy and other mysterious sciences'. Odoevsky also dedicated 'Zhivoi mertvets' and 'Kosmorama' ('The Cosmorama') to the Countess, who shared his theosophical interests. 'Letter IV' comprises a viable short story in its own right ('an excellent subject for a tale of terror', as Odoevsky puts it) and is notable too for featuring Count Saint-Germain, a legendary but historical figure used by Pushkin in 'Pikovaia dama' (1833) and who has recently resurfaced in Umberto Eco's occult extravaganza, *Foucault's Pendulum*.[9]

'Zhivoi mertvets' is a striking tale of out-of-body experience, based ultimately this time on dream, which influenced Dostoevsky's later fantastical stories, 'Bobok' and 'Son smeshnogo cheloveka' ('The Dream of a Ridiculous Man': see Chapter Two). It is of interest for its exploitation of mixed narrative techniques – largely proto-stream-of-consciousness, alternating with dramatic diaglogue – and linguistic register (including thieves' argot), but is also notable as the clearest statement of Odoevsky's philosophical preoccupation with cause and effect: the ultimate impact on a single life and on posterity of every action and even every thought. This theme, which is present also in 'Kosmorama' and 'Salamandra' ('The Salamander'), was later taken up by Tolstoy in *Fal'shivyi kupon (The False Coupon)* and *Smert' Ivana Il'icha (The Death of Ivan Ilyich)* and is implicit too in the philosophy of *Voina i mir (War and Peace)*.

The main Gothic meat of this particular selection, however, and of Odoevsky's literary production, is to be found in three major tales, traditionally seen as the most significant and the most elaborate of what have been termed his 'works of mystical content': 'Sil'fida', 'Kosmorama' and 'Salamandra', all written in a particularly productive period at the end of the 1830s.

'Sil'fida' is subtitled 'from the notes of a reasonable man' (Odoevsky was ever suspicious of reliance on reason per se) and begins with seven letters from one Mikhail Platonovich to his friend and eventual editor, the 'reasonable man', who has little grasp of the artistic spirit (ironically, the 'authorial' confession, with which the tale ends, displays great rationality, both by purporting to understand 'nothing in this story' and by mangling the protagonist's name as 'Platon

Mikhailovich'). Bored with provincial life, the protagonist discovers the cabbalistic books and folios of his deceased uncle's secret library and immerses himself in the pursuit of sylphs. The reasonable man's account of the 'saving' of his friend for marriage and a conventional provincial lifestyle frames the extracts from Mikhail Platonovich's journal, in which the poetic saga of his relationship with a sylph (involving an alternative artistic vision – indeed an alternative reality – and the separation of time and space, leading to 'the soul of the soul' where 'poetry is truth'), gradually descends from the sublime to become incoherent jottings.

'Kosmorama' represents Odoevsky's most overt fictional depiction of his interest in the concept of dualism (or *dvoemirie*), drawn from his study of such mystical thinkers as Jacob Boehme, John Pordage, Swedenborg and Saint-Martin. The construction of a 'cosmorama' occurs in one of Odoevsky's children's stories, while it appears that he himself possessed some such 'toy', as he recorded in his travel notes (Mainz, 1847): 'In the steamship cabin an Englishman and a Belgian did not know how to work my travelling *kosmorama*; each time they wanted to see by looking into the magnifying lens, instead of the frosted glass'. With the mystical powers bestowed upon it in this tale, the cosmorama takes on a capability comparable to that of Borges's 'Aleph' (in his story of that name) – itself said to be 'one of the points in space containing all points' and 'the microcosm of alchemists and cabalists'. The cosmorama, however, is only the starting point for the visions of the protagonist Vladimir, which in fact reach their most extravagant Aleph-like quality after the destruction of the allegedly magical device. The scope of Vladimir's perception, both of the dissolution of space and time and the apprehension of an inner or parallel world, may be seen as counterpoint to the purely mechanistic powers of Kipriano, the Improvisor from *Russkie nochi*, while his visions, together with those portrayed in 'Sil'fida' and 'Salamandra', come disturbingly close, as romantic writing occasionally could, to what has more recently been labelled 'near-death experience'.

'Kosmorama' is Odoevsky's most full-blown romantic tale: perhaps this is why, from its original publication in 1840, it had to wait until 1988 for a reprinting (even Odoevsky himself unaccountably omitted it from his 1844 *Sochineniia*).[10] It includes as full a gamut of occult and Gothic paraphernalia as may be encountered in any work of Russian romanticism: the walking dead, crime and torture, amorous intrigue, second sight, supernatural arson and spontaneous human combustion. This grotesque phantasmagoria is, however, skillfully interwoven between vision and 'reality', accompanied with a slight edge of undercutting irony. Indeed, unlike 'Sil'fida' or 'Zhivoi mertvets', it cannot be conclusively explained in terms of madness or dream (although insanity remains one strongly plausible interpretation): riddles still remain, as we are warned in the 'publisher's preface', not least the mysterious personalities of Doctor Bin and the unfortunate Sophia (the evolution of whose name from 'Sonia' is undoubtedly to be seen in occult terms). The promised sequel to 'Kosmorama' never materialised, although there is some evidence that one had been seriously intended.

'Salamandra' is, *Russkie nochi* as a totality excepted, Odoevsky's longest work of prose fiction and the nearest he came, at least in finished form, to writing a full-scale novel. Indeed, 'Salamandra' has a curious bi-partite structure, termed by Odoevsky a 'dilogy' (as compared to the far more common 'trilogy' form), which, while comprising a genuine continuation in narrative terms, signals a radical break in the work as regards narrational mode, chronological leap, and generic emphasis. The first part (first published separately as 'The Southern Shore of Finland at the Beginning of the Eighteenth Century') has many of the characteristics of the historical novel and could almost have been entitled 'The Finn of Peter the Great' (as opposed to Pushkin's *Arap Petra Velikogo* ['The Blackamoor of Peter the Great']). Another striking attribute is the pervasive presence of Finnish folklore, derived from the researches of Odoevsky's friend Iakov Grot and his translations into Russian from *The Kalevala* (which had made its first appearance in Helsinki only in 1835).

In its second part, 'Elsa', 'Salamandra' (the overall title being imposed in 1844 on the work's first integral publication) shifts dramatically into the genre of Gothic tale. The main characters continue, but the magical folkloric elements are transferred to an alchemical search for the philosopher's stone. And yet, as in all things occult, there remains a mysterious connection. The first part uses omniscient first-person narration. 'Elsa', however, switches abruptly to a seemingly authorial narrative, and is mainly a flashback from the nineteenth century; the sub-narrator (the apparent author's uncle) is the real Odoevskian figure: a characteristic self-parody in the guise of an elderly eccentric and slightly impatient adept in all matters arcane. This type, indeed, owing something to Irinei Gomozeiko (from *Pestrye skazki* and other Odoevskian developments of his favoured type of the middle-aged encyclopedic pedant), anticipates many a psychic doctor to come in subsequent European Gothic fiction. The central character, Yakko the Finn (Peter the Great's former favourite, now fallen on hard times), is transposed from hero to villain and, with his affirmation that 'all is permitted to a rich man', he takes his place in a long line of Russian moral delinquents, stretching from Pushkin's Hermann to Dostoevsky's Raskolnikov and various Karamazovs. Again, a goodly range of Gothic and alchemical appurtenances are on display and the tale reaches a rousing finale.

Odoevsky's propensity, revealed in a number of tales, for open, multiple, or alternative endings shows his natural instinct for the pure fantastic: not just in the use of Gothic detail and thematic content, but in classic Todorovian and romantic terms of ambiguity and hesitation, the representation (and frquently the reconciliation) of opposites and the inadequacies of language to express a deeper reality. Notable too is the exploitation of various of the devices associated with romantic poetics: romantic irony, distancing by means of varied and multiple forms of narration and use of the fragment or manuscript, as well as other forms of fragmentary composition.

## IV

In addition to the stories already discussed above, or even merely alluded to, there are perhaps three further – albeit lesser – Odoevsky tales that warrant at least some comment under the rubric of Gothic: 'Orlakhskaia krest'ianka' (The Peasant Girl from Orlach), 'Neoboidennyi dom' ('The Uninhabited House') and, more particularly, 'Prividenie' ('The Apparition' or, to give it its title as translated, 'The Ghost').

Let us take these in reverse order of composition, or at least of publication. 'Orlakhskaia krest'ianka' (1842, but dated 1838) follows 'Kosmorama' in certain respects as a philosophical-romantic tale, with its epigraph from Swedenborg and its reflection of the ideas of Pordage and Saint-Martin.[11] A society setting (once again) frames the narration of a certain Count Valkirin (a favourite recurring name in Odoevsky), who is an adept in the philosophy of these occult theosophical mystics. His narrative proceeds to recount the story of Anchen, a peasant girl from Orlach, whose consciousness, or subconscious, is the battle-ground for a spectral struggle of possession, to resolve a four-hundred-year-old crime of multiple murder. The dead here speak through the living and the story is based on a supposed actual occurrence, reported in the 1830s from Germany, involving a peasant girl named Magdalena Grombach. This story is the only completed item in a projected further cycle of 'mysterious' tales dealing with the phenomenon, in its various forms, of 'possession'.

'Neoboidennyi dom' (1842, written 1840) is another story lurking somewhere on the fringes of Gothic, although Odoevsky himself preferred to regard it as deriving rather from folk legend. An old woman sets out through a forest to go to a monastery about ten kilometers away. Lost in the woods, she enters what, in modern par-

lance, would be regraded as a time warp: she calls three times within
the day at the same house, only to find that decades have elapsed
since her previous call. Such a plotline would seem to have more in
common with *Rip Van Winkle* than with classical Gothic, but even
that story receives consideration, at least under broader definitions of
the genre, or style, in question.

'Prividenie' (1838) is superficially closer to mainstream Gothic,
though, not unusually for Odoevsky, of a tongue-in-cheek variety.
Not untypically of its author, or the genre, it provides a classic case of
embedded narrative; the authorial narrator is riding in a carriage with
none other than Irinei Modestovich Gomozeiko (here revived from
*Pestrye skazki*) and two other passengers. Within the carriage ride (in
itself an unusual and whimsical chronotope for the emergence of a
ghost story), Gomozeiko recounts a round of supernatural storytelling
(involving premonitions, apparitions and 'dancing chairs'), to which
he had been a party; the ensuing story is the narrative of one of the
participants of this circle. Antics of mystification which allegedly took
place in a nearby castle supposedly led to tragic consequences; how-
ever, an alternative dénouement is supplied by another participant,
claiming the involvement of an actual apparition, while the original
storyteller is allegedly afflicted by a curse (on tellers of that very
story!). The reader is left guessing, as even Gomozeiko does not
reveal all. The pastiche element in this story is heightened by the tone
in which the 'ancient castle' is described: 'with all those odd features
of so-called Gothic architecture, which we laughed at then, but which
now, with the collapse of good taste, are coming back into fashion'.[12]
At the same time, Odoevsky is satirising the 'romantic' stories of the
'young, fashionable writers in the journals', as well as making his
usual social sallies, while producing something in the nature of a
spoof version of Hoffmann's 'The Entail'.

# V

While there may be no comprehensive or universally accepted def-
inition of Gothic as such, both narrower and wider guidelines can be
indicated. In particular, main themes or features of the Gothic can be
proposed. Chris Baldick, to name just one authority in the field, enu-
merates several such qualities. Firstly, he suggests:

> For the Gothic effect to be obtained, a tale should combine a fearful
> sense of inheritance in time with a claustrophobic sense of enclosure in
> space, these two dimensions reinforcing one another to produce an
> impression of sickening descent into disintegration.

In more concrete terms, he continues, we expect the Gothic tale to invoke 'the tyranny of the past' (a curse, archaic forms of despotism or superstition), the stifled liberty of heroine or hero, and the Gothic house, castle or mansion, reverberating with 'associations which are simultaneously psychological and historical': indeed, 'we could just say that Gothic fiction is obsessed with old buildings as sites of human decay'.[13] It should by now be apparent that Odoevsky uses, plays on or parodies all these Gothic features, and no doubt others too, in many of his works, but particularly in the body of fiction outlined in this chapter.

Odoevsky lacks, it has to be conceded, the masterly concision of Pushkin, the stylistic elegance of Lermontov and the sheer linguistic verve of Gogol (although at the height of his fame, in the 1830s, his reputation was not so very far short of theirs), but, on the other hand, his relative verbosity brings him closer, arguably, to the English style of writing of the first half of the nineteenth century. His themes too are close to the romanticism of both European and the English-based literatures; comparisons can be made, not only with Hoffmann, but with Charles Brockden Brown and of course Poe, Mary Shelley, Maturin, and (Odoevsky's near contemporary) Sheridan Le Fanu. Particularly intriguing is the proximity between Odoevsky's 'Sil'fida' (1837) and 'The Diamond Lens', a story written some twenty years later by the Irish-American author Fitz-James O'Brien (just about explicable, conceivably, in terms of the utilization of common alchemical sources). This matter, however, is explored in detail in the final chapter.

It is only comparatively recently, with the revival of critical interest in romanticism in the latter years of the Soviet Union, that a number of Odoevsky's best works have again seen the light of day. It is hoped that the renewed availability of the Russian texts, together with an English translation of most of these tales, will help to mark a new stage in promoting the resurrection of the Russian Gothic.

# Notes

This essay is a revised and enlarged version of the introduction to Vladimir Odoevsky, *The Salamander and Other Gothic Tales*, trans. Neil Cornwell (London, 1992), adapted from the form in which it appeared in *Rusistika* 3, June 1991.

1. See for example such studies as: Robert Reid (editor), *Problems of Russian Romanticism* (Aldershot, 1986); Amy Mandelker and Roberta Reeder (editors), *The Supernatural in Slavic and Baltic Literature* (Columbus, Ohio, 1988); Neil Cornwell, *The Literary Fantastic: from Gothic to Postmodernism* (New York and London, 1990). The one book-length study that does address itself specifically to this area is unfortunately disappointing: Mark S. Simpson, *The Russian Gothic Novel and its British Antecedents* (Columbus, Ohio, 1986). See also, however, V.E. Vatsuro, 'Iz istorii "goticheskogo romana" v Rossii (A.A. Bestuzhev-Marlinsky', *Russian Literature*, 38, [1995], pp. 207-26).

2. Valentin Korovin (editor), *Russian 19th-century Gothic Tales* (Moscow, 1984).

3. See Neil Cornwell, *V.F. Odoevsky: His Life, Times and Milieu* (London, 1986).

4. V. F. Odoevsky, *Povesti i rasskazy*, Moscow, 1988.

5. See Chapters 7 and 4 of this study on *Pestrye skazki* and *Russkie nochi* respectively.

6. Vladimir Odoevsky, *The Salamander and Other Gothic Tales*, trans. Neil Cornwell (London, 1992). The Russian texts of most works mentioned here ('Kosmorama' apart, see below) are to be found in V. F. Odoevsky, *Sochineniia v dvukh tomakh* (Moscow, 1981), vol. 2.

7. David Lowe's translation of 'Kniazhna Mimi' may be found in *Russian Literature Triquarterly*, 9, 1974; in *Russian Romantic Prose: An Anthology*, ed. Carl R. Proffer (Ann Arbor, 1979); and in *The Ardis Anthology of Russian Romanticism*, ed. Christine Rydel (Ann Arbor, 1984). 'Kniazhna Zizi' has yet to be translated. *4338-i god* is included in *Pre-Revolutionary Russian Science Fiction: An Anthology*, ed. and trans. Leland Fetzer (Ann Arbor, 1982); and, in Alex Miller's translation, in Korovin's selection (see Note 2 above).

8. See the anthologies (noted above) edited by Proffer and Korovin.

9. For a study of Saint-Germain, see Jean Overton Fuller, *The Comte de Saint-Germain: Last Scion of the House of Rakoczy* (London and The Hague, 1988). See also the appendix to Neil Cornwell, *Pushkin's 'The Queen of Spades'* (London, 1993).

10. 'Kosmorama' was finally reprinted in *Povesti i rasskazy*, 1988 (see Note 4 above).

11. For information on Odoevsky's interest in Pordage and Saint-Martin, see Cornwell, *V.F. Odoevsky*, 1986, pp. 103-5.

12. Translated as 'The Ghost', in *Russian Tales of the Fantastic*, trans. Marilyn Minto (London, 1994), pp. 32-44 (see p. 38); also trans., under the same title, by Alex Miller in Korovin (see Note 2 above).

13. Quoted from the Introduction to *The Oxford Book of Gothic Tales*, ed. Chris Baldick (Oxford), pp. xix-xx.

*Chapter 9*

# PIRACY AND HIGHER REALISM

The Strange Case of Fitz-James O'Brien and
Vladimir Odoevsky

In a study of *The Literary Fantastic* (1990) I remarked on a surprising similarity between Vladimir Odoevsky's 'Sil'fida' ('The Sylph', published in 1837) and 'The Diamond Lens' (1858), the best known tale of the Irish-American writer Fitz-James O'Brien (1828-1862).[1] Both stories feature sylphs, observed with the naked eye in a vase of water (Odoevsky) or through a microscope in a drop of water (O'Brien). In both, the sylphs are surrounded by poetic worlds of great beauty; the protagonists fall in love with their sylphs and lapse into madness when they lose contact with them; moreover both stories are narrated in the first person and share a 'fantastic' ambiguity as to whether these alternative worlds are 'real', or the product of psychological ravings. There are also differences: in particular regarding O'Brien's modern scientific microscope, which in his own day attracted accusations of plagiarism (from a manuscript called 'Microcosmus' by one William North). Nevertheless, the similarities remain striking, to say the least.[2]

I had first come across a brief reference to O'Brien's story in Brian Aldiss's *Trillion Year Spree* ('The Diamond Lens' having generally been treated as early science fiction, rather than romantic-Gothic)[3] and had found the text in two anthologies of American short stories.[4] Only with some difficulty and much more recently did I manage to get hold of a fuller collection of O'Brien's tales.[5]

Some sort of an influence of Odoevsky upon O'Brien did immediately seem a possibility. Both French and German translations of

Odoevsky's stories had taken place before O'Brien's tale was written. However, the texts of both stories referred to alchemical sources, in particular *Le Comte de Gabalis*. This source, together with Paracelsus and others, had been known, directly or indirectly, to Hoffmann, Poe, and other Gothic writers with whom O'Brien would have been familiar. This fact, together with any researches into alchemy and elemental spirits that O'Brien may have conducted, might well have been sufficient to account for the similarities; at the same time, there were the differences too. After all, it was highly unlikely that O'Brien would have known Russian and his knowledge of other languages was also an unknown quantity.

When I was invited to present a paper at the Leiden October Conference (in 1991, on the sources and origins of Gothic), it seemed to me that the alchemical tradition feeding into similar and parallel stories of sylphs and their manic human admirers in St Petersburg and New York, through the quill pens of Odoevsky and O'Brien respectively, might make a suitable topic. The importance of such authorities to this literary genre was of course well known. In 1932 Joyce Tompkins wrote of the Gothic tale that 'a fantastic element enriched the confusion in the stories of occult powers ... on the confines of magic and science, of moral idealism and charlatanry', and went on to mention Rosicrucianism, Freemasonry, and Illuminism as sources of such activity.[6] We could of course add to this list Mesmerism, Galvanism, and other burgeoning pseudo-scientific teachings, while pointing out too the existence of more than one type of charlatanry. Leslie Fiedler remarks on 'the convention of treating magic as science and thus reclaiming it for respectability in the Age of Reason'.[7] A more recent commentator, Camille Paglia, has remarked that 'English Gothicism of the 1790s is equivalent to the medieval alchemy and occultism in [Goethe's] *Faust*'; 'Gothic is a style of claustrophobic sensuality', she continues: 'art withdraws into caverns, castles, prison-cells, tombs, coffins';[8] and – one might add in relation to our two writers – lenses and retorts, the vase, or even drop, of water. One is reminded here too of Blake's line from *Auguries of Innocence*, 'To see a World in a Grain of Sand', which is followed by the couplet:

Every Tear in Every Eye
Becomes a Babe in Eternity.

Paglia aptly remarks that 'microcosms are dangerous in Blake because they are separatist and solipsistic'.[9]

The decade and a half, from about 1829 until the appearance of his three-volumed Compositions (*Sochineniia*) in 1844 and his subse-

quent virtual retirement from literature, saw the flowering of Odoev-
sky's literary achievement in various styles. One of the best known
of his romantic-philosophical compositions is his tale 'Sil'fida' of
1837, ironically subtitled 'from the notes of a reasonable man'. This
story has already been outlined in the previous chapter.

The prose of Odoevsky has been said to lack the masterly conci-
sion of Pushkin, the elegance of Lermontov, and the linguistic verve
of Gogol (although at the height of his fame, in the 1830s, his repu-
tation was not so far short of theirs), but his relative verbosity brings
him closer, arguably, to the English style of writing of the first half of
the nineteenth century. His themes too are close to the romanticism
of both European and English-based literatures: comparisons can be
made with, not only Hoffmann, but with Charles Brockden Brown
and of course Poe, as well as Mary Shelley, Maturin, and Sheridan
Le Fanu. Particularly intriguing, though, was the clear proximity
between Odoevsky's 'The Sylph' and 'The Diamond Lens', the story
written some twenty years later by a certain Fitz-James O'Brien.

O'Brien was born in Cork in 1828. After occupying himself with
poetry and journalism, first in Ireland and then London, he squan-
dered a healthy family inheritance and left for New York at the end
of 1851, where he found immediate success as a prolific contributor
to the *New York Times, Putnam's, The Atlantic Monthly, Harper's* and
other journals.[10] He published poetry, fiction and plays, including a
successful two-act piece called *A Gentleman from Ireland*. He sup-
ported an extravagant bohemian lifestyle by his writings and
achieved a peak of lionisation with his story 'The Diamond Lens',
published in January 1858. In 1861 the Civil War broke out and
O'Brien joined a regiment of the National Guard of New York; cited
for bravery at Bloomery Gap, he was wounded in February 1862 and
died in April. His stories and poems were collected in 1881. Since
then collections of his work have been at best sporadic, but 'The
Diamond Lens' (frequently termed O'Brien's 'masterpiece') and one
or two other favoured stories have been frequently anthologised.

Of his other stories, fleeting mention may be made of 'What Was
It? A Mystery' (1859), singled out by H.P. Lovecraft as 'the first well-
shaped short story of a tangible but invisible being, and the proto-
type of de Maupassant's *Horla*';[11] and 'The Wondersmith' (also 1859)
which, with its theme of the infusion of the souls of 'demon' children
into wooden manikins, bears a superficial (but, I think, coincidental)
resemblance to Odoevsky's tale of girls converted into dolls, 'Skazka
o tom kak opasno devushkam khodit' tolpoiu po Nevskomu
prospektu' ('A Tale of Why it is Dangerous for Young Girls to go
Walking in a Group along Nevsky Prospect' of 1833). One recent
commentator picks out four elements in O'Brien's plots which, he

claims, shaped subsequent fantasy: the animated mannikin, the lost room, the invisible creature and the microscopic world.[12] While the quality of the microscopic, in Russian literature at least, seems to anticipate in particular the work of Zamiatin, in fact all four of these motifs can also be found in stories written in the 1830s by Odoevsky. We shall return to another of these later.

'The Diamond Lens' is a first-person narrative recounting the protagonist's progression from boyhood enthusiast for microscopes to the status of 'constructive microscopist' and on to his final position as 'Linley, the mad microscopist'. This obsession with microscopy leads Linley to seek the perfect lens, in pursuit of which he consults through a medium the spirit of the Dutch naturalist Anton van Leeuwenhoek (who had lived from 1632-1723). He then murders his French confederate in order to steal a one-hundred-and-forty-carat diamond from which to fashion the required lens. With his now perfect instrument, Linley is able to discover and observe, within a single drop of water, a sylph of unparalleled beauty and a whole new and poetic world which greatly exceeds the possibilities of his own world, even as embodied in its most gracious ballerina. However, Linley neglects the laws of evaporation and returns to his vision only to find his sylph dying of suffocation (or, rather, dehydration). The shock is such that he collapses, thus wrecking his perfect lens, and falls into apparent madness, from which state his account has presumably been written.

In these stories, as already suggested, resides an ambiguity as to the supposed actuality of what has been observed, in terms of its derivation from either another reality or from the delusions of brainstorms, or 'crazed imagination'; Thomas Clareson sees this quality as crucial in making 'The Diamond Lens' O'Brien's finest story.[13] Both stories therefore share a quality of what is termed, in a Todorovian sense, 'the literary fantastic'.[14] Furthermore, Odoevsky's protagonist gets into his situation due to the legacy of a deceased uncle; O'Brien's Linley is enabled to pursue his career in microscopy thanks to 'a small fortune' bequeathed by his 'poor Aunt Agatha'. Linley murders to achieve his aims, it might be argued, whereas Mikhail Platonovich does nothing more antisocial than standing up his fiancée. However, another Odoevskian protagonist, Yakko in 'Salamandra' ('The Salamander') follows the example of Pushkin's Hermann of 'Pikovaia dama' ('The Queen of Spades') in being willing to kill in the pursuit of occult secrets; the example of certain Poe characters, though, represents a more probable precedent for O'Brien.

Such structural similarities, or for that matter reversals, are however relatively superficial compared to the use in both stories of the figure of a sylph and the proximity of the poetic worlds described in association with such a creature. This near identity of vision between

Odoevsky and O'Brien is far more striking than any distinction which can be made between Mikhail Platonovich's naked-eye vision of a sylph in a vase of water, emanating from the action of sunbeams on a turquoise ring, and Linley's more 'scientific' and scaled down version through a microscope.

The two following passages may be compared:

> But hardly was the water in motion, when once again green and pink threads extended from the rose and flowed together with the water in a variegated stream and my beautiful flower appeared once more at the bottom of the vase. Everything calmed down but something had flashed across the middle of it. The leaves opened little by little and – I couldn't believe my eyes – between the orange stamens there reposed – I wonder whether you'll believe me? – there reposed an amazing, indescribable, unbelievable creature: in short, a woman, barely visible to the eye! How am I to describe to you the joy, tinged with horror, which I felt at that moment! This woman was no child. Imagine the miniature portrait of a beautiful woman in full bloom and you will get a dim notion of the miracle which lay before my eyes. She reposed casually on her soft couch and her russet brown curls, wavering from the rippling of the water, now revealed and now concealed from my eyes her immaculate charms. She appeared to be immersed in a deep sleep and I, my eyes fixed avidly on her, held my breath, so as not to disturb her sweet composure. (Odoevsky, 'Sil'fida' [St Petersburg, 1837]: my translation)

> It was a female human shape. When I say human, I mean it possessed the outlines of humanity, but there the analogy ends. Its adorable beauty lifted it illimitable heights beyond the loveliest daughter of Adam.
>
> I cannot, I dare not, attempt to inventory the charms of this divine revelation of perfect beauty. Those eyes of mystic violet, dewy and serene, evade my words. Her long, lustrous hair following her head in a golden wake, like the track sown in heaven by a falling star, seems to quench my most burning phrases with its splendours. If all the bees of Hybla nestled upon my lips, they would still sing but hoarsely the wondrous harmonies of outline that inclosed her form.
>
> She swept out from between the rainbow-curtains of the cloud-trees into the broad sea of light that lay beyond. Her motions were those of some graceful naiad, cleaving by a mere effort of her will, the clear, unruffled waters that fill the chambers of the sea. She floated forth with the serene grace of a frail bubble ascending through the still atmosphere of a June day. The perfect roundness of her limbs formed suave and enchanting curves. It was like listening to the most spiritual symphony of Beethoven the divine to watch the harmonious flow of lines. This, indeed, was a pleasure cheaply purchased at any price. (O'Brien, 'The Diamond Lens' [New York, 1858])

Indeed it is the presence of the apparently modern microscope in 'The Diamond Lens' that caused this story to be seen more in terms of early science fiction than the nature of its vision, deriving rather from the much older occult and Gothic forms, perhaps warrants. However, the balance has been partially redressed by connections recently made between O'Brien's vision and Poe's aesthetic of beauty. O'Brien's story, it has now been pointed out, 'is finally concerned not ... with the ethical ramifications of an obsessive scientific interest, but, rather, with the inevitable failure of man's longing for ideal beauty'.[15] In fact, comparisons with Odoevsky help to reinforce the link with Poe, as well as to draw us back to what would be earlier common sources. Odoevsky, like Poe, with whom he later came to recognise a kinship,[16] could be said to have felt 'trapped by a hopelessly inadequate language system and equally trapped by the physical limitations of his own mortality'.[17] The possibilities for the true poetic imagination were near enough the same – for Odoevsky, as for Poe, as for O'Brien; however, Odoevsky's sylph, it must be said, is not shown dying (it is lost to its admirer merely through the intervention of unsympathetic philistines), whereas the demise of O'Brien's sylph re-enacts Poe's precociously decadent dictum that 'the death, then, of a beautiful woman is, unquestionably, the most poetical topic in the world'.[18]

Odoevsky is unlikely to have been familiar with Poe before the end of his own career as a fiction writer; however, Hoffmann immediately arises as an influence common to these three later writers. More interestingly, though, the question arises as to whether and how O'Brien could have known Odoevsky's work. 'Sil'fida' had, as a matter of fact, been translated into German as early as 1839 and into French in 1855.[19] Nevertheless, the explanation for the main similarities between the sylphs of Odoevsky and O'Brien could perhaps be much simpler and merely reside quite overtly within the text of each, in the form of references to the pre-romantic and pre-Gothic esoteric and alchemical traditions.

Odoevsky alludes to alchemical sources in a number of his fictional works and his own scientific and pseudo-scientific interests are well known. In 'Sil'fida', Mikhail Platonovich discovers in his late uncle's sealed cupboards 'the works of Paracelsus, *The Count of Gabalis,* Arnold of Villanova, Raimondo Lulli and other alchemists and cabbalists'. In 'The Diamond Lens', Linley too refers to what he calls 'the Count of Cabalis' [*sic*], 'the Rosicrucian'. Fouqué's *Undine* (1811), another source certainly common to Hoffmann, Odoevsky, Poe and O'Brien, derived, we are informed by H.P. Lovecraft, 'from a tale told by ... Paracelsus'.[20] The most clearly specific common ground, though, is *The Count of Gabalis.*

*The Count of Gabalis, or Discourses on the Secret Sciences,* a book on elemental spirits and their relations with humans, was written and published anonymously in Paris in 1670 by the Abbé Nicolas de Monfaucon de Villars (1635-1673). The Abbé de Villars's book, which was reprinted several times, enjoyed a considerable readership and influenced many a European writer, and especially Hoffmann (in such stories as 'The Golden Pot' and 'The King's Betrothed'). In English literature we have only to look at Pope's *The Rape of the Lock*. This passage, quoted from an English translation last printed in 1886, has obvious relevance to the stories of Odoevsky and O'Brien:

> You need but shut up a glass fill'd with Conglobated Air, Water or Earth, and expose it to the sun for a month; Then separate the element according to art, which is very easie to do, if it be Earth or Water. 'Tis a marvellous thing to see, what a virtue every one of these purified Elements have to attract the *Nymphs, Sylphs* and *Gnomes*. In taking but never so little, every day, for about a month together, one shall see in the air the volant republic of the *Sylphs* .... Thus venerable Nature teaches her Children how to repair the Elements by the Elements. Thus is Harmony reestablished. Thus man recovers his natural Empire, and can do all things in the Elements, without *Daemon*, or unlawful art. Thus you see, my Son, that the *Sages* are more innocent than you thought.[21]

Similar passages may be found in the *Liber de nymphis, sylphis, pygmaeis, et salamandris, et de caeteris spiritibus* and elsewhere in the writings of Paracelsus. Odoevsky, we may note, retains, in 'Sil'fida' at least, the 'white magical' innocence of such experimentation. In the hands of O'Brien, the treatment is more daemonic and, thanks to the microscope, afforded a scientific veneer. Both writers, to varying degrees and in a Hoffmannian or Poe-like manner, poeticise – or romanticise – the vision.

O'Brien could, then, have developed an interest in sylphs either directly from the alchemical sources or through a variety of literary intermediaries. He wrote at least one other alchemical story, 'The Gold Ingot' (1858). In the case of Odoevsky, we can trace his sources back from contemporary romanticism and the philosophical system of Schelling, via the theosophical, Hermetic, and cabbalistic traditions, to the original alchemical writings and even earlier – via such luminaries as Saint-Martin, John Pordage, and Jacob Boehme to the Neoplatonists.[22] Lovecraft claims that there is a kind of imaginary or Gothic history of the occult, connecting the magi of the Renaissance directly with the necromancers of the Middle Ages,[23] and, indeed, the influence of alchemical writings on the fantastic fictions of the nineteenth century can certainly not be ignored. Perhaps the most celebrated example is Mary Shelley's *Frankenstein* in which Victor Frankenstein, in the second chapter, invokes the works of Cornelius Agrippa, Paracelsus and Albertus Magnus. The legacy of the alchemists was felt in Gothic fiction not only upon its eastern and western peripheries, but also at its English and West European centre.

And there we might have been content to leave matters, crediting Fitz-James O'Brien with having created, from his awareness of common sources, an original story entitled 'The Diamond Lens', albeit one sharing certain remarkable intertextual similarities with the Russian story 'Sil'fida'. However, there is another detail within O'Brien's literary biography which provides cause for a rejection of this attitude. Further research on O'Brien brought to light what is probably the only book-length study to have been written on him: Francis Wolle's *Fitz-James O'Brien: A Literary Bohemian of the Eighteen-fifties* (published in 1944). This book provided the key information.

In September 1857, four months before the appearance of 'The Diamond Lens', O'Brien had published in *Harper's New Monthly Magazine* a story named 'Seeing the World'. A mere synopsis of this story, which O'Brien's biographer regarded as 'Poesque',[24] revealed it to be, to all intents and purposes, indistinguishable from Odoevsky's story 'Improvizator' – 'The Improvisor', or 'The Improvvisatore' as it is called in the English translation of *Russkie nochi* – down to the very names of the characters. Inspection of the full texts bears out what was already more than a suspicion. Here follows a comparison of the first page:

Loud applause resounded in the hall. The improvvisatore's success surpassed the expectations of the audience and his own expectations. No sooner was a topic suggested to him than lofty thoughts and tender feelings, decked in sonorous meters, poured from his lips, like phantasmagoric visions from a magic sacrificial vessel. The artist did not reflect even for a moment: in the same instant an idea was conceived in his mind and went through all the stages of its development and was transformed into expression. The intricate form of a piece, poetic images, elegant epithets, obedient rhymes, appeared at one stroke. Yet this was not all: two or three topics completely different in character were suggested to him at the same time. He dictated one poem, wrote another one, improvised a third, and each was exquisite in its own way: one brought about rapture, another moved you to tears, the third made you split your sides with laughter. And yet he gave the impression of being unconcerned with his work; he constantly joked and talked to his audience. All the elements of poetic creation were at his fingertips, like figures on a chessboard which he carelessly manipulated as needed.

Finally the attention and amazement of the audience was exhausted; they suffered for the improvvisatore. But the artist himself was quiet and cold – there was not a trace of fatigue in him. His face, however, did not reflect the lofty enjoyment of a poet, satisfied with his creation, but rather the simple, self-satisfied look of a juggler surprising the crowd with his skill. Full of mockery he watched the tears, the laughter he had produced; he alone of all those present neither cried nor laughed; he alone did not believe his words, and treated his inspiration as an indifferent priest, long accustomed to the mysteries of his temple.

The last of his audience had not yet left when the improvvisatore rushed to the man collecting the entrance fee, and began counting it with the greediness of Harpagon. The take was very large. The improvvisatore had not seen so much money in all his life, and was beside himself with joy.[25] (Odoevsky, *Russkie nochi*)

The hall reverberated with plaudits. The *improvisatore* surpassed himself. Scarcely was a subject given to him by the spectators than grand ideas, profound sentiments, clad in majestic verse, rolled from his lips, as if evoked by some magic. The artist did not reflect for an instant. In the twinkling of an eye his newly-born thoughts ran through all the phases of growth, and appeared clothed in the most exact expression. Ingenuity of form, splendour of imagery, harmony of rhythm, all were exhibited at the same moment. But this was a trifle. People gave him two or three subjects at the same time. The *improvisatore* dictated a poem on one, wrote a second, and improvised a third; and each production was, in its way, perfect. The first excited enthusiasm; the second called tears into the eyes of the listeners; and the third was so humorous that none could restrain their laughter. In the midst of this the *improvisatore* did not seem to be in the least preoccupied with his subject. He talked and laughed with his neighbours. All the elements of poetical composition seemed to be at his disposal, as the pieces of a chess-board, which he used when he needed them, with the most superb indifference. At last the attention and admiration of the spectators were exhausted. They were more wearied than the *improvisatore*. He was calm and cold. One could not trace on his countenance the slightest of fatigue; his features, in place of expressing the lofty joy of the poet content with his labour, displayed only the vulgar satisfaction of the conjuror who astonishes a stupid crowd. He listened to the laughter, and watched the tears tremble on the cheeks, with a sort of disdain; he alone neither laughed nor wept; he alone had no belief in his utterances. In the moment of divinest inspiration he had the air of a faithless priest, whom long habit had familiarized with the mysteries of the temple. The last of the audience had scarcely issued from the apartment when the *improvisatore* flung himself upon the pile of money received at the door, and commenced counting it with the avidity of Harpagon. The sum was large. He had never received so large a one in a single evening, and he was enchanted. (O'Brien: 'Seeing the World')

'Seeing the World', then, is the story of an ineffective poet named Cipriano who receives from a physician from India an irrevocable dual gift of poetic improvisation and a power to know and to comprehend everything. From then on Cipriano sees only the material, scientific bases of things: his beloved Charlotte is only an anatomical specimen; a picture is only canvas and paint. Despite his astounding performances of feats of poetic improvising, 'his mind revolts at his terrible gift, and his reason totters'. Wolle's book also confirms O'Brien's excellent knowledge of French and makes it plain that accusations of plagiarism, although unproven, were not uncommon during his career. We are therefore dealing here with something which goes beyond traceable common sources, beyond 'ideas in the air' transferred through anything like Lotman's semiosphere.

Both 'Seeing the World' and 'The Diamond Lens' were written in 1857. In 1855 a volume had been published in Paris entitled *Le décameron russe: histoires et nouvelles,* translated by one Pierre-Paul Douhaire; this included seven stories by Odoevsky, among which were 'Sil'fida' (under the title *L'alchimiste*) and 'Improvizator' (*L'improvisateur*).[26] We are therefore left with the inescapable conclusion that O'Brien's use of the alchemical tradition in 'The Diamond Lens' too masks his exploitation of a yet further and even older tradition, or perhaps rather a charge: one by no means entirely unknown before in Gothic fiction and one levelled at O'Brien not for the first time – that of plagiarism.

O'Brien's game, then, is now surely up – in relation to these two stories at least. So the charming Bohemian did chance his arm at a spot of plagiarism after all. But perhaps plagiarism is itself a form of fantastic realism? At least, until it is exposed. That it was not to be considered what Dostoevsky would have termed a 'higher form of realism' was, though, perhaps at least tacitly acknowledged by O'Brien himself. 'The Diamond Lens' was O'Brien's most acclaimed story. It was therefore to be expected that, in drawing up a list of his works for inclusion in a proposed collection a few months before his premature death in the Civil War, he should have intended calling it 'The Diamond Lens and other tales By Fitz James O'Brien'.[27] It is perhaps also revealing and, in view of the evidently more extreme degree of charlatanism involved in this case, not surprising that he should have omitted 'Seeing the World' from his list of twenty tales. The striking qualities of this tale, of course, prompted unsuspecting editors subsequently to restore it to his oeuvres.

# Notes

1. Neil Cornwell, *The Literary Fantastic: From Gothic to Postmodernism* (New York and London, 1990), pp. xiv, 65 and 235 n. 10.
2. For the text of 'Silfida', see V.F. Odoevsky, *Sochineniia v dvukh tomakh* (Moscow, 1981); and (in English) Vladimir Odoevsky, *The Salamander and Other Gothic Tales,* trans. Neil Cornwell (London, 1992).
3. Brian W. Aldiss, *Trillion Year Spree: The History of Science Fiction* (London, 1986), p. 94.
4. *The Masterpiece Library of Short Stories: The Thousand Best Complete Tales of all Times and all Countries,* ed. Sir J.A. Hammerton, vol. XV, *American* (London, The Educational Book Company, no date), pp. 103-22; *American Short Stories of the Nineteenth Century,* introduction by John Cournos, Everyman's Library (London, 1930, rep. 1982), pp. 102-29.
5. *The Fantastic Tales of Fitz-James O'Brien,* ed. Michael Hayes (London, 1977).

6. Joyce M.S. Tompkins, 'The Gothic Romance', quoted from *The Gothick Novel: A Casebook* (Basingstoke and London, 1990), p. 96.
7. Leslie A. Fiedler, *Love and Death in the American Novel,* revised edition (Harmondsworth, 1984), p. 139.
8. Camille Paglia, *Sexual Personae: Art and Decadence from Nefertiti to Emily Dickinson* (Harmondsworth, 1992), p. 265.
9. Ibid., p. 284.
10. See Francis Wolle, *Fitz-James O'Brien: A Literary Bohemian of the Eighteen-Fifties* (Boulder, CO: University of Colorado Studies [Series B. Studies in the Humanities, Vol. 2, No. 2], 1944).
11. Howard Phillips Lovecraft, *Supernatural Horror in Literature* (New York, 1973), p. 66.
12. Thomas D. Clareson, 'Fitz-James O'Brien 1828-1862', in E.F. Bleiler (editor), *Supernatural Fiction Writers: Fantasy and Horror,* vol. 2 (New York: Scribners, 1985), pp. 717-22 (722).
13. Ibid., p. 720.
14. See Cornwell, *The Literary Fantastic,* especially pp. 11-16.
15. Michael Wentworth, 'A Matter of Taste: Fitz-James O'Brien's "The Diamond Lens" and Poe's Aesthetic of Beauty', *American Transcendental Quarterly* 2(4), 1988, pp. 271-84.
16. Neil Cornwell, *V.F. Odoyevsky: His Life, Times and Milieu* (London and Athens, OH, 1986), p. 313.
17. Wentworth, p. 274.
18. Edgar Allan Poe, 'The Philosophy of Composition', *Selections from the Critical Writings of Edgar Allan Poe,* ed. F.C. Prescott (New York, 1909, rep. Gordian Press, New York, 1981), p. 158.
19. See Cornwell, *V.F. Odoyevsky,* p. 384.
20. Lovecraft, p. 45.
21. *Sub-Mundanes; or The Elementaries of the Cabala: being the History of Spirits* (Bath, 1886), p. 40. Reprint of *The Count of Gabalis; or the Extravagant Mysteries of the Cabalists Exposed, in five pleasant discourses on the Secret Sciences.* Trans. into English P.A. Gent. London, no date.
22. See Cornwell, *V.F. Odoyevsky,* pp. 104-5.
23. Lovecraft, pp. 18-19.
24. Wolle, p. 149 (synopsis is on pp. 149-50). The story was originally published as: 'Seeing the World', *Harper's New Monthly Magazine,* September 1857, XV, pp. 542-6.
25. Odoevsky, V.F., *Russian Nights,* trans. Olga Koshansky-Olienikov and Ralph E. Matlaw (New York, 1965). Includes 'The Improvvisatore', pp. 132-45.
26. See note 19 above.
27. Wolle, pp. 230-31.

# SELECT BIBLIOGRAPHY

Apart from a basic list of the main editions of Odoevsky's works, this bibliography is limited to works not found in Neil Cornwell's *V.F. Odoyevsky: His Life, Times and Milieu* (Foreword by Sir Isaiah Berlin. London and Athens, OH, 1986). Other works referred to throughout this study are referenced in the endnotes which follow each chapter.

## I. Main editions of Odoevsky's literary works

*Pestrye skazki s krasnym slovtsom.* ... (St Petersburg, 1833).
*Sochineniia kniazia V.F. Odoevskogo,* 3 vols (St Petersburg, 1844).
*Russkie nochi* (Moscow, 1913, rep. Fink, Munich, 1967).
*Romanticheskie povesti* (Leningrad, 1929, rep. Meeuws, Oxford, 1975).
*Deviat' povestei* (New York, 1954).
*Povesti i rasskazy* (Moscow, 1959).
*Russkie nochi,* 'Literaturnye pamiatniki' (Leningrad, 1975).
*Povesti* (Moscow, 1977).
*Sochineniiia v dvukh tomakh* (Moscow, 1981).
*Poslednii kvartet Betkhovena* (Moscow, 1982, and rep.).
*O literature i iskusstve* (Moscow, 1982).
*Povesti i rasskazy* (Moscow, 1985).
*Povesti i rasskazy* (Moscow, 1988).
*Pyostryye skazki,* ed. Neil Cornwell ('Durham Modern Language Series', University of Durham, 1988).
*Pestrye skazki s krasnym slovtsom...* (Moscow, 1991, facsimile of 1833 original edition).
*Pestrye skazki / Skazki Dedushki Irineia,* 'Zabytaia kniga' (Moscow, 1993).
*Pestrye skazki,* ed. M.A. Tur'ian, 'Literaturnye pamiatniki' (St Petersburg, 1996).

Mnemozina: Sobranie sočinenij v stichach i proze, I-IV (Moscow, 1824-25), rep. with Foreword by Wolfgang Busch (Hildesheim, 1986). [Edited by Odoevsky and Küchelbeker, this almanac includes a number of Odoevsky's early texts – fiction and non-fiction – never otherwise reprinted.]

# II. Odoevsky in English

V.F. Odoevsky, *Russian Nights,* trans. Olga Koshansky-Olienikov and
Ralph E. Matlaw (New York, 1965; rep. with Afterword by Neil
Cornwell, Evanston, IL, 1997).

*Russian Romantic Prose: An Anthology,* ed. Carl R. Proffer (Ann Arbor, 1979).

*Pre-Revolutionary Russian Science Fiction: An Anthology,* ed. Leland Fetzer
(Ann Arbor, 1982).

*The Ardis Anthology of Russian Romanticism,* ed. Christine Rydel (Ann Arbor,
1984).

*Russian 19th-century Gothic Tales,* compiled by Valentin Korovin (Moscow,
1984).

Vladimir Odoevsky, *The Salamander and Other Gothic Tales,* ed. and trans.
Neil Cornwell (London and Evanston, IL, 1992).

*Russian Tales of the Fantastic,* trans. Marilyn Minto (London, 1994).

# III. New Odoevsky Criticism/Materials

*Katalog biblioteki V.F. Odoevskogo* (Moscow, 1988 ). (Chastnye sobraniia v
fondakh Gosudarstvennoi Biblioteki SSSR imeni V.I. Lenina. Katalogi).

Andrew, Joe *Narrative and Desire: Masculine and Feminine in Russian
Literature,* 1822-1849 (Basingstoke and London, 1993).

Brown, William Edward *A History of Russian Literature of the Romantic
Period,* 4 vols (Ann Arbor, 1986).

Campbell, J.S. *V.F. Odoyevsky and the Formation of Russian Musical Taste in the
Nineteenth Century* (New York, 1989).

Cornwell, Neil 'Gothic and its Origins in East and West: Vladimir
Odoevsky and Fitz-James O'Brien', in *Exhibited by Candlelight: Sources
and Developments in the Gothic Tradition,* ed. Valeria Tinkler-Villani and
Peter Davidson (Amsterdam and Atlanta, GA, 1995).

Cornwell, Neil 'Vladimir Odoevskii and the Society Tale in the 1820s and
1830s', in *The Society Tale in Russian Literature: from Odoevskii to Tolstoi,*
ed. Neil Cornwell (Amsterdam and Atlanta, GA 1998).

Glówko, Olga 'Mysli Vladimira Odoevskogo o vere i religii (*Russkie
nochi)*', *Opuscula Polonica et Russica,* 1, 1994 (15-36).

Glówko, Olga [Gluvko, Ol'ga] 'Simvolika knigi v "Russkikh nochakh"
Vladimira Odoevskogo' (conference paper: in press).

Glówko, Olga *Idee romantyzmu w 'Nocach rosyjskich' Wlodzimierza
Odojewskiego* (Lódź, 1997).

Grekov, V.N. 'Zhizn' i mirazh (O skazkakh V.F. Odoevskogo)',
introduction to *Pestrye skazki / Skazki Dedushki Irineia* (Moscow, 1993).

Ivanova, T.A. 'Zefiroty V.F. Odoevskogo i L.N. Tolstogo', *Russkaia rech',* 5,
1988 (24-8).

Levina, L.A. 'Avtorskii zamysel i khozhestvennaia real'nost' (Filosofskii
roman V.F. Odoevskogo "Russkie nochi"', *Izvestiia Akademii nauk SSSR,*
Seriia literatury i iazyka, 49, 1, 1990 (31-40).

Levitsky, Alexander 'V.F. Odoevskij's *The Year 4338:* Eutopia or
    Dystopia?', in *The Supernatural in Slavic and Baltic Literature: Essays in
    Honor of Victor Terras,* ed. Amy Mandelker and Roberta Reeder
    (Columbus, OH, 1988).
Medovoi, M.I. 'Izobrazitel'noe iskusstvo i tvorchestvo V.F. Odoevskogo',
    in *Russkaia literatura i izobrazitel'noe iskusstvo XVIII - nachala XX veka*
    (Leningrad, 1988).
Nemzer, A. 'V.F. Odoevsky i ego proza', introduction to *Povesti i rasskazy*
    (Moscow, 1988).
Reid, Robert (ed.) *Problems of Russian Romanticism* (Aldershot, 1986).
Sakharov, V.I. *Stranitsy russkogo romantizma: kniga statei* (Moscow, 1988).
Semibratova, Irina 'Neizvestnye i zabyte materialy o kniaze V.F.
    Odoevskom', *Rossica* 1, 1996 (96-116).
Tur'ian, M.A. 'Irinei Modestovich Gomozeika', in the collection
    *Peterburgskie vstrechi Pushkina* (Leningrad, 1987).
Tur'ian, M.A. *Skazki Irinieia Modestovicha Gomozeiki,* supplement to *Petstrye
    skazki* (Moscow, 1991).
Tur'ian, M.A. '*Strannaia moia sud'ba...*'. *O zhizni V.F. Odoevskogo* (Moscow,
    1991).
Turian, Marietta 'Neizvestnaia "kavkazskaia" stranitsa biografiia V.F.
    Odoevskogo', *Zvezda,* 6, 1993 (167-85)
Vatsuro, V.E. 'Sud'ba "russkogo Fausta"', foreword to M.A. Tur'ian,
    *'Strannaia moia sud'ba ...': o zhizni Vladimira Fedorovicha Odoevskogo*
    (Moscow, 1991).

# INDEX